The Fire and the Cloud

Robert F. Reiland

A Hearthstone Book

Carlton Press Corp. ❖ New York

Copyright © 1996 by Robert F. Reiland
ALL RIGHTS RESERVED
Manufactured in the United States of America
ISBN 0-8062-5056-9

To all those who love the Lord,
and to all those who will then
love Him when they meet Him.

Acknowledgments

We are grateful for copyright permission granted from the following publishers for the works listed:

— *Biblical Archaeology Review, March/April 1983*—Copyright © **BIBLICAL ARCHAEOLOGY SOCIETY.** Reprinted by permission. *Subscription inquiries should be mailed to:*
Biblical Archaeology Society, 3000 Connecticut Avenue NW, Suite 300, Washington D.C. 20008

— Scripture quotations marked (NEB) are from *The New English Bible.* Copyright © The Delegates of the **OXFORD UNIVERSITY PRESS** and The Syndics of the **CAMBRIDGE UNIVERSITY PRESS**, 1961, 1970. Reprinted by permission.

— *Holy Bible—From the Ancient Eastern Text—George M. Lamsa's Translation from the Aramaic of the Peshitta*—Copyright © **HARPER & ROW, PUBLISHERS, INC.** Reprinted by permission.

— *The Works of Josephus*—Copyright © **HENDRICKSON PUBLISHERS.** Reprinted by permission.

— *Will The Real Jesus Please Stand?*—Copyright © **THE INSTITUTE OF JUDAIC-CHRISTIAN RESEARCH.** Reprinted by permission.

— *Encyclopedia Judaica*—Copyright © **KETER PUBLISHING HOUSE JERUSALEM LT'D.** Reprinted by permission.

— *The Coming Prince*—Copyright © **KREGEL PUBLICATIONS,** Division of Kregel, Inc. Reprinted by permission.

— Scripture quotations marked (NASB) are from the *New American Standard Bible,* © **THE LOCKMAN FOUNDATION 1960, 1962, 1963, 1968, 1971, 1972, 1973, 1975, 1977. Used by permission.**

— *The Babylonian Talmud*—**THE SONCINO PRESS, LIMITED,** Quincentenary Edition—1978. Used by permission.

— *Midrash Rabbah—Third Edition*—Copyright © **THE SONCINO PRESS LIMITED.** Reprinted by permission.

— Scripture quotations marked (NIV) are from the *Holy Bible, New International Version.* Copyright © 1973, 1978, 1984 International Bible Society. Used by permission of **ZONDERVAN BIBLE PUBLISHERS.**

— Certain quotations are taken from *Cruden's Complete Concordance,* by Alexander Cruden. Copyright © 1949, 1953, 1955, 1968 by **ZONDERVAN BIBLE PUBLISHERS. Used by permission.**

Contents

List of Figures	xi
Preface	xiii
Introduction	xv
Chapter 1 — "His" Story	1
Chapter 2 — The "Happening"	8
Chapter 3 — Impressions	17
Chapter 4 — Archaeological Comments	24
Assumptions	25
The Open Gate	26
What "City"?	27
Where Was the "Miphkad Altar"?	27
Who Shut Which Gate?	34
Oregano & Red Stuff	37
Please Stay Downwind!	39
The Line of Departure	41
Where the "Fault" Lies	43
The Truth About Watergate	47
Some Obvious Arguments	48
Chapter 5 — Some Updated Bible Stories	52
Why Gethsemane?	52
Now, What About This "Jesus"?	57
What Judeans and Romans Were Thinking	59

Where Was the Crucifixion?	60
Evidence in the Temple	64
Not Your Ordinary "Vail"	66
If You Had Been There	67
Keeping His Schedule	75
Caiaphas, "Good-Guy" or "Bad-Guy"?	76
Standing-Tall, but Bowing-Low	77
The Character of God	79
Chapter 6 — Prophecies Relating to This Event	**81**
More "Heifers" for the Unclean	81
The Closed Door Policy	84
Fulfilling the Feasts	88
When Did Those "Two Days" Start?	100
Olivet, a Holy Mountain	103
The Divine Number	106
What If Israel Had Repented?	107
Chapter 7 — "Signs and Wonders"	**109**
Signs of the Jewels	110
Signs Above the City	112
A Sign to Be Seen, but Not Heard	112
A Time of the Signs	113
A Woe in the Darkness	114
The "Sign" of the Disappearing Signs	117
"Drawing the Lots"	119
"The Crimson Strap"	120
The Two "He-Goats"	121
"The Westernmost Candle"	123
"The Logs for the Altar"	123
"The Breads"	123
"The H'ekhal Doors"	124
How the Jews Regarded the Signs	124
Is "The World" Learning?	128
Chapter 8 — The Controversy	**141**
The Accusations	141
The Resistance	145
Some Missing Pieces	148
You Shall Know the TRUTH!	152

Chapter 9 — The Debate 157
   Ezekiel's Prophecy of the Glory Withdrawal 157
   Whose "House"? 160
   The Rending of the Veil 169
   What, Then, Did the Centurion See? 173

Chapter 10 — Will the Real "Chosen People" Please Stand? 177
   Can a "Jew" Love the Lord? 181
   Father, Forgive Us! 185
   Messiah—Son of Joseph—and a Carpenter! 188

Chapter 11 — The Debate Continues 192
   So, Who Believes in Signs? 192
   "THE" Unanswered Question 195
   Understanding the Cohens and the Trinity 197
   How Many "Gods" Did You Say? 198

Chapter 12 — Closing Remarks 199
   A Messenger's Plea 199
   But . . . How Can We Be Sure? 201
   Some Questions for the Skeptics 202
   So, That's What "They" Want! 205
   So, Now What Should We Do? 207
   Let's "Get-It-Together" 207

Appendix A — Josephus Excerpt 212

Appendix B — Midrash Excerpt 214

Appendix C — Josephus, "Lover Of Truth" 223

Glossary 226

References 231

Index of Biblical References 234

Index 239

List of Figures

Chronology of Principal Events Referenced in this Work	xix
Map of Jerusalem Old City	xxi
Summary of Scriptural / Historical / Archaeological Evidence	51
Checklist for Locales of the Crucifixion	74
Sketch 1 — Plan of Second Temple	131
Sketch 2 — Isometric View of Second Temple	132
Sketch 3 — Detailed Elevation of Second Temple	133
Sketch 4 — Elevation Profile of Temple and Temple Mount	134
Sketch 5 — Elevation Profile of Temple Mount, Kidron Valley, and Mt. Olivet	135
Sketch 6 — Jerusalem	136
Sketch 7 — Detail of Second Temple	137
Sketch 8 — The Sanctuary of the Second Temple	138
Sketch 9 — Mount of Olives as viewed from the Temple on the day of The Crucifixion	139
Sketch 10 — Detail of the "pit" or "cavity" in the face of the Mount of Olives	140

Preface

We must all remember this is not my story. This story belongs to Almighty God, the great "I AM." He lived it. This work became a book without my realization or intent. It began with the questions: What ever happened to the Shechinah? What impact was felt by the Jews at the time of His departure from the Temple? When did this happen?

The answers to these questions came together during a long search that started even before the questions began to stimulate my curiosity. During the past several years I have become driven to a search for Christ as Messiah within Judaism. The pieces began accumulating and fitting together with a "snow-balling" effect. Before I knew it, this wonderful story emerged—one which could no longer be withheld from those who would be open to hearing it.

We are indebted to Beth, my wife, for her wise counsel, for her strength, sacrifice, patience, love, and stenographic skills; to Dave and Harriet Sanford for their encouragement and many prayers; to my anonymous Jewish friend who translated critical Hebrew segments; to Professor Ernest Martin for exposing this Holy Event in his works; and to the unrivaled Temple Israel Library, and especially, librarians Elsie Leviton and Adele Sayles for their kindness and unflagging assistance during my search for Messiah through dozens of Judaica volumes.

Much of the credit for any value or quality this book may possess must be assigned to the entire staff of Carlton Press Corporation. We also are grateful to Ms. Billie Young and Mr. Kevin Orr. Their assistance has greatly contributed toward attempting to present fair treatment of some extremely sensitive material. Simply stated, I could never have done this work without their guidance, patience and skills.

We owe our thanks to several friends who read and critiqued the earliest manuscript, giving many new thoughts, questions and comments to enrich our text. We are also grateful for the endurance and attention received from our earliest critical reviewers, who would obviously prefer to remain anonymous. These are of the conservative clergy, who regrettably are not yet able to recognize the significance of this Event. Nevertheless, a few did not ignore me and actually supplied the arguments we have addressed. For this, we owe them our thanks and prayers, that they and all our readers will see the Glory of God in this story.

All of us, Jews and Christians, certainly owe our gratitude to Flavius Josephus and to the hundreds of Rabbi sages who witnessed, felt, and recorded for us the many beautiful and spiritual thoughts and facts which not only "made" this story, but which serve so stalwartly to make this an exciting and personal story of The Creator.

Introduction

This book is about truth—the truth about the withdrawal of the Shechinah Glory from the Temple in Jerusalem.

Whatever happened to the Glory of the Lord—His visible Divine Presence—the Shechinah who dwelt in the Temple? Unless you are a really "deep" scholar, you may never have thought about this. Some may even be surprised to know the Glory was Almighty God in person. (The Great "I AM" who spoke to Moses from a "burning" bush.)

The event discussed here is, in my opinion, perhaps the most important Biblical event since the Holy Spirit was manifested as tongues of flame on the Day of Pentecost, forty days after The Resurrection. Strangely, the Shechinah withdrawal has gone virtually ignored for all this time, despite the fact that it has been documented by eye-witness accounts from three highly respected Judaic sources. Furthermore, since very few Christians or Jews or Muslims have ever heard it before, this story will cause a "shock" reaction from all three faiths because we have been taught a completely erroneous story for 1,900 years.

As you can easily understand, this would cause it to be a very controversial story. Readers who are inclined to regard only Biblical information taught from their own Sunday School, church, or synagogue, may have difficulty accepting this report. However, when we recover from the initial "shock" to our traditional "security blankets" and look at the evidence, Scriptural and secular, we see a very beautiful, God-glorifying story. But, above all, this story is true.

Since there are so many dates relating to events and persons discussed in this work, a chronological chart has been provided as an aid to our readers in assessing relative periods in history. Further aid to readers is provided by a glossary of terms used in this study.

As you read, you will see several rather unfamiliar names: "Parah," "Shekalim," "Middoth" and others. These are Hebrew titles for "tractrates" or divisions of the Babylonian Talmud, which is frequently referenced in this study. The Talmud was written by the Rabbis and Sages as an interpretation and explanation of the Law which Moses received from the Lord. Each tractate is comprised of a "Mishnah" (or ruling), which is usually accompanied by a "Gemara" (or discussion). The Hebrew Midrash is also referenced. The Midrash is actually a commentary that also was written by various councils of Rabbis concerning the Jewish Bible (Tenach).

We must remember that ancient Hebrew writings in the Talmud and Midrash are certainly not of any divine inspiration. These are merely the works of men, and must be viewed only for what is said by these writers themselves. They are not speaking for the Lord; although, in some of their discussions and laws, we can see the Hand of God as we view these ancient records *in the light of Scripture.*

It is my prayer and hope that "open-eyed" Jews, Christians, and Muslims will read and evaluate this work. It is also my prayer and hope that, by considering Scripture and the simple facts, even those who do not yet "believe" will be able to "see" the Glory of the Lord through this story. I have been thrilled by what I have found and I fervently wish to share these blessings with others. I believe the reader will find at least a few surprise blessings, especially in the later chapters and Appendix B. If you love the Lord, this book will make you cry; and it will also make you shout with joy.

*The only thing new in the world
is the history you don't know.*
—President Harry S. Truman

```
JEREMIAH                                         4000 B.C. ─┼─ ADAM
586 B.C. ─┼─ BABYLON CAPTIVITY
EZEKIEL         SOLOMON'S TEMPLE DESTROYED

HAGGAI, ZECHARIAH ─ SECOND TEMPLE
      500 B.C. ─┤

                                                 3000 B.C. ─┤
       NEHEMIAH
       MALACHI
       400 B.C. ─┤
                                                 2500 B.C. ─┼─ FLOOD, NOAH


       300 B.C. ─┼─ SIMEON, THE RIGHTEOUS        2000 B.C. ─┼─ ABRAHAM
                    JOHN HYRCANUS

                                                 1500 B.C. ─┼─ MOSES
       200 B.C. ─┤                                              ISRAELITES ENTER PROMISED LAND
                  ─ MACCABEAN REVOLT, 167 B.C.
                                                 1000 B.C. ─┼─ KING DAVID
                                                 ELIJAH, JOEL  SOLOMON'S TEMPLE DEDICATED
                                                 HOSEA, AMOS
       100 B.C. ─┤                              ISAIAH, JEREMIAH
                                                  586 B.C. ─┼─ BABYLON CAPTIVITY
                                                  EZEKIEL      SOLOMON'S TEMPLE DESTROYED

                 \|/                                         \|/
                ─ ─                               ┌─────────┐ ─ ─
                 /|\                              │  BIRTH  │  /|\
        30 A.D. ─┼─ CRUCIFIXION                   │   OF    │
                    SHECHINAH WITHDRAWAL, 66 A.D. │  JESUS  │
                    SECOND TEMPLE DESTROYED, 70 A.D.└─────────┘
       JOSEPHUS                                             ─┼─ HILLEL II, JEWISH CALENDAR
       100 A.D. ─┤                                 600 A.D. ─┼─ MOHAMMED, RELIGION OF ISLAM

                                                 1000 A.D. ─┼─ CRUSADES

       200 A.D. ─┤
                                                 1500 A.D. ─┼─ PROTESTANT REFORMATION, LUTHER
                                                               POPE GREGORY XIII, CALENDAR

       300 A.D. ─┤                               2000 A.D. ─┤
       EUSEBIUS
```

CHRONOLOGY OF PRINCIPAL EVENTS REFERENCED IN THIS WORK

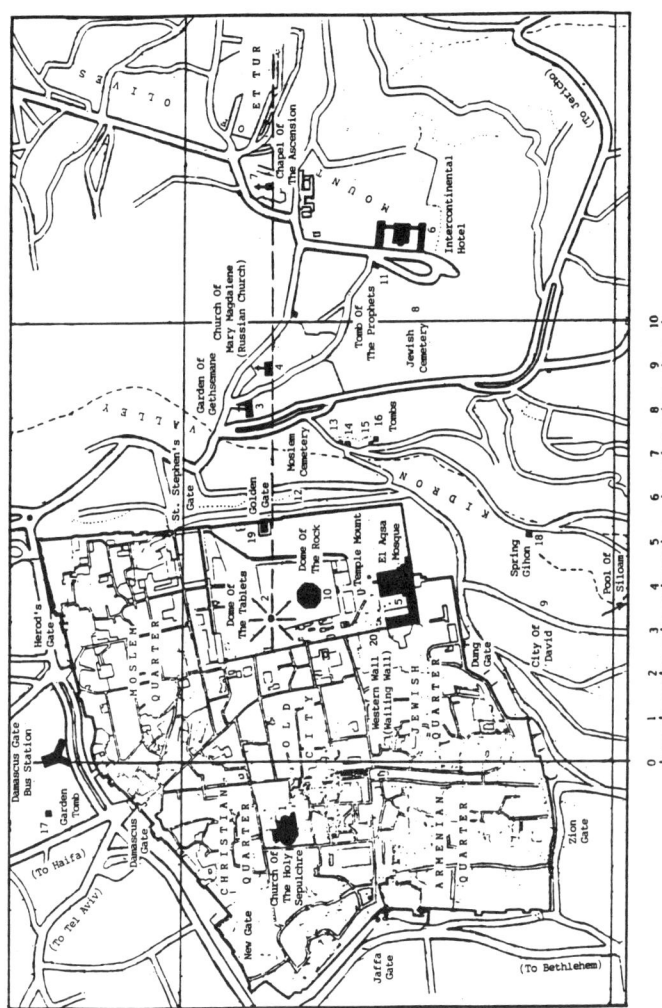

"OLD CITY" OF JERUSALEM & THE MOUNT OF OLIVES

1 "His" Story

- When did the Shechinah Glory leave the Temple?
- What was the reaction of the Iraelites to that event?
- How does this event link Judaism and Christianity?

The answers to these provocative questions have been well documented and have been available for more than 1,900 years. However, these things are not generally known or discussed except, perhaps, among the most diligent and informed scholars. Neither are these answers directly available from Scripture, since only the prophet Ezekiel describes the departure of the Glory of the Lord, but without addressing any of those issues listed.

Our purpose is to offer answers to these questions and to provide new insight through recent archaelogical discoveries in Jerusalem.

This story tells what really happened to the Lord's Divine Presence (Shechinah), who first appeared to Moses and later dwelt in the Temple. This story refutes the traditional lore we have been hearing for 1,900 years. It presents Scriptural evidence and ancient documentation of this event in order to corroborate the real story.

Almighty God Himself dwelt among the Iraelites in the Temple as a visible Presence, the Shechinah Glory. Through eyewitness accounts, we shall "see" the events leading up to and including His

1

dramatic withdrawal from the Temple, followed by the Ascension of Shechinah from the Mount of Olives forty years after the Ascension of Jesus Christ from that same mountain.

Let us briefly review the history of the Shechinah Glory as provided in the Old Testament:

1500 B.C. The Glory appeared first to Moses as a brilliant light. Moses' face shone from the "brightness" after confronting this light. (Exodus 3:2 and 34:29, 30)

The Glory led the Israelites forty years throughout the Sinai as "... a pillar of cloud by day ... and a pillar of fire by night...." (Exodus 13:21)

The Israelites heard the Lord speaking to Moses from His great "fire" and from the "cloud." (Exodus 19:9)

The Glory dwelt in the Tabernacle, in the Holy of Holies, over the Ark of the Covenant during the forty years of wandering in the Sinai and later in The Promised Land until the First Temple was built by King Solomon.

1000 B.C. In Solomon's Temple, the Glory dwelt within the Holy of Holies, just as He did in the Tabernacle. He was seen once each year on Yom Kippur (Day of Atonement) and then only by the High Priest within that chamber. (Leviticus 16:1–17 and 16:34)

586 B.C. It is not known what happened to the Glory after King Nebuchadnezzar destroyed Solomon's Temple and during the subsequent Babylonian Captivity, 606 B.C.–536 B.C. Nevertheless, the Glory must have departed from the Temple before the first destruction. One of the Apocryphal Books (II Macabees) states that King Nebuchadnezzar gave the Ark of the Covenant to the Prophet Jeremiah for safekeeping. It was then sealed within a cave on Mount Nebo. (God alone knows.)

515 B.C.	Zerubbabel completed the Second Temple. No Ark of the Covenant (not even a replica) was in the Holy of Holies (Ref. Jeremiah 3:16)
20 B.C.	King Herod (the Great) began remodeling the Second Temple to achieve the grandeur it possessed at the time of Jesus.
30 A.D.–100 A.D.	Two New Testament verses testify to the contemporary dwelling of Shechinah in the Temple during Jesus' lifetime and afterward. The first is from the Gospel in Matthew 23:21:

> "And he who swears by the temple, swears both by the temple and by Him who dwells within it." (New American Standard Bible)

The other is proclaimed by the Apostle Paul in Romans 9:4:

> "They are Israelites: they were made God's sons; theirs is the splendour of the divine presence, theirs the convenants, the law, the temple worship, and the promises." (New English Bible)

Thus, Shechinah was in the Second Temple. Jesus declared it and so did Paul. Yet, most of the writers of the New Testament seem to have left this for granted, as if to say: "Of course Shechinah dwells in the Temple! Everybody knows that! He is part of Israel! Where else would He be?!"

Such brief and "obscure" disclosures should not surprise us since none of the New Testament writers would have been permitted to enter the Holy of Holies to stand before the Divine Presence. By the Law, only the High Priest was authorized for such a visit each year on the Day of Atonement (Leviticus 16:2).

In addition to the Scriptural statements, considerable Rabbinical comment in Midrash and Talmud indicates Shechinah was dwelling in the Second Temple. Although there is no mention of the specific return of Shechinah to the Temple in the Old Testament, considering the tone, the emotion, and spirit conveyed through these verses, it would seem that the Lord could hardly reject the pleas from Nehemiah and the People asking for His Blessing and Presence. (See Nehemiah, Chapters 8–12, especially 12:43.) One century earlier, Haggai was told to encourage Zerubbabel by Promising him: "I will fill this house with Glory" (Haggai 2:7). Talmud states that "forty years before the Temple was destroyed" (70 A.D. minus "forty" equals 30 A.D.!), "signs" in the Temple indicated that Shechinah was going to depart. (See "SIGNS AND WONDERS," Chapter 7.)

At this point it should be mentioned that what our English Bibles refer to as "The Glory of the Lord" has been identified by several names: "The Sheckinah (or Shechinah) Glory," from the Hebrew "Shechinah" meaning Divine Personage, The Father of the Triune God: "I AM," "Elohim," "Yahweh," "Jehovah," and others. The Shechinah (or Divine Presence) is the visible form of Almighty God Himself, who appeared to the Jews in the Sinai and dwelled in the Tabernacle and in the Temple in the Kodesh Ha-Kodashim (Holy of Holies). And, as also regarding God's Holy Spirit, the Shechinah or Glory should never be mentioned as "it" but as "He" since He is God, a personal being (not an inanimate object).

A cloud of doubt drifts into the minds of some Believers who will say, "But why do you refer to this Shechinah as 'He'? Is this a person?" Many Christians who have studied the Bible only from a traditional teaching position do not realize that "I AM" was "Yahweh" or "YHWH"—Almighty God Himself. They don't comprehend, or maybe accept, that God actually spoke to Moses and to the "children of Israel" and was visible to them as a "fire" and as a "cloud." Furthermore, many are not aware that the same "fire" or "cloud" was actually in the Temple—including during the time of Jesus.

Since very little interest exists in Christian teaching concerning Shechinah, most preachers and Sunday school teachers never seem to talk about the fact that the Divine Presence actually dwelled among the Jews! But, not among the Gentiles! This is difficult for many Christians to swallow. (You mean God loved "them" more than us?! And after what "they" did?!)

Most Christian believers, including myself (until recently), have never even thought much about the Glory of the Temple. Most Jewish worshipers are probably resigned to the fact that the Temple is gone, the Shechinah is gone, and they are now awaiting Messiah. Like the Gentiles, the Jewish people have not been told about this sad, remarkable, and glorious event. Scholars have known of it for many centuries, but now we "troops" can hear this fascinating story plus some additional facts that emerge as a result of recent archaelogical discoveries.

This event has important bearing on Biblical archaeology, Jewish evangelism, and even on the written Gospel of Jesus Christ. Much of the controversy arises because this story reveals certain facts and timing of events that are contrary to some of the "traditional" teaching in those areas.

Many believe that the Glory withdrew "sometime" before the time of Jesus or the Glory departed when "the veil was rent in twain." Others maintain that the Glory departed when Ezekiel "saw" Him withdraw and that He never resided in the Second Temple. But most ministers have never really thought about when or how this spectacular event occurred. As we will demonstrate, these traditional views are at great variance not only with each other, but also with recorded history. All three traditional concepts are at variance with recorded details of the Second Temple and, in some ways, even contradict Holy Scripture, including the Gospel of Jesus Christ.

Christian scholars have ignored (?), overlooked (?), or misunderstood (?) the Event, especially since it is recorded by Jewish historians. They are "suspicious" of Jewish historians, except those who recorded all the books of our Bible! Christian teachers suspect the credibility of the Talmud and Midrash because they are not Divinely inspired of the Holy Spirit. Of course not! But, that doesn't mean we should ignore such works. It would appear that very little, if any, of our most treasured secular literature was inspired by the Holy Spirit. We regard it as the works of man and separate the wheat from the chaff. We don't ignore it!

The history, tradition, and "Law" of the Talmud and other Judaica have many beautiful "pictures" of Christ that are tragically unseen by some, but have rich blessings for those who have eyes *and heart* to see within these writings.

Christians who are uninformed concerning Jewish Law and tradition not only are missing a lot of rich blessings, but also are missing great opportunities to more fully understand and appreciate the Gospel of Jesus Christ. Jesus was the greatest Jew of all time. Many of His parables and teachings were drawn directly from Jewish tradition, the "Law" and Judaic teaching of that time. Should not we obtain more blessings by learning more about the base from which our Lord teaches us?

Jesus is the "bridge" between Jews and Gentiles as well as the bridge between God and man. Jesus, of course, was crucified for claiming to be that "bridge." In discussing this story with friends, Jewish and Gentile, I have found that anyone who claims to understand and appreciate both Judaism and Christianity is apt to be misunderstood and condemned by many of both faiths. Paul was such a man.

Most of the Apostolic Fathers (all, save John) died horrible deaths as they tried to "bridge" both faiths. I certainly don't compare myself with any of those saints; however, I have already experienced some amount of "stress" from both sides as I attempt to point out the bridge revealed throughout this story. There are still a few Pharisees out there, even in our day, who absolutely close their minds (and hearts) to anything pertaining to the other faith—be it Judaism or Christianity.

Having reached the time of Jesus in reviewing the history of the Shechinah Glory, we can end the suspense and get on with the story. But wait! What does the Bible say about this event?

The only Biblical description of the departure of the Glory from the Temple was given as a vision to the prophet Ezekiel about 591 B.C. Ezekiel saw the Glory leave the Temple and go the Mount of Olives. (Ezekiel 10 and 11.)

Please keep in mind that Ezekiel was a prophet of the Babylonian captivity and therefore could not have seen the Glory "in person," besides, Ezekiel describes it as a vision (Ezekiel 11:24). So, did the departure of the Divine Presence occur before or after Ezekiel's vision? Was it a report or a prophecy? I had always assumed the vision had reported this to Ezekiel and that he was the only man who saw the event. I had also supposed that the Glory just sort of faded away one night while nobody was watching. After all, the Israelites had become sinful and were acting as if the Lord didn't exist (much less that He dwelled in their Holy Temple!). So it was easy for me to assume God would just "pout" (as I would have done) and go out the back, slam the door, and not come back. So, there! (I'd show 'em!)

I had even imagined a little scenario in which I speculated about the shock, dismay, yes . . . heart-break! felt by that one unfortunate High Priest the next Yom Kippur as he entered the Holy of Holies to plead before the Lord's Presence, offering atonement for Israel's sins, and: "Oi! . . . He's gone! . . . The Shechinah . . . Where is He? . . . Oh, NO! . . . The Lord's Presence has deserted his Holy Abode in His Temple . . . This is terrible! . . . What will I tell the King? . . . How can I tell the people?

But I was wrong—just not thinking. Because we know all prophecy in God's Word must be fulfilled. We also know (or should have known) God would not just "sneak-out" in a "pouting" farewell. (Not HIS Style!) Also, it is not likely that the brilliant light ("fire") or cloud would depart through the corridors and along the walls of the Temple and over to the Mount of Olives without having been observed by priests, attendants, and guards. This is exactly how Ezekiel described each movement in Chapters 10 and 11.

Thinking back on this now, it seems almost ridiculous to suppose Ezekiel was the only person who witnessed the departure of Almighty God from His Earthly dwelling. This Glorious Event had to have been seen by the entire populace, regardless of when it happened. Ezekiel was in Babylon when Solomon's Temple was destroyed. He saw the departure of the Glory of the Lord as a vision—a prophetic vision of a future event.

So, we know Ezekiel's prophecy (God's Word) had to be fulfilled. We know there was no Temple after 70 A.D. Therefore, there can now be no question that Shechinah departed, was seen "publicly" in fulfillment of Ezekiel's prophecy, and that it had to have occurred in either 586 B.C. or 70 A.D. Perhaps it was even fulfilled both times, although we have only the 70 A.D. Event as documented history.

Since Ezekiel was very precise about dates, we know his prophetic vision was given 591 B.C., about five years before the first Temple was destroyed. But this does not prove the fulfillment occurred only before Solomon's Temple was destroyed. Plenty of prophecies have had (or will have) more than one fulfillment.

Since this was a "public" event, did no one record this in some patriarchal document? This event must have made a profound, if not frightful, impression on those who witnessed it. Why haven't we heard about this in churches or synagogues or from Jewish history? (A very interesting question.)

Perhaps no one can answer this "why" question, but we can certainly see what has been recorded about the event and, as far as most of us are concerned, has been lying dormant for almost 2,000 years. It has certainly not been hidden—perhaps not even really suppressed—but certainly not "advertised" either. In the next chapter we shall discuss and describe this remarkable event as it actually happened.

2 The "Happening"

The question regarding "when?" and curiosity concerning the Jewish reaction to the withdrawal of Shechinah persistently came into my mind. For a few years, however, I was never able to locate any book on that subject in Christian, Jewish, or secular libraries. Then recently, in Professor Ernest L. Martin's scholarly and controversial book, *The Original Bible Restored*,[1] I came across his brief, though comprehensive reporting on this event.

There are three ancient documents that report the event, all of which are greatly respected and available. The renowned first century Jewish historian, Josephus, documented much of the story, but omitted (or was unaware of) some interesting details. Also, the Midrash, exegesis (a Hebrew Bible commentary), and the Babylonian Talmud (Jewish interpretation of The Law and Jewish tradition) provide a good description of most of the story, but omit some items reported by Josephus.

Thus, from the complementing statements of these three documents and supporting Scriptural statements, we can obtain a good accounting as to when it happened and how it happened. Then, with the benefits of Dr. Kaufman's discovery of the Temple site[7] and with some rudimentary surveying techniques, some interesting archaelogical observations surfaced. These subjects are discussed in

Chapter 4. (We should remember here at this same time, and indeed from 30 A.D. until 70 A.D., many other strange "signs" were reported by Josephus and by the Talmud. These events are discussed in Chapter 7.) The Jewish Talmud mentions the event, but does not provide as much detail as the other sources. The Talmud also takes what is considered a more "traditional" view, as we shall point out later.

Summarizing collectively and chronologically from Josephus, the Talmud, and the Midrash, the Shechinah withdrawal occurred as follows:

1. About 3 A.M. on the 8th day of Nisan (approximately April), 66 A.D., as several (perhaps twenty or so) priests were preparing, spiritually and physically, for the Passover Feast, the Divine Presence came out from His position inside the Holy of Holies and into the Holy Place and then to the threshold of the Temple. (Sketch 1)

2. Next, He moved back again into the Holy of Holies as if to bid farewell and to have just one more last look before leaving.

3. Next, He passed over the Altar of Sacrifice to the East Gate, all within the space of about half an hour. (Sketch 2)

4. From the gateway He went to the roof of the Temple and remained until the Feast of Pentecost.

5. On Pentecost (approximately June) He went back into the Temple just once more, weeping and speaking a saddened farewell, caressing His "Precious Vessel." Returning to "kiss" the walls and the Altar, He says "Good-bye, My Temple. Good-bye, My Precious Vessel. Good-bye!"

6. From the Temple, the Divine Presence moved through the East Gate and across the Kidron Valley, weeping and calling out to the "city" below (with many voices), "Let us remove hence."

7. The Divine Presence next arrived at the summit of the Mount of Olives and remained for 3½ years, quoting from Scripture and pleading to the Israelites (as "naughty" children) to repent and "return to the Lord." But they would not.

8. Finally, toward the end of the year (approximately December), 69 A.D., perhaps ironically during Chanukah, the Festival of Lights, the Divine "Light" ascended into Heaven from the summit of the Mount of Olives saying: "I will go back to My Place." (Hosea 5:15)

References:
Josephus: Wars, 6 / 290–300
Midrash, Lamentations (Eichah) Section 25 (Proems)
Talmud, Tractate Rosh Hashanah 31a.
(Also see Appendix A and Appendix B.)

Just a few months later, spring 70 A.D., the Roman Army under Titus began that final siege of Jerusalem,[5] which ended with destruction of the Temple and "scattering" of the Jewish people to "the four corners of the earth." (Isaiah 11:12)

Note:
Talmud presents a version somewhat different than the Midrash. Talmud Rosh Hashanah 31a says that after He appeared on the Mount of Olives, Shechinah "tarried for Israel in the wilderness six months in the hope that they would repent," but a lament is given over the fact that they did not repent. However, Talmud and Midrash both agree that Shechinah returned to "His Place."

But that isn't the end of this story. As a result of recent archaeological discoveries, some interesting facts emerge.

For many centuries it was believed that the site of the Temple was beneath The Dome of the Rock, No. 10 on the map of the Old City of Jerusalem. This created a difficult situation, because that mosque is the third most holy shrine for the religion of Islam (Muslim faith). Then, in 1978, Dr. Asher Kaufman[7] discovered the Foundation Stone of the Temple, the bedrock on which the Ark of the Covenant rested in the Holy of Holies, the threshing floor of Araunah (Ornan) the Jebusite. (II Samuel 24:24–25) The Temple site is now determined to be about 100 meters north of The Dome of the Rock.

Dr. Kaufman has shown that the East Gate of the Second Temple was *exactly* due east of "The Dome of the Tablets," the position of the Temple Foundation Stone. (See Sketch 1.) The Dome of the Tablets, (or sometimes "Dome of the Spirits") has been plotted on the Jerusalem map. Now, refer to the map and watch what happens. A straight line is extended from The Dome of the Tablets directly eastward to the summit of the Mount of Olives. This line indicates the reported farewell route of the Shechinah Glory according to Ezekiel, the Talmud, and the Midrash, also as supported by the Temple orientation determined by Dr. Kaufman.

Precisely at the intersection of the extended line at the Mount of Olives Summit is The Chapel of the Ascension (No. 7 on the map). Most of the local Jerusalem guides casually point to this site saying: "According to tradition, that is the place from which Jesus ascended into Heaven." But notice, the guides never mention that the Shechinah Glory also ascended to Heaven from this summit. (They haven't heard this story yet!) Could both have ascended from the same location?

The line, thus oriented and extended from "The Dome of the Tablets," continues across the summit of the Mount of Olives and passes through the Arab village, Et Tur (The Mountain). Now, if this analysis is correct, and if you stood at The Chapel of the Ascension or if you walked through the village of Et Tur along the line shown on the map, you might be treading on Holy Ground; for this is the area from which the Lord Jesus and Shechinah both ascended into Heaven.

Well, we don't really know the exact spot location for either Ascension, but we can be almost certain it was along the line shown. Why? We have Scriptural confirmation of this because such a route is outlined in Ezekiel's prophecy of the withdrawal. Chapters 10 and 11 of Ezekiel's narration indicate: "from the altar (of incense) to the threshold" and "from the threshold to the gate." A path so described passes directly along the center-line of the Temple, or directly eastward, continues to the summit of the Mount of Olives, and passes through The Chapel of the Ascension (see map of Old City, Sketches 7 and 8). The place of the Ascension of Jesus and for the Ascension of Shechinah is most likely the same point from which Jesus wept over Jerusalem (Matthew 23:37) and the same point where Messiah's feet will stand (again) on that Great Day when He returns in power and glory. "And His feet shall stand in that day upon the Mount of Olives...." (Zechariah 14:4)

Now, after almost 2,000 years, we are able to more accurately locate this "Holy Ground," the last earthly position of our Lord and our God. That position is somewhere along this line, at most only a few meters from the "traditional" site of Jesus' Ascension. We cannot prove this is the location, but . . . look at the odds!

So, it is possible for each of us to climb that summit today and,

The Dome of the Tablets

Recently identified location of the Holy of Holies in Solomon's Temple and in the Second Temple—identified by Dr. Asher Kaufman, 1978 (See Reference 7.)

The Threshing Floor

The Foundation Stone in the Holy of Holies, where the Ark of the Covenant rested in the Temple. This flat, level granite bedrock is sheltered by The Dome of the Tablets.

if elevated sufficiently for an unobstructed view of The Temple Mount, to align oneself due east of The Dome of the Tablets with the aid of a compass. Once aligned, you would probably be standing at or very near the point where those precious feet will stand on that Great Day.

But, if you are at Jerusalem on that Great Day, be sure you don't stand at that spot or anywhere along the line shown. Because the prophet Zechariah says:

> ... and the Mount of Olives shall cleave in the midst thereof toward the east and toward the west, and there shall be a great valley; and half of the mountain shall move toward the north and half of it toward the south.

With access to the geologic fault line detail of Mt. Olivet and the Kidron Valley, it would be interesting to compare such data with the east-west line plotted on the map as the apparent departure route of the Divine Presence. (More about this in Chapter 4.)

There are some interesting thoughts we should now consider. From the timing involved, considering the Ascension of Jesus in 30 A.D. and Ascension of the Glory of the Lord in 69 A.D., it is evident that the Jews of the first century knew this point on the Olivet Summit was the same point from which followers of Jesus had claimed the risen Savior had ascended into Heaven in 30 A.D. These same disciples could not have pre-selected that spot. But lo-and-behold, about forty years later, in 69 A.D., the Divine Presence apparently ascended from that very same point! And everyone has kept pretty quiet about that fact all these years.

It is important, also, for us to remember this departure was not a secretive movement. The Lord didn't just "sneak" away, sulking into the night! He went, displaying His Glory in full public view, beginning with a large group of priests in the Temple that first night. Then, in even more public "style," He remained on the Mount of Olives for three and one-half years. He must have been seen and, yes, even heard by literally thousands of Jews, Christians, and Romans.

With some help from Professor Martin, just try to appreciate the predicament of the Jewish people at that time. While in the Sinai wilderness they knew that when the "fire" moved from the Tabernacle, they were to move also. So, here they had just recently completed the Temple (64 A.D.) and now the Glory moves out! They couldn't just move the Temple! "But, what shall we do?! The Lord commanded us 'to move out' when He moved His great 'fire' or 'cloud.' What can we do?"

To the serious-minded, this meant that God was abandoning His abode in Jerusalem and leaving it behind. He even had left the gate open, leaving the Temple as a "gift" to whomever wished to have it. The Temple was now just another building without a tenant—no more sacred than any other building. Meanwhile, as all of this is happening, the Romans are marshaling legions for that final brutal siege, which was to result in unspeakable cruelties on both sides. So, is it any wonder this story has been shunned for all these years? This is the kind of story where, especially in those times, it was customary to kill the messenger! (I pray to be spared.)

All of these events must have been most puzzling, especially to the Jews: "Could that young Rabbi, who was put to death, actually have been the Son of God? Now Jerusalem and the Temple are destroyed. Are we abandoned? Our troubles are just beginning! We don't have time to argue or discuss 'signs'—we must survive!"

And survive they did—Jews and Christians. The wisest Jews and Christians saw the departure of the Divine Presence from their midst as a signal from God that they should "move out of the camp." These wisest, therefore, "scattered" themselves away from Roman Judea where hundreds of thousands of Judeans, Jews and Christians (it mattered naught to the legions), would, in a few more months, be slaughtered without restraint.

Professor Martin explains that this warning was, to a large measure, responsible for preserving Christianity and Judaism for their coming ordeals through the Church Age. Since the Romans didn't discriminate between Jews and Christians in the postsiege slaughter of 70 A.D., those Judeans who recognized this event as a warning "got out of camp" before the slaughter. And, since they were evidently "serious" believers, they were presumably selected by God to preserve both faiths in the ages to come. Satan, of course, would have destroyed both faiths at a single stroke (by the hand of Titus) but for the escape of these blessed "fruit," who were "harvested" via God's own warning. (See commentary note 9 on Midrash Eichah Narrative, Appendix B.)

Another thought we must develop involves the relationship of Jesus to the Temple. It is obvious, from Matthew 23:21 and from the Midrash and Josephus, that the Shechinah Glory dwelt in the Holy of Holies during the time of Jesus. Please consider for a moment that the New Testament records about four or five occasions when Jesus entered the Temple. Knowing the Divine Presence resided in the Temple must have been a great wonder to the disciples, especially to Peter, James, and John, after having seen Jesus transformed bodily and reflected in the Glory of God, The Father, at the Transfiguration; yet, they later were with Jesus when He entered the outer courts of the Temple where His Father's Presence also dwelt in the Holy of Holies!

Also, can we just imagine for a moment the indignation of the Jews at the claims of this man, Jesus of Nazareth? The Divine Presence (the Father) dwelled within the Holy of Holies at that time; and here is this "man" who claims, "I and my Father are one." (John 10:30) Jews had then, and still have today, no concept of more than one "God" although, at times, they called Him "Elohim" —indeed, a plural name. (Or how about, "Let us remove hence"?) Small wonder that unbelievers and legalizers called Jesus a blasphemer. How could this "man" be God, while everyone knew God was in the Holy of Holies. In fact, God is everywhere! How could He be God?

Christians have been smug in judging the Jewish people for missing/rejecting their Messiah. Awareness of some of the things discussed here could help us to be more understanding. How could this humble son of a carpenter be God?—Could he be that same God who could strike a man dead for coming uninvited into His Presence, into the Holy of Holies? If you had been a Judean at that time, what would you have thought?

It just might be appropriate to think about this for a while the next time we try to explain the Holy Trinity. Even the disciples did not understand the Trinity until after Pentecost 30 A.D. Perhaps some did not understand until after Chanukah 69 A.D. (More about this in Chapters 6 and 11.)

3 Impressions

The **withdrawal of** Shechinah from the Temple may qualify as the most important Biblical event since Pentecost. It is of importance, if for no other reason, because it is a well-documented fulfillment of Ezekiel's prophecy.

After learning of this event (1,900 years late), one must ask: "Why aren't Bible believers informed about this story? Why has this story been ignored for nearly 2,000 years, even though the event has been thoroughly documented by at least three respected and authoritative historical sources during that same length of time?"

There are no simple answers to these questions. Many people do not want to hear of this event because they do not want it to be true! They do not want to know that God continued to show compassion, patience, and mercy toward the Jews forty years after The Crucifixion. "After what they did, how could He show mercy?" Judge not lest ye be judged!

Most modern Christians have been misled while being brought up on what Vendyl Jones describes[4] as "Replacement Theology"—i.e., "God is finished with the Jews. The Old Testament is just 'Jewish' history. We need not concern ourselves with all those 'Jewish' Laws and customs, etc. We (Christians) are His new and 'faithful' Chosen People, etc., etc."

Such thinking might have originated during the Crusades. Nevertheless, many Christians today (especially since World War II) truly love God's Chosen People; but, unfortunately, many are just not interested in Judaism, Jewish history, tradition, archaeology, etc., unless it pertains directly to Jesus.

If we really study our Bibles, we will come to realize that some knowledge of Judaism is important to all Christians, because much of the symbolism in Jewish rites, feasts, traditions, etc., pertains to Messiah. Much of the Old Testament Law (Torah), all of the Feasts of Jehovah, and most prophecy is, of course, Christ-centered and is therefore important to all Christians and should not be ignored.

Many modern Jewish people have very weak hopes concerning their Messiah. (Just as many professed Christians do not believe Jesus is really going to come back to this earth.) Besides, the departure of the Lord's Presence from their midst just before desolation came upon them was just not a very positive occasion for the Jewish people. One can easily understand why they might not wish to call attention to the event—if they knew about it.

Even more understandable is the Jewish resistance to anything "Christian." The Shechinah Event was a Jewish event. How can we say it related to Christianity? Jewish scholars were well aware this happened after The Crucifixion and that it could be interpreted as a judgment against them. They were also aware of the obvious implications of the fact that Jesus and Shechinah both ascended from Olivet summit. Traditional Jews do not want to hear this! Neither do the Jews want Christians to throw this in their faces to remind them of why it happened. So, they have not told this story.

The Christian objection to this story is a bit more complex and more difficult to understand. Most Christians view any "religious" information with suspicion unless that specific item is mentioned in the Holy Bible. Further, they paradoxically choose to ignore any Jewish information written after The Crucifixion, yet they must surely revere highly the New Testament which was definitely written by Jews after The Crucifixion.

At least three different traditional versions of the Shechinah departure have been taught within Christianity, because few, apparently, are willing to accept what Jewish historians (and Scripture!) have related. Nor are any of these groups willing to agree with any of the others, primarily because all of these theories are merely based on opinion. None of them has even one shred of evidence as a basis. But, as we know, tradition is a powerful force and is not easily set aside or overcome.

- The most popular conservative/fundamentalist/evangelical view has been that Ezekiel "saw" the Glory withdraw before Solomon's Temple was destroyed by the Babylonians. They add that since the Lord was so displeased with the decadence of the Jews, He never returned His Divine Presence to reside in the Second Temple. Ignoring that Scripture (Zech. 1:16) says He did reside, they base their argument on a claim that no known record exists. They assume, therefore, He did not return. This group further insists that God would never have "defiled" Himself by residing in "Herod's" Temple and that Jesus called it "a den of thieves."

- Liberal Christianity just never thought much about this. They appear to assume the Shechinah maybe just sort of "drifted away."

- Middle-of-the-road Christianity seems to hold to the belief that the Glory of the Lord left the Temple when "the veil was rent in twain."

There may be even a few more "theories" bouncing around out there. However, all three of these groups have formulated these concepts from their own imaginations, based on assumptions, without any attention to historical accounts, eye-witness descriptions, or literal statements from Scripture.

Scholars of Christian theology then, have virtually ignored the Talmud and Midrash and have formulated three completely different versions of the Shechinah Withdrawal. All three versions are based on assumptions; none agrees in any way with any other version and none is supported by literal Scripture or by recorded history. The documented Jewish version is supported by both of these. It was written by "Jews" and the Jewish story says the Christian theologians are mistaken. Some Christians just don't want to hear this.

In summary, we see that Jews don't want to hear (even from Jewish historians) a story that says the Lord "scolded" them because they failed to recognize their Messiah. Christians don't want to hear a story (especially from Jewish historians) that says their Christian version is totally in error. Both groups are, therefore, understandably embarrassed and have withheld and/or suppressed information about this beautiful and Holy Event from the grass-roots laity of their "flocks."

In modern times this might be called a "cover-up," but I do not believe modern Jewish or Christian scholars are intentionally suppressing this story. More likely it is that they have been hearing their own "traditional" versions for so many centuries that any "new" information just cannot penetrate that traditional prejudice.

This human appetite for tradition is just one of several manifestations of man's resistance to "change." This attitude and tendency probably has been with us since man first walked this planet. Human adherence to traditional concepts is a very powerful and emotional trait. It must be respected even when we assail it in order to let truth prevail.

The renowned Roman poet of the first century, Ovid, has said:

> Nothing is stronger than custom (i.e., tradition).

Tradition is still at least as strong as it was in Ovid's time; however, we moderns have much more accumulated information to evaluate in our quest for TRUTH than did those of earlier societies. The data presented in this work has not really been "hidden." We just haven't been looking for the truth. Instead, we have been content to take the easier course by "sticking" with the traditional Bible stories.

I realize I am getting into a perilous situation by challenging "Bible stories." However, I am challenging them on the foundation of what Scripture says, instead of what "everybody has been telling us it says." Moreover, we shall present historical and physical (archaeological) evidence that agrees with Scripture, whereas the traditional stories cannot be supported either by Scripture or by the physical evidence. As you read this account, we pray that you will see what Brother Ovid failed to see—that Scripture and truth are stronger than tradition or custom. Our Lord wants us never to settle for less than the truth.

Apparently the Lord just wasn't ready for us to know all of these things before now—(because we weren't ready?). But, now . . . who knows? Could it be that now He is preparing "Believers" among His people for His "imminent" arrival at the summit of the Mount of Olives?

> And in that day His feet will stand on the Mount of Olives. . . .
>
> Zechariah 14:4

> ... they will look upon Me whom they have pierced and they will mourn for Him, as one mourns for an only son. ...
>
> Zechariah 12:10
>
> And one will say to Him, "What are these wounds in your hands?" Then He will say, "Those with which I was wounded in the house of my friends."
>
> Zechariah 13:6

(Above verses quoted from NASB.)

Some skeptics and critics will say, "Well, this is all very interesting, but how do we know it's true?" Indeed, this is not just another "Indiana Jones" story. (But it would certainly be terrific for a movie!) My favorite answer to this criticism is provided by the Rabbis of the first and second century in the Midrash texts. These men were writing a commentary on the Book of Lamentations. Their lament was certainly appropriate in light of the fulfillment of Israel's tragic destiny as foretold by many of their prophets. It is evident that the Rabbis recognized the tragedy of this event, not only for unrepenting Israel, but also in the pathos seen and heard in the Lord's movements and in His voice(s).

Thus, can anyone seriously believe those Rabbis "invented" this tragic drama just as "entertainment" for future Jewish generations to "enjoy?" Does anyone seriously suggest that the Rabbis of 100–200 A.D. would intentionally select, for the Glory Ascent, the very same site that had already been recorded in New Testament writings for the Ascension of Jesus of Nazareth?

Rather, it seems surprising they recorded this event at all. One might think they would have preferred to forget all about it. But how could they possibly "just forget about it"? You've got to be kidding! Added to this is their dedication to detail—right down to each and every movement of the Divine Presence as well as His pleadings and farewell remarks. (They *couldn't* forget it.)

There was always, of course, a reviewing and regulatory authority to determine what was accepted for such documents as the Midrash, Talmud, etc. If the story was not true, witnessed by several other Rabbis and/or persons of integrity, this material would have been rejected and those Rabbis contributing such a "fish story" would have been discredited, dishonored, or possibly even "defrocked." It is no small wonder that modern Judaism has avoided /

ignored this story; both in their own synagogues and in general publication. However, it surely must have been intended to be related to all of us, eventually, as a "lesson" from the Lord.

It is my opinion that this story shows two basic lessons from God to be noticed and studied by *both* Christians and Jews:

> Christians: God did indeed forgive the Jews (and the rest of us) at the Cross. He did not terminate His Everlasting Covenant with His Chosen People. Rather, He fulfilled another Promise to them; which most of them failed to recognize and accept, because to a large extent they were (and are) "blinded" by tradition. Perhaps the Lord may forgive Jews for failing to recognize Jesus as Messiah. But, He will not forgive their sins unless they yearn earnestly for Messiah and observe the Law that surely points to His sacrificial death and blood offering for their sins.

> Jews: The Lord gave another "sign" in the fact that His Divine Presence ascended from the same place at which the earliest Jewish followers of Y'shua ben Yosef of Nazareth witnessed His Ascension forty years earlier. He did not cut you off from Himself at the death of His Innocent, as many Christians have been saying for centuries in order to justify their persecution of your people. But, He did "go back to His Place" and He has smitten and scattered you for almost "two days"; but not before He spoke to you again, just as He did through the "fire" and the "cloud" during the Exodus from Egypt.

We must especially take notice of the importance of this event to Jews and Christians in that the most faithful and obedient of both faiths were warned by this startling Event to "get out of camp" before the destruction of Jerusalem and the Temple. Both groups of serious Believers were obedient to God's Word in the command given in Exodus 40:36–38, knowing that when the "fire" or the "cloud" withdrew from the Tabernacle, they were to move "the camp." This warning did much to preserve those who deserved to survive the slaughter to follow in 70 A.D. as well as guide both "flocks" through the Church Age.

Indeed, we see a tragic irony in that some of both groups knew, at that time, that the Shechinah Withdrawal had a personal meaning for each of them. Bittersweet irony emerges in this day as neither group wants to hear this story. Both sides need to know these truths. It is becoming increasingly important that Jews and Christians draw closer together against the worldly onslaughts of Satanism, anti-Judaism, Humanism and a general decline of so-called Judeo-Christian ethics.

Truly, this story brings about a convergence of Judaism and Christianity "at a point"; yes, both figuratively and literally (on the Mount of Olives). But it should cause us to question ourselves once more: "WHY does God even bother with us? WHY does He go to so much trouble to get through to us? He doesn't need us. We need Him! Why should He weep and lament over leaving His earthly abode?" Again, why should God even concern Himself over us?

Part of the answer is, of course, that God not only has infinite power and infinite riches: He also has infinite patience, infinite wisdom, and infinite time. He gives infinite love and infinite mercy. He gives all this to us, asking nothing from us but our love for Him and for each other. He gives all things to us despite our persistent inclination and surrender to every kind of sin. In fact, God can do no less than "infinity" in anything. God is all!

4 Archaeological Comments

As a somewhat seasoned engineer, Bible student, eschatology student, and Biblical archaeology "enthusiast," I was immediately inspired upon first reading of Dr. Kaufman's discovery of the Temple site.⁷ Having recently been intrigued by Ezekiel's prophecy concerning the departure of the Shechinah Glory, I plotted a line on my Jerusalem tourist map to see just where a line, passing due east from the Dome of the Tablets, would intersect at the summit of the Mount of Olives. I was not surprised when this extended line passed straight through The Chapel of the Ascension at the summit of the Mount of Olives. Notably, however, we must surely be impressed by the fact that—after two millennia—this "traditional" position for Jesus' Ascension has remained intact.

Even so, just in the past few years, a perplexing thought has persistently entered my mind: "When, where, how, and what ever happened to the Shechinah Glory?" The answers to those questions (although few persons know of it) are of course a matter of record as we have already discussed. But, there is much more—and the material and thoughts developed are of such detail that it was considered better to present these detailed discussions separately from the main story. Additionally, there was the consideration that too much detail would dilute the main story—which, I believe, urgently needs to be heard by "the man on the street."

The quest for answers began first with The Holy Bible (and a concordance) and next, the library, for some searching through *Encyclopedia Judaica and The Universal Jewish Encyclopedia*, as well as the Talmud and other Judaica. Having become interested in the traditions of Jewish rites (weddings, purification, feasts, etc.), I also took note of anything along that line, especially the sacrifice of the Red Heifer. This interest was stirred initially by reading about Reverend Vendyl Jones' search for the urn containing the Red Heifer ashes.

Meanwhile, for reasons known only to God, I finally decided to discipline myself to read a book on entirely different subjects, which I had received months earlier as a gift from an evangelical scholar. My quest regarding the Shechinah Glory then received a "quantum jump." Professor Martin opened the way for this whole story to fit together by revealing the documentation of the departure of the Glory of the Lord from the Second Temple.[1] Here, the details relating to Biblical archaeology are presented, because this information provides important background to the overall discussion of the event.

ASSUMPTIONS

The analysis made here concerning the line of travel for the departure of the Divine Presence from the Temple is based on the following assumptions. However, presented later in this discussion are some arguments regarding these assumptions and possible conclusions from the analysis. I hope that scholars will have a "field-day" in criticism of this discussion, although, I don't intend any conceit by flattering myself with such an expectation. I sincerely hope and pray that such scholars will improve the analysis of this unheralded but historic event. The assumptions are:

1. Facts based on Biblical references used in this analysis are reliable as the infallible Word of God.

2. The records provided by Flavius Josephus, the Midrash, and Talmud are reliable. (See Appendices A, B, and C.)

3. The locations of the Foundation Stone and the orientation of the Second Temple as discovered by Dr. Asher Kaufman[7] are accurate.

4. The Divine Presence moved along a straight line extending from the Foundation Stone, along the center axis of the Temple, through the east gate of the Temple, and on to the summit of Mt. Olivet. (See Sketches 1 and 6.)

5. The surveyed map locations of the Dome of the Tablets and the Chapel of the Ascension are accurate.

THE OPEN GATE

The description by Josephus[2] of the mysterious opening of the east Temple gate (Sketch 2) has interesting areas for archaeological investigation as well as theological interest.

Josephus (Appendix A) explains: "at the sixth hour of the night" (about midnight) this gate "was seen to open of its own accord." He expresses a certain amount of wonder at this by describing, in some detail, the gate hinge structure and floor mounting and that it "had been with difficulty shut by twenty men." One of my friends, upon first hearing of this, immediately remarked, "Just like He rolled away the stone." (Read more about the miracle of this gate in Chapter 7.)

It would seem that theological interest could be addressed from some archaeological (and engineering) fact-finding. Specifically, it would be interesting to find:

(a) Detailed sketches of this "brass" gate. Was it ornate? What figures or decor were present? What of its construction, thickness, dimensions, etc.? Such information should be stimulating both to engineering and to archaeological minds; especially with respect to this incident.

(b) The description: "... rested upon a basis armed with iron, and had bolts fastened very deep into the firm floor, which was there made of one entire stone..." invites at least one archaeological search. Could those "very deep" (and likely, very large) bolt holes be visible even now in the bedrock of the Temple Mount somewhere on a line east of the Dome of the Tablets?

(c) If such details are available from ancient Jewish or Roman writings and/or from archaeological study, a few engineering calculations for weight, size, friction, etc., would give better understanding as to why twenty men closed it "with difficulty." Such data would provide means for investigating the "great noise of its turning hinges," which is reported in the Talmud. Since only a few measurements are available concerning the gates and the courts of the Second Temple (Sketch 7), it is not certain whether this "one entire stone" was bedrock or a large slab floor piece at this entrance. Without more detailed information, on the basis of sound engineering and construction practice I prefer the bedrock option. But this one will, of course, have to wait, because the present Muslim authorities, who have jurisdiction over the Temple Mount, would prohibit even a "peek" at that bedrock.

What "City"?

There was at first some confusion (at least for myself) regarding just what was considered to be the "city" mentioned by the prophets Ezekiel and Micah. (See comments in Appendix B.) Professor Martin explains[12] that because of crowding of Jerusalem's overnight accommodations during feast days, and in order to enable pilgrims to remain within the Talmudic travel laws on the Sabbath, the official city boundaries were extended "a Sabbath day's journey" (Acts 1:12), 2,000 cubits, or about $^1/_2$ or $^2/_3$ of a mile from the Temple, depending upon actual cubit measurement. (See "Oregano & Red Stuff.") There is perhaps a more definite answer to this query within the intricacies of Talmudic Law dissertations—and, therefore, it may or may not be applicable in this question.

Where Was the "Miphkad Altar"?

According to an article in *The Jerusalem Post*,[11] Dr. Asher Kaufman stated that part of his search for the Temple site involved reasoning from Ezekiel 8:16, that the site of the Red Heifer sacrifices (on the western slope of Mt. Olivet) might offer a clue toward locating the Temple. It didn't work out that way, because to this day the Red Heifer site (or Miphkad Altar) is known only in an approximate way. This most important sacrifice was commanded in Numbers, Chapter 19.

The name "Miphkad" is the Hebrew word meaning an assembly or a group, but more specifically a "muster"; i.e., an "accounting." This particular definition of the term may be reflected in the Law that pertains to the ritual of the burning of the Red Heifer. Parah

3:10 requires the High Priest to hold up each of the three materials to be tossed into the fire and to ask the bystanders: "Is this cedarwood?" and repeat: "Is this cedarwood?" Each time the crowd replies, "Yea." The Priest then continues by asking, two times: "Is this hyssop?" and then: "Is this crimson wool?" The group replies each time, "Yea." In this way the materials that must be added to make the burning complete have been, as they say, "mustered." Hence, the name "Miphkad."

Encyclopedia Judaica, under "Mount of Olives," estimates that this sacrifice site was located "somewhere above Absalom's Pillar" (No. 14 on the Jerusalem map in the Kidron Valley). It appears that a somewhat more specific location for this altar can be determined through application of some elementary geometric principles along with a detailed study of Talmudic Law and other ancient records. Talmud, Middoth 2:4, states that all the Temple walls were built high except the eastern wall, which was lower than all the others so as not to obstruct the priest's view of the Sanctuary when burning the Red Heifer at the top of the Mount of Olives. The same observation is also recorded in the tractate Yoma 16a. Thus, location of the Miphkad Altar at Olivet summit is verified to a large extent by application of Judaic Law plus the archaeological and geometric principles discussed in this study.

It can be seen from the map that the locale just described should be along the line extended from Dr. Kaufman's Temple site to the Olivet summit. The Red Heifer site, then, can perhaps be located by examining soil samples (see Oregano & Red Stuff) along the line described, if this can be done without desecrating graves. The aforementioned conclusion is, of course, right in line with Dr. Kaufman's Biblical observation. According to Middoth 2:4, the priest standing at the Miphkad Altar on Olivet, by "directing his gaze carefully," must be able to look across the Kidron Valley, over the City Wall, over the Beautiful Gate, and through the East Gate of the Sanctuary and see the doors of the H'ekhal as he sprinkles the heifer's blood "directly before the Tabernacle . . . seven times."

This implies that a rather small sight-picture required the priest to "direct his gaze carefully" in order to see the doors of the H'ekhal through the East Gate. The *Universal Jewish Encyclopedia*[9] and Josephus indicate that no lintel rested across the top of the Beautiful Gate and that it had no "doors." In other words, it was really just an opening in the outer wall, rather than a "gate," per se. The eastern gate in the city wall was much lower than the Temple gates. (See [6] and Sketch 4.)

In the interest of scholarly attention to detail and honesty it should be noted that Middoth 2:4 neglected to mention that the Veil was drawn across the doors at the front of the H'ekhal. The priest, therefore, would actually be looking to see the Veil, not the doors, but they probably just presumed everyone already knew that!

We have observed from Middoth 2:4 that the High Priest must "direct his gaze carefully" to be able to see the front of the H'ekhal (and the Veil) as he stands at the Miphkad Altar "on the top of the Mount of Olives." All of this means that careful positioning is required for the High Priest during the Red Heifer sacrifices in order that he will be able to see the Veil through a rather small viewing aperture. This "tight" aperture (or "sight picture") results because the view is directed through the open doors of Nicanor's Gate or East Gate. (See Sketches 2, 3, 4, 5.)

Field of view is reduced because the viewer is at a much greater distance from the gate than the Veil is from the gate, at a ratio of approximately 14 to 1. (See Sketch 5.) The Veil is almost 30 feet wide. Then, using proportions from similar triangles, this means an observer with a 14:1 aperture is viewing at a very small angle of vision through the gate. The priest must therefore be located within a distance of 8.54 ft. (2.50 meters) left or right of the center axis, since the gate opening (or aperture) is about 45 feet wide. Moreover, Talmud teaches us that the Rabbis were not "sloppy" or so careless as to permit the Veil to appear off-center. The priest must therefore be standing where he will see the Veil centered perfectly within the gate opening. From this we can observe that the priest must not be pacing back and forth. He must stand in place in order to "direct his gaze carefully."

Further evidence from Talmud, Parah 4:2, alludes to a requirement for strict precision on the part of the High Priest while standing at the Miphkad Altar at the burning. The priest is commanded to dip his finger in the heifer's blood and sprinkle the blood directly toward the Tabernacle. He is required to do this exactly seven times. If he forgets to dip his finger, if he loses count of the sprinkles, if he flinches or miscasts off to left or right, if he loses his balance, stumbles, falters, or whatever, the whole ritual is "invalid." The whole deal is off! Back to square-one! A new heifer—everything!

Considering the severity of the Law in this sacrifice, it is to be expected that the priest must also have a perfect sight-picture of the Veil as he sprinkles, while he must "direct his gaze carefully to see the door of the H'ekhal." (Middoth 2:4) Remember, it says "directly before the Tabernacle" or it is back to square-one!

Using dimensions of Nicanor's Gate and the Veil as provided in the Talmud and by Josephus, it might be feasible to survey the location of the Miphkad Altar within just a few meters. We have also explained that this may be very near the position of The Cross of Jesus.

So, again—knowing elevations of the intervening gates along the line-of-sight, using basic surveying methods, we could re-create the "sight-picture" that the priest would have had while facing the Temple and standing at the Miphkad Altar near Olivet summit. Since the burning took place "without the camp" (2,000 cubits), it had to be near Olivet summit. (See Sketch 5.) Such a sight-picture would result when viewed from Olivet just below the summit and directly above Gethsemane. Professor Martin[12] suggests that Gethsemane of 30 A.D. was much nearer that summit than the present olive grove bearing that name. If this conclusion is valid, some intriguing theological questions emerge; not the least of which is: WHY did Jesus pray at Gethsemane? When we answer *this* question, it appears even more likely that Prof. Martin's conclusion is correct. (See "Why Gethsemane?" in Chapter 5.)

Nevertheless, another Gospel question arises, which may provide additional insight concerning the location of this important sacrifice. Since the Veil was several meters back under the overhanging Portico (porch) of the Temple, it would be difficult to see the Veil from Olivet summit during any hour at which the Veil would be in the shade. So, at what hour would the Red Heifer burning be planned in order that the High Priest could see the Veil as he sprinkled the heifer's blood "directly before the Tabernacle?"

Most tourists visiting Jerusalem are eager to get a snapshot (or a video) of the Old City before their luggage is even delivered to the room. However, those who are patient enough to wait for their tour guide to schedule that marvelous sight will find that he has wisely scheduled a trip to Olivet summit for the next morning—first thing! The reason is, of course, from that vantage at that time the Old City, the Dome of the Rock, the East Wall, etc., will be painted in bright, golden sunlight just as the sun rises over Olivet summit behind their backs.

In fact, the best "photo-opportunity" occurs at about 9 A.M. when the earliest and best light appears after burning off the early morning mountain haze. This is also about the only time when the priest would be able to see the Veil through the open East Gate. As we explained earlier, in saying that the High Priest must "direct his

Temple Mount Viewed from the Chapel of the Ascension

The Dome of the Tablets stands to the right to the Dome of the Rock about one-hundred meters. It is standing just in front of the four arches in the center of the picture.

Could this be the Miphkad Altar Site?

The flat, level clearing in the midst of rugged terrain and thick undergrowth was located using crude surveying techniques, just below Olivet summit and on-line with the Chapel of the Ascension and the Dome of the Tablets. The actual location of that sacred place must be only a few meters from this spot.

gaze carefully" to see the door of the H'ekhal, this implies that he is "sighting" through a rather small opening.

This implied situation, then, has been somewhat verified by our examination of gate details and topography of Olivet and the Temple Mount. The sun must not be too high or the Veil is shaded by the Portico above—too low and it becomes shaded by the lintel across the top of the East Gate in front. Ideally then, the sun should be up at about a 45 degree angle at 9 A.M., beaming into the court in front of the Temple. (See Sketches 3, 4, 5.)

Further, he would need to select a time of year when the sun would be directly behind him; i.e., due east. This was necessary in order that he would have the sun's rays passing straight through the East Gate and against the Veil under the Portico. Otherwise, if he chose to conduct this rite in, say, December—the sun would be too far to the south; or in June—too far in the north. Thus, in either case the Veil would be partially shaded on the right or left by the wall extending to the sides of the East Gate. Then yes, the sun must be directly behind him and in good weather—preferably in the spring rather than in autumn—actually at the time of the Vernal Equinox.

All this alignment in order to avoid a shadow is not based upon any frivolous principle. It would have been considered "profane" to have "sprinkled the blood" while a shadow was being cast on the Veil or even across the steps approaching the H'ekhal entrance. (See Sketches 2, 3, 4, 5.) (There is much "hidden" in this picture that will be discussed in later chapters.)

We can now observe, from all this precision, that the designers and architects who built the Second Temple followed the Law by very "religiously" adhering to the geometric / astronomical / Talmudic requirements noted here. The prophet Ezekiel detailed many other specifications that were implemented in the Second Temple and will be discussed later in Chapter 6.

Additional information from Talmud further underlines the precise location, timing, and opportunity one must have had in order to see the Veil. The Mishnah of tractate Shekalim 8:4 details that each time a new Veil was woven (twice a year) it was displayed atop the Temple colonnade roof "so that the people might behold its fair workmanship." Here, "the people," so considered were: women and girls, underage lads, and of course, all lepers. These had limited chance to see this beautiful curtain, because none of these would ever be permitted to tread beyond Nicanor's Gate. They might be able to crane their necks and push through the crowds to "peek" at times when the gate was open, as it was on Sabbaths, New Moons, and Feasts. However, we know the Veil would be at least partially shaded unless one gained this opportunity at around 9 o'clock in the morning.

The Miphkad Altar was also "off limits" because it was "a clean place." All of these "people" had their only good opportunity to see this "fair workmanship" from almost any location on the western slope of the Mount of Olives, but only twice per year and not while the Veil was hanging in its rightful place before the Temple doors. This semiannual display also provided the only opportunity for "strangers" (Gentiles) to behold Israel's beautiful curtain.

From the analysis I have been able to perform to date with the present dimensional data, it appears that the priest would be able to see the full forty-cubit height of the Veil. According to analysis of the elevation profiles available, Sketches 3, 4, 5, and 7, the full Veil would be visible through the gate and beneath the lintel across the top as viewed from Olivet summit at a range of about 2,000 cubits. However, more work is needed in this area before any conclusion can be formed concerning the priest's exact "sight picture" when viewed from the vantage point described.

Professor Martin has stated his conclusion, placing the Red Heifer site at the Olivet summit. Nevertheless, I would like to check it out via the "sight-picture" technique earlier described. If the elevations of the Temple walls and portals were known with infallible accuracy and detail relative to the Dome of the Tablets, it would be relatively simple to "sight-it-in" in much the same way as a survey instrument operator would do.

Who Shut Which Gate?

> Then the man brought me back to the outer gate of the sanctuary, the one facing east, and it was shut. It must not be opened; no one may enter through it. It is to remain shut because the Lord, the God of Israel, has entered through it. The prince himself is the only one who may sit inside the gateway to eat in the presence of the Lord. He is to enter by the portico of the gateway and go out the same way.
> Ezekiel 44:1–3 (New International Version)

Some prophetic scholars, at least until James Fleming's discovery,[6] have pointed to Suleiman the Magnificent as the one who (unwittingly) fulfilled one of Ezekiel's best-known prophecies; because

Suleiman ordered the eastern gate (Golden Gate) to the City mortared shut when he heard of the prophecy that the Jewish Messiah would enter through that gate.

Such teaching is seen to be incorrect, because of the Scriptural identification of the gate in the prophecy. The "gate" to be shut was the outer gate of the sanctuary. Obviously this was not the gate in the city wall, but more likely it was Nicanor's Gate, the immense brass (or bronze) gate to the Temple (sanctuary) court. This gate was probably "shut" when the Roman soldiers razed the Temple, 70 A.D. (Read much more about this prophecy in Chapter 6.)

Dr. James Fleming discovered what appears to be the arch of a gate in an earlier wall, which is directly beneath the sixteenth-century Suleiman's Gate (Golden Gate) in the outer wall of the City. (In our discussion we shall refer to this as the "City Wall.") Fleming's discovery resulted when the rain-softened soil gave way beneath his feet, dropping him a few meters down into a Muslim grave just outside of Suleiman's gate in the City Wall. It is likely that top remnants of Fleming's wall were actually used as the foundation for the present City Wall. (See Sketch 4.)

It is possible that some teachers may now speculate, albeit incorrectly, that Fleming's "Lower Gate" may be "the gate that was shut." Further confusion exists concerning which wall was built low, in order that the High Priest would have a clear view of the front of the H'ekhal as he sprinkled the Heifer's blood. The footnotes of Middoth 2:4 confirm that three walls stood between the Holy of Holies and the Mount of Olives: (1) the east wall of the Temple Court, (2) the east wall of the court of Women, and (3) the City Wall. (See Sketch 5.) Since all these gates and walls are so closely related, and since they are important to this study, some clarification is necessary to eliminate or reduce the confusion.

First, since the prophecy said "the outer gate of the sanctuary" would be shut, this could not be the gate in the City Wall because that was not the outer wall of the sanctuary. Also, the reference would not be to the gate in the outer wall of the Temple courts, i.e., "The Beautiful Gate," because this was an opening into the Court of Women. According to Josephus, there were no "doors" in that gate and there was no "portico" above it. The prophecy must therefore refer to the East Gate of the Temple, which was also called Nicanor's Gate, as already stated.

Continuing, if James Fleming indeed saw the top portion of the first-century City Wall, then the wall was already much too low to have caused any obstruction of the High Priest's view. Most scholars agree that even the present City Wall would have to be much taller to pose that kind of problem. However, this fact led at least one scholar, F. J. Hollis (referenced in the footnotes of Middoth 2:4), to conclude that the wall between the Court of Women and the Court of the Israelites was built lower to provide the view from Olivet.

However, that wall could not be a factor in this problem, because Nicanor's Gate in that wall would have been opened so the Priest could see the H'ekhal. The wall that was lower then, was the east wall of the Court of Women. This may also be the reason there were no "doors" and there was no lintel over the Beautiful Gate. (See Sketches 2 and 5.)

In summary, perhaps the clearest settlement of this matter is found in the Mishnah of Middoth 4:2, where this lower wall is identified to be the east wall of the Court of Women, since that wall bounded the easternmost limits of the Temple. (See Sketches 1, 2, 3, 4, 5, and 7.)

Obviously, not all archaeologists and theologians agree with Prof. Kaufman's conclusions. Indeed, it is most difficult to persuade against the traditional belief that the Dome of the Rock (Arabic: *es-Sakhra*) is the Temple site. This belief has been in place for at least thirteen centuries and persists even today among some of our most respected scholars, despite the facts involved.

Although Kaufman's proposal cannot yet be proved incontrovertibly, it is in fact easy to disprove any claim for *es-Sakhra* as that Holy Place, based solely on the Talmudic laws pertaining to burning of the Red Heifer and considering simple geometric specifications for the Temple.

Briefly, the geometry of the Temple courts and gates, in concert with the Law and with the contour topography of Olivet and the Temple Mount, produce a profile criteria for this landscape that is undeniable. The priest at Olivet summit *must see the Veil* at the door of the Temple as he sprinkles the Heifer's blood. If the priest stood east of *es-Sakhra* at one Sabbath Limit from that rock, he would not be able to view the Veil, simply because he would be too far over the brow of the hill and behind Olivet. There is considerable geological evidence (tombs, etc.) indicating that this region of the Olivet profile has not been altered significantly during the past 1,900 years. The geometry we see today is therefore essentially the same as it was during the first century.

Moreover, the probable Eastern Gate of the first-century City Wall; i.e., Fleming's "Lower Arch," is several meters north of a Temple axis as proposed through *es-Sakhra*, whereas, Fleming's arch is directly east of the Dome of the Tablets, the location of the Holy of Holies as proposed by Prof. Kaufman.

There are other factors in the category of common sense that indicate against *es-Sakhra* as the Holy of Holies. The most glaring of these is the fact that the Holy of Holies was in fact "a threshing floor," (II Chron. 2:1) and there is not a level place on *es-Sakhra* much larger than a man's hand. In its present configuration, at least, it could never be considered as "a threshing floor." Contrastingly however, the Dome of the Tablets is a flat, level granite slab of at least six feet in diameter. There can be no denying—in every way, it resembles "a threshing floor!"

Now, from literal interpretation of Scripture, from archaeology, from Jewish historical data, from Temple Mount / Olivet topography, and from Jim Fleming's "fortunate accident," Suleiman's Gate is not the gate the prophet was writing about. And Suleiman didn't shut the gate—God shut it, centuries before Suleiman, "because the Lord had entered through it."

Applying some elementary logic: The gate has been shut since 70 A.D.; therefore, the God of Israel (Messiah) must have "entered through it" before the gate was shut. It shouldn't take anybody very long to come up with a pretty good guess as to WHO that was and when HE "entered through it." Some additional signs were given in the Temple "forty years before the destruction of the Temple," according to the Talmud. (See Chapter 7, "Signs and Wonders.")

OREGANO & RED STUFF

> And the priest shall take cedar wood, and hyssop, and scarlet and cast it into the midst of the burning of the heifer.
>
> (Numbers 19:6)

Most laymen can readily identify cedar, but what is "hyssop?" The dictionary, by several routes, will eventually tell us the hyssop is an oily herb and is related through various botanical "families" to oregano. The "oregano connection" is, in fact, revealed in the botanical Latin name for this ignominious weed: "Origanum syriacum."

It would be interesting to know more about this hyssop plant, which was (and perhaps is yet) indigenous to the Sinai wilderness and to Israel. (See reference 18.) There must be some Biblical and /

or practical reason for the command to use hyssop. More "Law" and detail is given regarding this lowly plant in the Red Heifer sacrifice than is presented for any of the other materials used in that most important Holy rite of Judaism. In Jewish tradition, the "scroungy" hyssop is a symbol of humility and the stately Lebanon cedar is a symbol for haughtiness.

The scarlet (or crimson) was red wool, apparently dyed or dipped in some sort of material that produced red smoke when incinerated; and this was evidently intended to represent blood. The Red Heifer itself—pure, un-yoked, innocent, and "without blemish"—of course, is interpreted by many Christians to be representative of the Messiah, as is the Paschal lamb. More study of *Encyclopedia Judaica* reveals that the Red Heifer sacrifice resembled the purification of recovered lepers, because cedar, hyssop, and crimson "stuff" were also used for that rite. It is further stated that the red smoke "alludes to the power of blood to overcome death." (Interesting thought . . . yes?)

It is worthwhile here also to note that these heifers were "purchased at a very high price" because the animal's coat had to be so near perfection, by Talmudic Law, that no more than two hairs of the entire coat could be other than red. Any herdsman who owned a prize heifer that would meet the qualifications could expect, therefore, to receive a pleasant remuneration.

Talmud, Parah 3:8, offers an interesting clue as an ash ingredient as well as reflecting a poignant "picture" in the Gospel of Jesus Christ. Along the roadway Jesus used on his Triumphal Entry, The Descent of the Mount of Olives, palm branches (or fronds) were strewn by the excited citizens of Jerusalem. Interestingly, dried palm fronds were used to kindle the blaze for burning the Red Heifer at the Miphkad Altar immediately along this eastern approach to the Heifer's Gangway Bridge.

Now, as a challenge for archaeology, it would seem that cylindrical coring samples of soil from regions identified along the extended line-of-sight from the Temple site may yield the probable location of this sacrifice. A few feet beneath the surface, there may be found in that soil, some trace ash residue from the animals, mixed with ash from cedar and hyssop and the other woods, plus wool and whatever the scarlet material was. *Encyclopedia Judaica* refers to this material only as "red-stuff."

Parah 3:5 states that a total of seven heifers were burned. Depending upon known persistence of the materials involved, there may be some evidence remaining even after all this time. Talmud[21] offers us some very definite encouragement toward finding some of the Heifer's ash residue. In Parah 3:11 the Mishnah relates that if there were large chunks of charred remains, such as the skull, bones, etc. separated by the sifting, these materials were then "hammered" into powder. This granulated residue was then divided into three parts, equally distributed as follows: one part to the twenty-four orders of the priesthood, one part to the "ramparts" or walls of the Temple compound, and one part to be deposited on the Mount of Olives!

At any rate, with so many burnings, even after nineteen centuries, there may be one location along that line that shows trace residue of all ash products involved. Professor Martin makes an excellent case[12] for the location of this sacrifice at a distance just slightly greater than 2,000 "cubits" from the Dome of the Tablets.

Now, if we believe in the aforementioned line established and if we know "What's a cubit?," we could survey to a position very close to the Red Heifer burning site, which Professor Martin identifies as the Miphkad Altar. Professor Kaufman determined the Second Temple cubit as 43.7 cm (17.204 in.); whereas, Professor Martin used a 21 inch cubit (53.34 cm).

Measuring from the Dome of the Tablets, then, 2,000 of the former value locates a position of 874 meters, somewhat below the summit; which may have been the 30 A.D. position of the olive grove called Gethsemane. The latter value places the site well up on the Olivet summit at 1,067 meters (in the middle of the main road). Within these areas, using "high-tech" organic chemistry sleuthing, might be found ash from wool, "red stuff," pine, spruce, fig, palm fronds, with cedar and hyssop ash mixed with ash from incinerated heifer flesh, bone, horns, dung, hooves, and hide.

PLEASE STAY DOWNWIND!

> While He (Jesus) was in Bethany, reclining at the table in the home of a man known as Simon the Leper. . . .
>
> Mark 14:3 (NIV)

Professor Yadin[14] points out, from the Midrash, that during the Second Temple period it was believed leprosy was transmitted through the air as well as by bodily contact. Lepers who lived in the area of Jerusalem and leprous pilgrims who journeyed there to worship were therefore housed at Bethany, which is east of Olivet summit and about two miles east of Jerusalem. Yadin makes the point that Bethany was founded there because the prevailing winds (off the Mediterranean Sea) are from west to east and Bethany was therefore established as a "safe" place to quarter "the unclean." The Rabbis were so strict on this point, in fact, that it was forbidden to even walk or stand east of a leper! Oi!

On Holy feast days there would be a large influx of Jewish worshipers coming into Jerusalem. Therefore, in order to provide additional space for their accommodations, even in tents, the city limits of Jerusalem were extended a "Sabbath Day's journey" or 2,000 cubits. This measure also insured that these pilgrims would be able to adhere within the travel laws of the Sabbath.

But how about the lepers? At a distance of about two miles east, Bethany was located significantly greater than a Sabbath Day's journey from Jerusalem. You may have questioned (as I did) just how this would have eased the lepers' compliance with Sabbath travel laws. Professor Yadin offers no explanation; however, he deserves our sympathy because the maze of Talmudic travel laws would probably have challenged even the best of Pharisee "lawyers."

A partial explanation of at least one legal loophole is provided in the footnotes under tractate Hallah 1:8, as the "Erub of Cooked Foods." In a family or a group of persons, if each contributes to a supply of food, enough for up to two meals each may be placed in a container and cached in advance at a point that is a Sabbath limit from the intended destination. Then, on the Sabbath day they may travel any distance from home to arrive and consume that food which is each person's "legal domain" in the Law. Each person may then proceed a Sabbath Day's journey from that point, thus "keeping" the Law. This was a very practical and accommodating provision; however, one wonders if the Lord saw this as a practical necessity or as legal "squirming."

Now, some interesting pictures develop:

(a) As Professor Yadin observed from Mark's understatement: Jesus didn't just visit overnight with Simon the Leper. Virtually the entire Bethany population were lepers!

(b) And yes, this also means that Lazarus, a "Bethanite," was probably a leper and complications from that ravaging disease may have caused that death from which Jesus raised him. No wonder his sister Martha said, " . . . Lord, by this time he stinketh...." (From John 11:39) Bad enough a leper! But in the tomb four days?

(c) When Jesus rode into Jerusalem, He probably passed right by the Miphkad Altar and He may have done something unseemly before the Pharisees that aroused their displeasure. In fact, Professor Martin[12] has proposed that incidents in this area of Mt. Olivet, including the Triumphal Entry, may have been used in prosecution of Jesus as a "criminal" against Judaism and, further, against Rome herself. (More about this in Chapter 5.)

THE LINE OF DEPARTURE
A more comprehensive depiction of first-century Jerusalem relative to subjects in this study is offered with the details of Sketch 6.

When approaching this investigation, I will freely admit there was initially a tendency (through my own ignorance or carelessness) to assume the line of departure made by the Shechinah was to be established through the Dome of the Tablets and the Eastern Gate (Suleiman's Gate) in the City Wall. This assumption was clearly in error of course, because, from Dr. Kaufman's analysis, the Second Temple was not aligned with the gate in the present City Wall. Rather, the Temple axis was aligned 6.20 degrees southward of that line and facing due east.

In addition, we observe from Scripture (Ezekiel 10:19) that the prophecy refers to the east gate of "the Lord's House." (See Sketch 1.) Further, we know from Scripture (Ezekiel 8:16) that the Temple faced eastward, as was pointed out so dramatically by Dr. Kaufman.[11] An even more direct statement from the New Testament "clinches" the fact that the Temple faced eastward.

When He was sitting on the Mount of Olives facing the Temple. . . .

(From Mark 13:3 NEB)

There can be no doubt that the Temple faced east. Nevertheless, an interesting archaeological question arises now concerning the location of the eastern (city) gate of the Second Temple period. James Fleming's discovery[6] of the "Lower Arch" may at first be assumed to be directly (center-for-center) beneath the corresponding arch of the ground-level observable Suleiman's Gate. But what if—for some strange reason—Fleming's Arch, being directly beneath Suleiman's south entry arch, is actually the north entry arch in the wall of the Second Temple period? Or there may even have been three arches in the City Wall of 70 A.D., as in the Hulda Gate. If there are two more "Lower Arches" south of Fleming's arch, the center arch would be approximately online with the center axis of the Temple as outlined by Dr. Kaufman, Sketch 1.

Sketch 5 presents the recent (1986) terrain contour of the profile extending due east from the Dome of the Tablets to Olivet summit at the Chapel of the Ascension. In the accompanying profile, the 70 A.D. contours have been estimated considering information from Fleming's Lower Arch and other features. Some "filling" of the Kidron basin has likely resulted from tumbling rubble produced by dozens of seiges and more than as many earthquakes and landslides during nineteen centuries.

This is a question that needs answering, although it does not appear to have any obvious direct bearing on either the Second Temple location or this Shechinah withdrawal story. However, remnants of the western end of the "Heifer's Gangway" bridge may presently be buried somewhere beneath Suleiman's Gate in the vicinity of Fleming's Lower Arch. (See Sketches 5 and 6.) Importance of this bridge is discussed under "Signs and Wonders," Chapter 7. Nevertheless, this question will have to wait for an answer, because Muslim authorities will not presently permit excavation to investigate the Lower Arch (or "arches").

The line of departure for the Shechinah then, is presently established by a line extended due east of the Dome of the Tablets. This determination is based on Dr. Kaufman's location of the Kodesh Ha-Kodashim at the Dome of the Tablets. However, a more definitive basis for this line could be claimed if just one more authenticating point could be located, rather than depending solely upon a surveyed due easterly location.

Location of such a point not only would establish the line of departure, but also would provide a secondary verification of sorts for the Temple site. As discussed previously, the Miphkad Altar site is perhaps the best candidate for such a point. Some slight encouragement for the accuracy of Dr. Kaufman's analysis is already provided by the very accurate alignment of the extended easterly line from "The Dome of the Tablets" to the "traditional" site at The Chapel of the Ascension. (See Map of The Old City and Sketch 6). However, it is understood here that the Chapel of the Ascension can hardly be considered as a verified archaeological site.

I certainly don't mean to suggest it is significant whether the Chapel of The Ascension is at the exact location of Jesus's Ascension. Rather, it appears to be much more important that Dr. Kaufman's location of the Temple site appears to be substantiated, at least to some extent, by establishing a line that can be extended to pass very closely to the traditional site of Jesus' Ascension in 30 A.D. Jesus probably ascended from somewhere along that line (we do not know where), but most likely at a point on or very near the Olivet summit. We have attempted to show that this is also likely the same location from which the Shechinah Glory ascended in 69 A.D. Finding the Miphkad Altar would just about "close-the-book" for most scholars concerning the location of the line of departure and the Temple site.

Where the "Fault" Lies

> ... and the Mount of Olives shall cleave in the midst thereof toward the east and toward the west, and there shall be a very great valley; and half of the mountain shall remove toward the north and half of it toward the south."
>
> (Zechariah 14:4)

In other words, on that Great Day, there is going to be a terrific earthquake, splitting the Mount of Olives to produce "a very great valley." Recently some geologists were reported to have been surprised when they located a seismic fault line that passed through the Mount of Olives, extending from east to west. (Imagine that!)

Geologists[22] indicate the landslides at the midst of Olivet reveal a fault that has existed since the time of King Uzziah. (Zechariah 14:5) Increased soil porosity produced by repetitive landslides enhances growth of trees, shrubs, and weeds, especially in an arid climate. Olivet's western slope exhibits an obvious proliferation of growth, especially "in the midst thereof" and heading directly toward the Temple Mount platform area.

But, there is much more to the geological/seismic quest that pertains to this Holy ground. Please read what Ezekiel and Zechariah say about that "very great valley." In Ezekiel 47:1–10 you will see that a "very great" river of "living waters" will run right past the south side of the Temple. In fact, the Kidron Valley will apparently become a large lake or inland sea. The river will extend from Jerusalem to the Mediterranean, also to the Dead Sea, and then southward to the Red Sea. (Zechariah 14:8) The desert village of En Gedi will become a prosperous fishing village(?)! You *can* believe it! (More about this river in "The Truth about Watergate!")

Nevertheless, it would be interesting to see if that seismic fault extends in a straight line across the Temple Mount, passing 250–300 "cubits" south of the Dome of the Tablets. Why 250–300 cubits? From Ezekiel 42:16–20 the prophet describes the Temple boundaries as being 500 cubits square by outside measurement of its court walls. Thus, the river edge must be about 250–300 cubits south of the center line of the Temple, which is the east-west axis passing through the Holy of Holies (Kodesh Ha-Kodashim) at the Dome of the Tablets.

Now, if we examine the Jerusalem map, we can see that 250 cubits (approx. 125 yards) or roughly 115 meters places the "riverfront" right through the Dome of the Rock (No. 10 on the map). As discussed in Chapter 2, until recently (1978) this revered Muslim shrine was thought to be occupying the same location where the Temple once stood on the Temple Mount. This brings us to another interesting prophetic observation from Revelation 11:2.

> But the court which is without the temple leave out, and measure it not; for it is given unto the Gentiles: and the Holy City shall they tread under foot forty and two months.

During the time of the first and second Temples, the Court of the Gentiles was needed as a barrier to keep Gentiles from entering, thereby defiling the Temple grounds. However, during the Millennial reign of Messiah on Earth, such a "barrier" would indeed be superfluous, because all nations and peoples will at that time be required to worship and honor Him at Jerusalem on the Feast of Tabernacles. (Zechariah 14:16–19) Therefore, no longer will it be necessary or appropriate that there should be any "Court of the Gentiles." In that day "the time of the Gentiles will be fulfilled." At that time all inhabitants of Earth shall worship the Lord together, united as one Church.

So, our Lord told John not to bother measuring that part of the Temple Mount, because it isn't going to be there after the Gentiles "tread" there for that last $3\,^1/_2$ years, "until the time of the Gentiles be fulfilled." The Gentiles' part of the Temple Mount is just going to be "river-bottom" after our Lord returns to reign from that Mount with His Kingdom.

(We really need to examine those fault lines.)

Chapel of the Ascension

This contested Christian/Muslim site is marked by the small minaret and dome just to the right of the lofty spire of the Russian Tower, dominating the skyline of the Mount of Olives.

Church of Mary Magdalene (Russian Church)

This is one of the most beautiful landmarks on the Mount of Olives. The thick forested growth at the center of the mountain attests in some measure to the seismic fault-line found in this area.

The Truth About Watergate

> ... and behold, waters issued out from under the threshold of the House eastward ... and the waters came down from under the right side of the House, at the right side of the Altar.
>
> From Ezekiel 47:1

You will no doubt be relieved to know the "Watergate" incident discussed here has not the slightest connection with the scandal. An archaeological detail exists concerning the "Water Gate" of the Temple, which has bearing on this seismic prophecy. (See Sketch 7.)

Talmud, Shekalim 6:3 asks, "... and the water gate. Wherefore was its name?" Rabbi Eleazer ben Jacob offers: "... because through it the waters trickled forth and in the hereafter they will issue out from under the threshold of the House...." Talmud refers to Ezekiel 47:1–2 concerning this statement.

We see that Holy Scripture supports this statement from Rabbi Eleazer. It is also exciting to note that in the last few years some evidence of an active aquifer exists in this very region under the Temple Mount. This aquifer happens to be on the south side, away from the Dome of the Tablets (on the "right side" of the House.)

Recently, Muslim authorities began accusing Israeli archaeologists of having undermined the El Aqsa mosque by diverting aquaducts to erode supports beneath the foundation. The El Aqsa mosque is located at the extreme south end of the Temple Mount platform above the Western Wall or "Wailing" Wall. (See Map of Old City and Sketch 6.)

At the same time, Jewish Orthodox scholars complained that Muslim custodians of the Temple Mount platform had diverted drainage circuits so as to cause water intrusion into those revered Jewish study areas deep underground, beneath El Aqsa mosque and beneath the Western Wall.

As accusations grew sharper and louder, tempers and patience shortened until Jerusalem civil officials stepped in to investigate. Hydrologists were engaged to determine the cause of this flooding, because each side swore to innocence. The hydrologists found an active aquifer in that region, having a very substantial source of water supplying it from "somewhere." (Now, how could Ezekiel have known about that?!)

Some Obvious Arguments

Even with all the analyses discussed here, there is of course still neither proof nor obvious conclusion to be reached. There are, however, at least two obvious arguments that deserve some thought.

First, some could say that the first-century Christians claimed the "traditional" site of Jesus' Ascension after Shechinah had Ascended. Remember, Jesus' Ascension in 30 A.D. was witnessed by only a small number of (perhaps eleven) disciples (Mark 16:14 and Acts 1:13), whereas the Temple Withdrawal and Ascension of the Glory of the Lord was certainly a very public event.

However, Jesus' Ascension was recorded as having occurred (30 A.D.) at the summit of the Mount of Olives (near Bethany) by at least one New Testament writer, during the first century, and a number of years prior to 69 A.D. (Luke 24:50, Acts 1:11,12). Also, it is significant here to note the Book of Acts must have been written no later than 63 A.D., because Luke (the apparent writer) was very close personally to Paul the Apostle and the book closes with Paul still imprisoned in Rome in 63 A.D. Luke would most certainly have reported Paul's death had he been writing after Paul's execution in 66 or 67 A.D.

Certain agnostic and atheistic criticisms of the Bible have charged that many or all New Testament books were written after 70 A.D. That criticism is certainly rendered impotent with the evidence of Shechinah's Withdrawal. It is obvious that New Testament writers would not have passed up such an opportunity to tell the Jews and the world how Christ was glorified by the Divine Presence as He implored the People to repent and then ascended from the very same point from which Jesus had ascended forty years before.

Secondly, there can be no doubt that Jesus' disciples, in their newfound zeal, would have immediately claimed the place of Ascension in 30 A.D. to all who listened. So, why—after forty years of banishment and persecution by their Jewish peers—would the disciples risk losing credibility by later claiming any different location for the Ascension of their Lord? They would surely have been "roasted" or stoned on the spot for claiming such a thing. It just doesn't figure.

If such a "blasphemous" claim had been made after-the-fact rather than before the Glory ascended, there would have been an "incident"; presumably one of sufficient turbulence that comment would surely have been noted, either in Jewish records or in the New Testament. One must then ask the question, "Isn't it strange how everyone knows that Jesus ascended from Olivet summit, but why do we never hear about the ascent of the Shechinah Glory?

There is some understandable doubt concerning the "exact" location of the Ascension(s) because the Bible does not say Jesus ascended from Olivet summit, but from the vicinity of Bethany—which was very near the Olivet summit. But then the narration terminates by saying that after the Ascension (Acts 1:12): "Then returned they unto Jerusalem from the mount called Olivet, which is from Jerusalem a sabbath day's journey." Now, we know that "a Sabbath Day's journey" is 2,000 cubits or about 900–1,000 yards from the Holy of Holies; actually on or very near Olivet summit (See Sketch 5.)

Many respected Bible teachers often say: "Let Scripture be interpreted by Scripture!" In this case we can gain new insight to this question by letting Scripture interpret itself.

The two angels of Acts 1:10–11 told Jesus' disciples: "... (He) shall come in like manner as ye have seen Him go into Heaven." We know from Zechariah 14:4 that His feet shall stand on the Mount of Olives upon His Glorious Return. Also, we know that *all* of Jerusalem will see Him and look upon Him whom they had pierced. In order to be seen by all, He must therefore descend to Olivet summit—*not* down in the Kidron Valley and *not* over the hill behind the summit.

Then, if He is going to return "in like manner," this means He ascended at that same place. Jesus therefore must have ascended from Olivet summit and on an easterly line extended directly from the Temple. We can know this because He will return "in like manner" as He ascended. (Literally, a "literal" interpretation of literal Scripture.)

As stated earlier, I believe that "exact" location (wherever it is) to be the same location where His feet will stand on that Great Day (Zechariah 14:4). I think God just does things that way.

These are obvious arguments, but still we have no proof. That will have to wait. However, most scholars would agree that on that Great Day:

Messiah's feet will stand on the Mount of Olives.

(Zechariah 14:4)

people will look upon Him whom we all have pierced.

(Zechariah 12:10)

Then, someone will ask Him, "What are these wounds in your hands?"

(Zechariah 13:6)

And He will say, "Those I received in the house of my friends."

(Zechariah 13:6)

SUMMARY OF SCRIPTURAL/HISTORICAL/ARCHAEOLOGICAL EVIDENCE

Prophecies indicate that Shechinah would occupy the Second Temple:
Ezra 6:12 (Lamsa Bible)—"And the God whose name we have found to be here, there shall He dwell."
Haggai 2:4–9 (KJV)—"Yet now be strong, O Zerubbabel, saith the Lord, . . . and work, for I am with you, saith the Lord of hosts, . . . and I will fill this house with Glory, saith the Lord of hosts."
Zechariah 1:16 (KJV)—" . . . I am returned to Jerusalem with mercies: My house shall be built in it, saith the Lord of hosts, ..."

Scripture says Shechinah was in the Second Temple during and after Jesus' time:
Matthew 23:21 (KJV)—"And whoso shall swear by the Temple, sweareth by it and by Him that dwelleth therein."
Luke 24:52–53 (KJV)—"(Disciples) were continually in the Temple, praising and blessing God."
John 2:16 (KJV)—" . . . make not My Father's house an house of merchandise."
Romans 9:4 (New English Bible)—" . . . theirs is the Divine Presence, . . . "

Prophecies of the withdrawal of Shechinah from the Temple:
Ezekiel Chapters 9–11, Ezek. 11:23 (KJV)—"And the Glory of the Lord went up from the midst of the city, and stood upon the mountain which is on the east side of the city."
Hosea 5:15 (KJV)—"I will go back to My Place, . . . "

Historians' accounts of Shechinah Withdrawal, 66–70 A.D.:
Josephus, "Wars of the Jews" 6/290/300
Eusebius, "Proof of the Gospel" Chapter XVIII
Midrash Rabbah–Eichah (Lamentations) Section 25 (Proems)
Babylonian Talmud–Rosh Hashanah 31b

Archaeological Evidence:
Dome of the Tablets identified as Holy of Holies (Dr. A.S. Kaufman) Shechinah departure path (due-east) leads directly to traditional site of Jesus' Ascension at summit of Mount of Olives. (See Map & Sketch 6)

5 Some Updated Bible Stories

It is perhaps only natural that an engineer with an enthusiastic interest in the Holy Word, especially concerning eschatology, archaeology, and Judaic customs, feasts, etc., relating to Messianic Promise, would want to "analyze" this fascinating event. Adding further intrigue to this analysis, several thoughts surfaced, concerning prophecy, Gospel writings, and "signs" appearing to the Judeans of the Second Temple period. I wish to share those thoughts with others, without diluting the "main story," which has been already too long neglected. There are meaningful aspects of the story that can enrich the hearts of those who hear of them. (These things are not taught in Sunday school!)

The story and implications surrounding this event bring about some revisions and "improved" blessings from several familiar Bible stories. Some of these are presented here. Maybe you will even think of some additional stories that should be "updated" as a result of this event and its meaning to Scripture.

WHY GETHSEMANE?
This question, in light of what is found in this study concerning the Miphkad Altar—the Red Heifer burning site—brings out a few other questions:

- Did that agonizing hour of discourse between Jesus and the Father require some proximity with the Miphkad Altar? That important but little known Jewish purification rite was certainly also representative of "cleansing" through that Greater Sacrifice of another Innocent being who was also "without blemish."

- Why this proximity with the Miphkad Altar?

- Would Jesus have deliberately irked the priests by treading on that sacred ground? (Maybe He would!)

As observed in Chapter 4, there is very likely some relationship between the Miphkad Altar and Jesus' Triumphal Entry into Jerusalem. This likelihood is based on the fact that the Miphkad Altar had to be on the line shown on the map and was therefore along His route into the Temple. (See Sketch 6.) Although, there is no reference to the possibility in any of the Gospels, it is interesting to explore the speculative thought that Jesus may have provoked the wrath of the Sanhedrin in other ways, in addition to letting His followers proclaim him a king, and later, by driving the moneychangers from His Father's House.

One can now speculate with some rationale that He may have performed some unacceptable act or made some remark concerning that Holy Ground (Miphkad Altar), which was later reported to the Sanhedrin as a blasphemous act. Remember, just a few days before, the Pharisee became irritated with Jesus because the Lord hadn't washed His hands before coming to the table ... tsk! tsk! (Luke 11:36–38). Or, even more likely, perhaps some of the lying "witnesses" fabricated some action or utterance that they falsely attributed to Jesus and used to prosecute this "blasphemer" at His trial before Caiaphas.

Jesus had said (Luke 6:5) that He was Lord over the Sabbath and also announced that He was sovereign over the Law. The "lawyers" were understandably incensed at such claims from this Galilean, especially when He repeatedly demonstrated this claim by healing many on the Sabbath. Now, what if Jesus had declined ritual cleansing after His exposure to lepers as a further demonstration of His sovereignty over the Law? Then He comes into the City and even the Temple!

Our imagination can extend to the Pharisee's reaction if He remarked about the significance of His blood. Jesus said (John 4:10) that He was "living water." This is a much-used expression in Jewish purification rites, especially in the Water of Purification mixed with the Red Heifer ashes. What if Jesus had dropped such "hints" as He sat astride that donkey crossing the Heifer's Gangway Bridge?!

Regardless, it seems altogether reasonable that the Miphkad Altar must have had some connection with His false trial and innocent death. After all, any believer (Jewish or Christian) should recognize the "unblemished" sacrificial heifer as certainly a "type" of the Messiah, whose blood washes away all uncleanness. In Jewish tradition it is said that, despite all his wisdom, King Solomon humbly admitted he did not understand the meaning of the Red Heifer sacrifice. So, maybe it is not so obvious to some, even though they "believe."

For example, although King Solomon was a devout Jew, He could not have known the symbolic reasoning for using dried palm branches to kindle the blaze at the burning of the Red Heifer. (Talmud, Parah 3:8) Palm branches on the Mount of Olives, "kindling the blaze" beneath *our* Red Heifer, Jesus! Of course! That dramatic and Triumphal Entry into the Holy City struck the spark that "kindled" the wrath of the Jewish religious "establishment" and incited them to plot the death of Jesus.

Christians today can see the significance immediately, but it is doubtful those excited Judeans were aware of this symbolism as they spread palm fronds along the Descent of the Mount of Olives and shouted:

> Hosanna! Blessed is the King of Israel that cometh in the name of the Lord!

> John 12:13

The name "Golgotha" (or Place of the Skull) has held a mystery of sorts concerning The Crucifixion because there seems to be no historical record of such a "place." This happens even in our modern society. Some names of persons, places, and things just never reach a status of acceptance into lasting folklore. Some streets and byways in your area, for example, have nicknames that are not on the map, yet they possess great contemporary popularity, especially among the "locals." Here in Palm Beach County we have State Road 710. Still, all of us call it "The Bee-Line"—nobody calls it Highway 710, not even local newswriters. Much the same type of semantic acrobatics may be involved with the meaning of Golgotha.

In this way a popular label may have arisen for the area of the Crucifixion, from the fact that when an animal is burnt, at least one part of its skeleton survives the blaze in recognizable form—the skull. With this reasoning in mind, it may be that "place of the skull" or Golgotha was the local nickname for the Miphkad Altar. A convincing discussion from talmud Rabbis (Yoma 68a, Zebahim 106a) indicates that the sin offerings of the bullocks and goats were *also* burned here. That place would have been strewn with literally thousands of animal skulls. And, Talmud says it was a place "where the ashes naturally pour down." It is easy to see why Olivet summit might be called "place of the skull." (See Sketches 9 and 10.)

Earlier we noted that Roman law required a crucifixion to be administered at the scene of the crime and/or the place of arrest. We know from Gospel Scripture that Jesus was pointed out by Judas in a garden called "Gethsemane" and was then arrested by the Temple guards. Also, we discussed the possibility that Gethsemane was likely much nearer Olivet summit than the present traditional Garden of Gethsemane. The summit location would have been at or very near the Miphkad Altar.

Now, we are getting some strong hints about why Jesus chose to pray at Gethsemane that grim night. It wasn't just because it was a pleasant setting with picturesque olive trees. And, it wasn't because Jesus had told Judas He would be there waiting for His betrayal. Well, maybe Gethsemane was just a nice quiet place where Jesus could speak in private with His Father. C'mon!—Jesus didn't have to come to Gethsemane for prayer. He could pray anywhere! Jesus was the greatest "pray-er" who ever lived!

Well, then why did Jesus choose to pray at Gethsemane? Maybe it was just a coincidence. He had to pray somewhere, didn't He?

Remember? Jesus came to fulfill the Law. Part of that assignment was to fulfill all of the Law concerning the Red Heifer sacrifice. Strangely, although we hardly ever hear a word about it, the Red Heifer burning is the most important of all the Jewish sacrifices. None of the other sacrifices, nor the priests—not even the Temple—can be valid without "cleansing" from Red Heifer ashes mixed with "living water."

Jesus knew exactly what He was doing. He knew all the precepts of Roman law and Herodian "puppet" statutes and certainly knew the Jewish Levitical Law. (His Father was the author!) Jesus, therefore, selected the vicinity of the Miphkad Altar as the place of His own Crucifixion by deliberately arranging to be arrested at that precise location. After all, Jesus is God! Would God just leave it to

Pilate or Caiaphas or Judas or some centurion to choose where His Supreme Sacrifice would be given?

It is interesting to note that in Jewish tradition the palm leaf is a symbol for victory! Jesus was our Red Heifer! Our burnt offering. Jesus had His Victory! Kindled by palm branches on Olivet.

Still, we do not know for certain why Jesus was arrested at Gethsemane or what specific "charge" was issued to warrant His capture. Jesus must have said or done something here (or was falsely accused of such). But what??? Some day we will know. One possible "affront" that can be postulated concerns the bridge that extended during the Second Temple period from the East Gate across the Kidron Valley to the Mount of Olives.

From the Talmud (Shekalim 4:2), it is stated this bridge was known as the "Heifer's Gangway." (See Sketches 5 and 6.) The eastern end of the bridge was just down the slope from the Heifer's burning site. The priest would carry the ashes across this bridge to the Temple.

In Jewish tradition and the Law, one becomes "unclean" if he touches or even walks across the grave of a dead person. It is then reasoned that one avoids defilement by being separated from the graves by dead air space or a "vault." (Talmud Parah 3:6) The double-vaulted bridge then was designed to provide a "clean" passage to the Temple from the Mount of Olives. The graves of thousands of Jewish dead in the valley below had to be "insulated" from the bridge traffic by those air-filled vaults.

These consecrated ashes, to be used later for "purifying" those who were "unclean" from having touched a leprous person or the dead (or even a grave), could then be carried across the Kidron Valley above the Jerusalem cemetery burial sites without the slightest exposure to that "uncleanness."

Another "act" that may have stirred anger among His prosecutors was the overnight accommodation Jesus apparently accepted in the home of Simon, the Leper—and in Bethany, the local leper colony! (See Chapter 4, "Please Stay Downwind.") If Jesus ignored the manmade "laws" about such a contact with "uncleanness," this would have added more fuel to the fire. Some of the locals interpreted the Law very strictly, it seems.

To illustrate, an amusing and exasperating story was related by Professor Yadin[14] pertaining to the strict adherences of the Essene sect. The Essenes of that day would not defecate on the Sabbath and for this reason one of the Western Gates of the city was sometimes called the "Essene Gate." This was so-named because these pious "hold outs" would come racing out of the Temple, "hastening" through that gate as soon as the Sabbath had ceased, since the latrines were outside the gates and northwest of the city. So, we can easily agree that some extreme "legalism" existed during the time of Jesus.

Lest we begin judging the Jews for their seemingly almost "paranoid" attitude toward "cleanness," we might reflect upon one of our own popular folk-sayings: "Cleanliness is next to Godliness." (I wonder who said that?) Well, it *may* have been Ben Franklin, but if he did originate that pearl of wisdom in our WASP-culture, he borrowed it from the Jewish Talmud!

Tractate Zabim ("they that suffer a flux") explains in the introduction that cleanliness in Judaism is regarded not only as next to Godliness, but as Godliness itself. Neglect of a person's health is regarded as a serious offense against the Lord, in whose image we are shaped. (Remember? Your body is, after all, a Temple to the Lord.) We should keep this tradition in mind as we consider our own personal health and the Jewish legalism that we will encounter in this study.

Now, What About This "Jesus"?

Very likely, this legalism was distorted by the priests (and by Pilate) in order to justify capital punishment of this innocent Nazarene. Let us examine, from the Jewish point of view, the incidents occurring just before, during, and after that Triumphal Entry into Jerusalem by this strange, gentle peasant.

> The night before (Saturday), He was a guest at the home of His friend, Lazarus, in Bethany—the local leper colony! (John 12:1–13)

> Next morning (Sunday), He instructs His followers to place Him on a burro colt to ride into Jerusalem as "mock-fulfillment" of Zechariah's prophecy. (Zech. 9:9, John 12:14–15)

> He begins His "royal" procession down the road called "The Descent of the Mount of Olives" and abstains from cautioning the adoring crowd against proclaiming: "Blessed is He who comes in the name of the Lord," a well-known implication that He was Messiah. (Such audacious blasphemy!) (Psalms 118:26 and Matthew 21:9–11)

> Then, with even more "arrogance," after some local church officials admonished Him for neglecting to discourage the adulation and Hosannas from the throng, He "boasts": " ... I tell you, if my disciples keep silence, the stones will shout aloud." (Luke 19:40, NEB)

He probably... "strutted" directly past the Miphkad Altar. We don't know what... "blasphemous"... act He may have committed at this sacred shrine. He had said many times before that He was "sovereign" over the Law. (Another "offense"!)

He continues His approach via The Heifer's Gangway, the two-tiered bridge over which the two he-goats, brought for the Day of Atonement offering, are marching into the Temple for the casting of lots. (Also see "Signs and Wonders.") Now, if Jesus didn't bother to have His... "impurity"... ritually cleansed after having spent the night in the leper colony, this would have been considered an offense, a defilement of this Holy bridge, which was built to avoid "uncleanness" as described earlier.

Only "Very Special People" were privileged to use this sacred bridge; another act of "presumption" and "mockery" on the part of this "pretender." (He probably didn't ask to use it.)

The next day (Monday), He enters the Temple and His anger "burns" at the bartering by the "businessmen" selling animals to religious pilgrims for their burnt offerings. He overturns their tables and literally runs them out of the Temple, actually calling the Temple, "a den of thieves."

Upon leaving the Temple, He declares that one day it will all be torn down, "... not one stone upon another." (Matthew 24:2) Later, He was reported by witnesses to have claimed that He could destroy and then rebuild the Temple in three days! (Matthew 26:60–61)

To the utter consternation of everyone, all during the week He insists on spending each night in that "leper-haven" up on the hill. He stays at the home of this Simon fellow and has expensive perfumed oil poured on His head. Only a few nights earlier, a sister of Lazarus (that "phony"!) washed His feet with the stuff!—Who does He think He is? (Matthew 26:6–7)

As if all this weren't enough, at His trial (facing death), this troublemaker, with unblushing temerity, still refuses to deny that He actually claims to be a king. (John 18:37)

Now, when we look at this Gospel narrative from the aspect of first century Judaic and Roman Law, the Gospel of Jesus Christ takes on new "light." After all, in order to obtain full appreciation for the Gospel, Christians need at least rudimentary knowledge of "the Law," because Jesus came to fulfill the Law (Matthew 5:17). Christians, therefore, can neither recognize these fulfillments nor experience the joy of such unless we know these "legal" details, even though we (Gentiles) are certainly not bound by the Law. Continuing, watch what happens.

What Judeans and Romans Were Thinking

The Triumphal Entry on the burro colt was a "mockery" to some, but to many this was a genuine and expected fulfillment. Why "expected"? Then (just as now), but especially then, Israel was expecting Messiah. The prophet Daniel had said Messiah, The Annointed One (the "Christ"), would appear exactly 483 years (seven plus sixty-two "weeks," each "week" of seven years) after "the commandment to go forth and rebuild the street and the wall." (Daniel 9:25–26) This commandment was indeed proclaimed to Nehemiah by the Persian King Artaxerxes exactly 483 years earlier.

They all knew "it was the time." But their Rabbis had taught a more "popular" theme in which he was to be a conquering Messiah—not a suffering, down-trodden . . . loser. The people had been taught traditionally that Israel was the "suffering" Messiah. So, they were expecting the "conquering" Messiah rather than a "suffering" Messiah—i.e., a radical, but meek Galilean carpenter's apprentice. Of course, with our 20/20 hindsight, it is very easy for us to see what most first-century (and modern-day) Jewish people were "blinded" from seeing. (Blinded by "traditional" teaching, not necessarily by disbelief.)

The priests and Pharisees were, of course, furious that this rabble-rouser would disrupt the commercialism being practiced in the Temple and then call it a "den of thieves." This larcenous operation was actually conducted by relatives of the High Priest, Caiaphas, as a family business! (Just imagine what would happen if you acted similarly by going up against the elders and "hierarchy" in some of our local churches.) And referring to the Temple as "a den of thieves" was certainly a major offense against the Holy House.

Both the priests and Pilate distorted the laws of the land at the "trial" in more than one way. But the claim of being a "king" was falsified, yet vital, to the cases of both prosecutions. So, they both distorted and twisted the testimony of Jesus and witnesses in order to make the case that Jesus had claimed to be King—an act of sedition against Rome. Jesus never claimed to be King of Judea, but the priests cleverly coaxed Pilate into making this charge, because to claim to be a King (of any sort) within Caesar's empire was an act of treason against Caesar and punishable only by death. In this way the priests twisted Jesus' admission that He possessed a kingdom ("not of this world") as a capital offense against Rome in order to "push" a reluctant Pilate into ordering the crucifixion of a man whom he knew to be absolutely innocent.

Remember, at the time of His arrest at Gethsemane, Jesus had not yet been charged under any Roman civil statute. (They did not even read Him His "rights" from a Miranda card!) He was picked up by the Temple guards. Herod's trivial civil authority was not even being invoked against this "criminal."

So, the priests actually goaded Pilate into finally bringing a grave civil charge (sedition) against this man. Also satisfying the priestly conspiracy, the charge of sedition against Caesar called for the death penalty under Roman law. Thus Jesus very likely made a point of announcing His "Kingdom" publicly at the precise location that He selected for The Crucifixion, because Jesus knew all about their laws and statutes and customs. He also had foreknowledge of exactly what, where, and how they would accomplish His entire Sacrifice. (Nothing was left to chance. Jesus was in control.)

Then Pilate, in order to "make it look good" legally (back home), ordered a sign to be placed on the cross saying: "King of the Jews." (John 19:19–22) Over the priestly protests at this abomination, Pilate stood his ground (this one time) and insisted: "What I have written, I have written." It was Roman custom to write the offense on the cross and to crucify the offender "at the scene of the crime." The "crime" and the execution therefore took place, as Professor Martin[12] has so brilliantly shown, at the Miphkad Altar or very close to that location, somewhere near Olivet summit.

Now, seeing all these events from the Jewish viewpoint, is it any wonder that Jesus was put to death? (It was all part of His Perfect Plan!) The Jews didn't kill Jesus. The Romans didn't kill Jesus. It's just that none of us prevented it! We couldn't have! It was planned an eternity earlier and by none other than the Lord himself!

WHERE WAS THE CRUCIFIXION?

Earlier in this chapter you probably jumped right up out of your chair at even the "suggestion" of The Crucifixion having taken place on the Mount of Olives! Rubbish! Why, everybody knows it was either at the Church of the Holy Sepulchre or somewhere over near the Garden Tomb . . . or . . . somewhere! ("Gee! I wonder which it really was!")

We should point out, as gently as possible, that no evidence has yet been found that would indicate either of those treasured and traditional tourist "attractions" as the actual location. Hallowed and precious as those sites are to millions of Christians, they both hold their "verification" based only on centuries of tradition. Sorry, no facts. However, we will present just some of the evidence here that backs up the untraditional location "on the other side of town."

Before any of you think I have just gone "off the edge" in my excitement, we can begin by presenting verification of the Olivet Crucifixion with just three passages from Scripture.

Ezekiel 8:16

> ... with their backs toward the Temple of the Lord, and their faces toward the east. ...

- Therefore, the Temple (and the "veil" faced toward the east. There can be no doubt!

Mark 13:3

> And as He sat upon the Mount of Olives facing the Temple. ...

- Therefore, Jesus faced the Temple (and the "veil") "as He sat upon the Mount of Olives." There can be no doubt!

Matthew 27:51–54

> ... the veil of the Temple was rent in twain ... the earth did quake ... and the rocks rent ... and the graves were opened. ... Now the centurion, and they that were with him, watching Jesus, saw the earthquake, and those things that were done. ...

- Therefore, the centurion and the others saw the "veil" rent-in-twain. In fact, they saw all "those things" from the top of the Mount of Olives. That is the only place from which they could have seen "those things." There can be no doubt!

As Professor Martin emphasized, the centurion and the others who witnessed this tearing of the Veil at the instant of Jesus' death could only have seen the veils (and/or Glory Brilliance) from a point directly east of the Temple on the slope of Mt. Olivet. In Chapter 4 we showed that the High Priest at the heifer burning "must direct his gaze carefully" in order to see the Veil through the aperture of the East Gate. Would not the centurion have to do likewise in order to see the Veil? He simply could not possibly have seen any of these things either from the Church of the Holy Sepulchre or from the vicinity of the Garden Tomb (Gordon's Calvary) near the Damascus Gate bus station, both of which are west of the Temple site. (See Sketches 4, 5, and 6.)

Further circumstantial evidence in favor of the Mount of Olives as The Crucifixion site is found in the traditions and Law surrounding the Jerusalem cemetery at that location. There are now, and have been for many centuries, literally a multitude of Jewish dead buried in that ground on the west slope of Olivet. This included many Old Testament Prophets and sages, some of whose tombs were opened when the centurion "saw those things."

According to Jerusalem tourist guides, Jewish tradition says: Many Jewish faithful from all over the world are buried at that cemetery because they look forward to *The Resurrection* when Messiah arrives at Olivet to rescue Israel from her enemies. They wish, therefore, to meet Him on the Glorious Day at that point and they don't want to burrow through the Earth in order to greet Him! (Sounds ridiculous?) Not to me. I rejoice that they want to greet Him!

Another point of law concerns the distance of an execution from the Holy of Holies. Yep! You guessed it! A "Sabbath Day's journey." Both traditional Crucifixion sites are located much less than two-thousand cubits from the Dome of the Tablets. The Romans also did their best to conduct such punishment where it would be seen by all—to keep the populace thinking about "staying in line." The summit of the Mount of Olives can be seen from almost anywhere in The Old City or the Temple Mount. Keep in mind, also, the fact that the populace would not have to squint into the sun at the time Jesus died, "the ninth hour"—3 P.M.

Another "new" thought develops in the Gospel when we contemplate that Sunday morning "foot race" between John and Peter. (John 20:4) If they raced from Jerusalem to a burial site on the near slope of Olivet, they ran indeed up a steep incline and it is a credit to the athletic prowess and eagerness of both young men that morning. Otherwise, it would have been just a little jog through the streets to the present "traditional" site at the Church of the Holy Sepulchre or the Garden Tomb. Nevertheless, even if John and Peter had spent the previous night at Bethany, they would have had a treacherous, rocky slope for a steep "downhill" course to the tomb. If you have walked on that Holy Mountain, you can have more appreciation for that contest knowing these things.

Tradition has overlooked another obvious factor that should apply the "coup de grace" to any thought for The Crucifixion taking place anywhere west of the Temple. All of the sacrifices took place in front (east) of the Temple. It just seems very unlikely that God would choose to offer His only Son for a burnt offering at just some "random" location behind the Temple! (He must surely get a good chuckle at some of "our ways.")

The prospect of Jesus' burial at Olivet and not in the Garden Tomb will be a "bitter pill" to many who have romanticized that beautiful site. However, when we look at the evidence truthfully, we may have to redirect our thinking and our "romance" to a different locale.

Recently *BAR Magazine* published an article[15] in which Mr. Barkay presents good evidence that dates the Garden Tomb to the eighth century B.C. The tombs found in that area of Jerusalem today would have been far outside the Jerusalem city walls of the eighth century B.C.; perhaps even in the environs of a neighboring village—a suburb of sorts. Thus, although the possibility is disappointing to many Christians (including myself), the evidence from Scripture, the Law, history, and logic just doesn't seem to add-up for the Garden Tomb (or the Church of the Holy Sepulchre) as the burial site of the Lord Jesus.

But, you say: "If they buried the dead west of the City in the eighth century B.C., why do you think they changed the cemetery location to the east during the time of Jesus? Perhaps that's only what *you* would call modern tradition!"

Zechariah's prophecy was the primary reason for moving the Jerusalem cemetery to the east side, although the proximity of the northwest latrines may also have had some influence on this decision. Zechariah's prophecy concerning the Glorious descent from the Heavens to the Mt. of Olives was pronounced about 516 B.C.—a couple of centuries after the period of burials in the Garden Tomb area. Thus, by the time of Jesus, 500 years later, the "rush" to be interred at the Mt. of Olives Cemetery was well established into the tradition of the Jews of the Second Temple. I am confident, therefore, that Joseph (of Arimathea), a very devout Jew and a member of the Sanhedrin, surely purchased the family crypt in one of the "choicest" locales on Mt. Olivet. It had to be the very BEST of tombs to be the resting place for the broken body of The Lamb of God.

Scriptural evidence proves that The Crucifixion took place on the

Mount of Olives. There is also a preponderance of evidence available from historical and archaeological sources that agrees with the Scriptural conclusion. As we proceed through the chapters to follow, much additional evidence, though certainly not all, will be presented.

Professor Martin has published a more recent book[25] that details a much more comprehensive and scholarly analysis of The Crucifixion site. His analysis is supported by many ancient documents, including early Christian historians such as Eusebius of the fourth century.[26] Professor Martin's work outlines several of the factors put forth in this discussion as well as several other items of evidence. In any case, these works display an overwhelming preponderance of evidence that indicates Olivet summit as the place of The Crucifixion.

Again, may we be reminded, not one strand of evidence, Scriptural or otherwise, has been found that would support even one of the traditional locations for The Crucifixion. I realize 1,900 years of traditional teaching by learned, respected, and well-intentioned scholars is difficult to "shake"—but, there it is—for all the world to see.

EVIDENCE IN THE TEMPLE

The tearing of the outer Veil (curtain) of the Temple at the instant when Jesus "gave up the ghost" has been the subject of some speculation. Scholarly evidence from Temple details, however, can improve our analysis of this subject.

Specifically, there were actually three veils (or curtains) in the Second Temple—not just the thick outer Veil that the centurion is reported to have seen "rent-in-twain." (More about that later.) Talmud, (Yoma 51) describes in some detail the two inner veils that separated the Holy Place from the Holy of Holies. These two inner curtains replaced the two cedar partitions, which provided the separation of these two holy chambers in Solomon's Temple as discussed in I Kings 6:16.

Moreover, we know from Ezekiel 8:16 and Mark 13:3 that the Temple faced eastward toward Olivet, and we also know it was placed high on top of the Temple Mount. The centurion at the Cross, then, would have to be well up the western slope of Olivet in order to "see" the Veil at the entrance of the Temple. He could not have seen it from below the City Wall at the floor of the Kidron Valley. (See Sketch 5.)

Even casual familiarity with Temple details would indicate that the massive East Gate of the Sanctuary (Nicanor's Gate) would have to be open in order for the centurion (or anyone) to see the Veil from outside the Temple court. (Sketches 2, 3, 4, 5.) No centurion or any other Gentile would be permitted even in the Court of the Women. The centurion therefore had to be standing near the Mount of Olives summit "when he saw these things that happened."

The East Gate provides even more drama to the occasion when we consider that it had to have been open. This massive and beautiful, bright golden bronze gate was opened for all Sabbaths, New Moons, and on Holy Days (feasts). (See Ezekiel 46:1 and Talmud, Sukkah 53b.) This gate, also known as "Nicanor's Gate," produced "a great noise" because of friction on its "turning hinges" according to Talmud, Yoma 39b.

On the eve of a Sabbath and the Passover, as when Jesus was crucified, this gate would have been opened with its "great noise" being accompanied by no less than forty-eight trumpet blasts from the ram's horn or "shofar." Details covering the exact hour of the gate opening schedule on the eve of Passover are unclear at this time. (Maybe it was opened about 3 P.M.!—Could be!) Notably, on the eve of Passover as The Crucifixion was taking place, "the great noise" of the gate and mixed staccato and squeals of the trumpet calls would certainly have added to the "spooky" conditions leading up to the eclipse, the earthquake, the opened graves, the tearing of the Veil, etc.

We just don't know whether the gate was being opened at that time (the "ninth hour," 3 P.M.) or if it had already been opened "at the third hour" as Jesus was being "lifted up." Or maybe it had "opened of its own accord" as it was to do forty years later. My own preference in this speculative question is that the third hour may have been the customary time for opening on the eve of the Sabbath. The gate opening at 9 A.M. would have been more in keeping with fulfillment of the Law concerning the "sprinkling" of His blood "directly before the Tabernacle."

It would seem that if the gate had swung open mysteriously at that moment, then the New Testament writers would have noted it. Such a miracle would seem to have been noted as one of "these things that happened." But this is not mentioned. We have already seen that those otherwise marvelous reporters seem to have omitted many details that now appear significant as we behold them with our 20/20 hindsight.

So, we can make all sorts of speculations as to exactly when it was opened or how it was opened, but it had to have been opened on the eve of the Sabbath and it must have been open if the Veil was visible—and it was—because Scripture says "he saw" the Veil rent. We can say for certain that gate was open when "he saw these things." From our detailed study of that gate "aperture" in Chapter 4 we also know the centurion had to be standing at precisely the same location where the High Priest stood when he "directed his gaze carefully" to see the Veil.

Not Your Ordinary "Vail"

We should point out here that we are not attempting to "update" Scripture by changing it even in the slightest manner. Rather, we are endeavoring to enrich Scripture by filling in pertinent and Glorifying details that are provided by secular historians of that same date and locale. Of course, I do concede that some of my own imagination has been sprinkled in here and there. However, again we are attempting to bring more appreciation for Scripture with local information on the events and details discussed.

Understandably, there has been a lot of attention directed toward the Veil of the Temple in this entire work. The Veil that receives most of this attention, is, of course, the thick Babylonian curtain that covered the front doors of the H'ekhal, the Holy House itself. We also know this is the "vail" which was "rent in twain" and is one of "those things" seen by those at The Cross at the moment Jesus died. We can have a bit more appreciation for the Biblical accounts concerning the Veil if we are better informed about Jewish tradition and the Law regarding the Veil.

Earlier in Chapter 4 we mentioned that the Veil was replaced two times each year with a new one exactly like the previous curtain. We also pointed out that it was customary to display the new Veil each time "so that the people might behold its fair workmanship" as they stood atop the Mount of Olives. But there is much more.

The Veil needed to be replaced at this interval because it would lose its beautiful colors after a time as a result of a number of factors. First, it was sprinkled with blood from some of the sacrifices as a Holy commandment of the Law. It had to be immersed occasionally for "cleansing" if defiled by anything "unclean." They did not have very many so-called fast color dyes in those times.

Moreover, it was exposed to sunlight and some amount of mountain weather and dust despite its position under the Portico. But, perhaps the strongest reason was because its great weight would cause the Veil to "creep" and to sag non-uniformly, thereby losing its majestic form and symmetry. The Jews were rightly proud of their Veil.

The Veil was not produced by "workman"-ship so much as by young "ladyship!" Talmud, Shekalim 8:5 informs us that it was braided by "eighty-two young damsels" using seventy-four cords of twenty-two threads each. This task probably kept these lasses occupied steadily all during those six months intervals because of the size of the task. The Veil was over three inches thick, about thirty feet wide and about sixty feet high. Three hundred priests were required to lift it for its immersion for purification. We detail this in order that a more realistic picture is available when considering the "rending." This was not just your ordinary religious drapery!

Its striking beauty came from its colors, which, according to Exodus 26:36, were blue, purple, and "scarlet." Can you just picture how it would appear to the High Priest as he "directed his gaze carefully" to view the Veil in the sunlight through the open East Gate?

If You Had Been There

It would be interesting now to place oneself in the position of that centurion at The Crucifixion. On the mount called Olivet, you and your men have been detailed to crucify, with two other criminals, a Judean who claims to be a king! You are to nail them to three crosses at a place the Judeans call "Golgotha"—their word for skull. Olivet in that area is piled deep in ashes and skull remnants from burned carcasses of bulls, rams, goats, lambs, etc. from what the Judeans call their "sin offerings." The place is a hideous and depressing scene and has an overpowering stench because they have been dumping *all* of their ashes, skulls, bones and charred remnants from *all* their sacrifices at this place for about 1000 years. (See Sketches 9 and 10.)

This is the place where their "Holy Book" tells them the ashes must be "poured out" (Leviticus 4:12) and where their "nit-picky" rabbis have further interpreted that this means the ashes must "naturally pour down from a place that is sloping." (Talmud Zebahim 105a) And, this place certainly is sloping; although, we actually are in a kind of shelf or pit that has been cut into the western slope.

The Judean "king's" cross stands centered between the other two and at the exact spot where witnesses have claimed He committed some sort of "abomination." This also is the same spot where their chief rabbi stands when they burn one of those red cows up here. You don't know just why all this is happening. You cannot get involved in religion or politics. You just have to do your job as you have been ordered.

Having arrived on the slope of Mt. Olivet at about "the third hour," you heard those weird calls of the Temple priest's trumpet and then that bone-chilling, ominous tone that was building up as the Temple guards opened that huge bronze gate in front of their Temple across the valley. All this happened just as you were "lifting up" this wretched Judean to be crucified for sedition against Caesar—something about claiming to be "King of the Jews" . . . HA!

It is now about "the ninth hour" (3 P.M.) and light of day has returned—after the sun had been mysteriously darkened since "the sixth hour." Presently, this Judean "crack-pot" astoundingly shouts a couple of sentences in His native Aramaic—and "in a loud voice." You are justifiably impressed at this, because you saw this fellow beaten nearly to death during the scourging at your barracks. And now, barely able to take a breath after hanging on that Cross for six hours, still He has strength and mental presence to actually shout two or three complete sentences. Unreal! You have seen many men, "bigger" and "tougher" than He, who didn't have the strength or breath to beg even for water after being suspended during crucifixion for that time.

All "those things" that you "saw," of course, took place very rapidly and at about the same time that this man suddenly died, after His display of inhuman strength and endurance. He just "up-and-died!" Even in their usual weakened state, some crucifixion victims suffer on that miserable "wiggot" for as long as seven days before finally "giving up the ghost." But this man, who earlier seemed to be doing much better than His two "companions," now dies suddenly and resolutely almost as if He had willed His own death—as if he were in control!

Now, some would think all this had "terrified" you and your men, convincing you at this point that this person was, as He had claimed, the Son of God. Well, not quite. He was evidently not an average man. He did have some impressive strengths, including a perfect physique. He didn't even let out so much as a whimper while He was literally stripped of His hide by that flagellum. Neither did He wince or blink His eyes when you drove those quarter inch diameter spikes into His wrists and feet. He just looked at you. And those eyes! All knowing, yet loving and forgiving, as you put

Him to death for a crime that nobody had committed. An unusual man, yes—but, maybe not a God.

Next, you feel a little earthquake and there is now light-of-day after the darkness that set in from about noonday until this time. The quake opens some of the graves around you there on the front slope of the mount called Olivet and some believe it was "these things" that frightened you and your men and caused you to think perhaps this fellow was a God. That just doesn't figure though, because you and your troops are hardened Roman foot soldiers, well accustomed to seeing "things" like earthquakes, dead bodies, graves, all kinds of unspeakable, unprintable gore, death, sieges, and disasters.

Then, some will say you were terrified when you saw the Veil tear from top to bottom. (Heavy and thick as that curtain was, it is difficult for me to understand why Roman infantrymen would be "terrified" by that.) The Bible goes on to say that not only were you terrified but also you, a Roman centurion—an officer in Caesar's army—said, "Surely, this man was the Son of God." Now that is especially hard to swallow. I can have no doubt that you were suddenly convinced of the Divinity of this Galilean, because Holy Scripture says it is so. But, it should take more than just "these things" as described in Scripture to bring you to terror and to this conclusion. What is missing? The Bible has intentionally omitted something subtle in this Event, which we have overlooked in our analysis.

You can see the Temple Veil is torn now. Or can you? Or would you even notice it is torn? It seems unlikely you would notice that kind of damage from that distance (800 to 1,000 yards) across the Kidron Valley.

Such detail would certainly be obscured since, at the time of Jesus' death (approximately 3 P.M.), the Veil, on the east side of the H'ekhal, would surely have been darkened by the shade of the Portico. (Sketch 2.) Also, while you were squinting into the 3 P.M. sun, the Veil would be especially difficult to see ... unless. . . .(!)

Temple Mount "At the Ninth Hour"

This telephoto view is from the estimated vicinity of the Miphkad Altar as seen at "the ninth hour of the day;" i.e. 3 P.M., and near the time of the Passover. Notice the darkly shaded City Wall. (Do *you* think the centurion could have seen that the Veil of the Temple was torn under just *these* circumstances alone?)

The Jewish Cemetery on the Mount of Olives

Multitudes of Jewish dead rest here awaiting Messiah, for: "...His feet shall stand in that day upon the Mount of Olives ..." (Zechariah 14:4)

Tomb of the Prophets

This well-known tourist stop is the traditional place of entombment for the prophets: Haggai, Malachi, and Zechariah, who *also await Messiah at the summit of the Mount of Olives!*

After all, there had just been an earthquake. This may have caused collapse of the Temple doors behind the outer Veil and the lintels supporting the veils or in some way caused all three veils to part simultaneously, at least for several moments. In this way, a view was provided from the Mount of Olives straight into the Holy of Holies. You would have been looking straight into the Earthly dwelling of the Divine Presence of Almighty God Himself! What a glorious sight that must have been! It also had to be very frightening as that brilliant "fire"—brighter than the sun!—lighted up the man on The Cross above you.

It would seem that the Lord had intended the sun to be in the centurion's eyes as he saw this flash. He knew it wasn't just a reflection from some soldier's burnished shield or helmet. It came from under that deeply shaded "front porch" of the Judeans' Temple—almost in the dark. Yet, although the sun was now shining brightly again, this light was even much brighter than the sun—and coming from inside the Temple—and through the torn curtain. What a sight to behold! Almighty God Himself "glowing" proudly yet painfully as He watched His Son, Jesus, lay down His Victorious Payment before the World!

Now I see why you and your squad were so terrified and were moved to believe at once as you did: "Truly, this man was the Son of God!" (See Chapter 9, "The Rending of the Veil.")

But, I still don't understand why the Bible didn't tell us all "these things."

Another theory could perhaps assume that the Shechinah Glory may have shone through the two more delicate inner veils (separating the Holy of Holies from the Holy Place). The discussion presented in Appendix B concerning the identity of the "Cherubim" would seem to discount the idea of a glow through the veils, however.

In either case, the centurion would have reason to be impressed because, even in daylight, a brilliant light from the Judean's Temple has just illuminated the man on the cross above him—like a spotlight or perhaps even lighting up the entire mountainside! This sight would understandably have "terrified" the centurion and his execution detail squad.

> Then, when the centurion and those with him who were guarding Jesus saw the earthquake and all that had happened, they were terrified, and exclaimed, "Surely he was the Son of God."

Matthew 27:54 (NIV)

CHECKLIST FOR LOCALES OF THE CRUCIFIXION

		Ch. of Holy Sepulchre	Vicinity of Garden Tomb	Olivet Summit
Temple faced eastward.	Exodus 38:13–15	+	+	+
Temple faced the Mount of Olives.	Mk. 13:3, Sketch 5, 6	+	+	+
Centurion *saw* the Veil *and* Jewish graves.	Matthew 27:51–54	o	o	+
Jewish graves on Olivet since 500 B.C.	Zechariah 14:4	o	o	+
Latrines were on NW side of Jerusalem. (Graves would *not* be next to latrines.)	"The Temple Scroll" Prof. Y. Yadin	+	o	+
Jesus fulfilled Zech. 12–14, including that He stood on the Mount of Olives.	John 19:37 Zechariah 14:4	o	o	+
Jesus fulfilled Law of the Red Heifer:	Matthew 5:17			
—Heifers were slain at Olivet summit	Talmud, Middoth 2:4	o	o	+
—Priest saw Veil as he sprinkled blood	Talmud, Middoth 2:4	o	o	+
—Sprinkled at 3rd hour toward Veil	Sketch 3, 4, 5	o	o	+
And, His Tomb must be "a clean Place":	Numbers 19:9			
—Must be an unused hewn stone chamber	Luke 23:53	+	+	+
—Must have air space beneath corpse	Parah 3:2, 3:6	o	o	+
Eusebius says Cross & Tomb on Olivet.	"Proof of the Gospel"	o	o	+
All sacrifices were *east* of the Temple.	Sketch 1, 5, 6, 7	o	o	+
Holiest sacrifices burnt "*outside camp*" about 1000 yards *east* of Temple at the *summit of the Mount of Olives*. Names, "Golgotha"–"Calvary" from "Place of the Skull," where *thousands* of skulls lay after burning these animals atop the *Mount of Olives*. Jesus fulfilled Law of:	Sketch 5, 6 Talmud, Yoma 68a, Zebahim 106a Matthew 5:17	o	o	+
—Atonement Goats	Leviticus 16:27	o	o	+
—Atonement Bullocks	Leviticus 16:27	o	o	+
—Bullocks for *daily* Sin Offerings	Exodus 29:14	o	o	+
—Bullocks for individual Sin Offerings.	Leviticus 4:11–12	o	o	+
Jesus fulfilled Law of Passover Lamb, which was killed "outside the camp"; i.e., 1000 yards from the Temple.	Matthew 5:17 Exodus 12:6 Sketch 5, 6	o	o	+
Criminals executed "outside the camp".	Numbers 15:30–36	o	o	+

+ qualifies according to Scripture and Talmudic Law
o does not qualify according to Scripture and the Law

Keeping His Schedule

We should not miss the opportunity to observe how the Glory of God is magnified in these events by His Precise Timing. Earlier we showed how the Lord "set up" His own sacrifice and fulfillment of the Law by arranging to be "lifted up" at "the third hour." This timing was necessary in order to fulfill the Law pertaining to the sprinkling of the Red Heifer's blood, which was done at the "third hour."

Jesus also exercised His own will, of course, in controlling His death on The Cross "at the ninth hour." It was no accident and that hour was not at the discretion of the centurion. The Lord died at that hour in order to maintain His Schedule.

He had to die as the Paschal Lamb of God on the eve of the Passover because, according to the Law, "You shall kill it (the Lamb) at evening." "Evening" began at about 3 P.M. In this way Jesus fulfilled the Passover. The next feast to be fulfilled was the Feast of Unleavened Bread. He therefore had to be off The Cross and in the tomb before the next day began (at sunset) because the bread must be "eaten" with the Lamb. Jesus had to begin "baking" as our Unleavened Bread of Life in the tomb. (Perhaps you knew that the name of His birthplace, little Bethlehem, is from the Hebrew: "beth" (house) and "lehem" (bread); i.e., "House of Bread.")

It was necessary to die at 3 P.M. on the eve of the Sabbath, in order that the East Gate of the Temple (Nicanor's Gate) would be open at that precise moment for the centurion to be able to confront the Divine Presence of Almighty God when the Veil was rent in twain from top to bottom. Perfect Timing! It had to be! The Law must be fulfilled—every "jot" and "tittle."

We would be remiss here to neglect another fulfillment of the Law if we did not mention His avoidance of the breaking of the legs, as suffered by the two thieves. (John 19:31–37) In order to hasten the death of crucifixion victims, sometimes their legs were broken in order that they would not be able to lift themselves to relieve their cramped, agonized, breathless position. And so it was on this day, as Passover was approaching. Everybody wished to "get it over with" and go home. However, when they came to Jesus to break His legs, the soldiers passed Him by because He was already dead. In this way, Jesus fulfilled His service to the Law of the Passover Lamb in Exodus 12:46,

> . . . neither shall ye break a bone thereof.

This was also a fulfillment of the prophecy in Psalms 34:20,

> He keepeth all His bones; not one of them is broken.

Of course, the "Divine Schedule" proceeded from there to fulfill all the other feasts and Law, which we cannot take time to discuss here. However, all was fulfilled on Schedule. Who but the Lord Himself could have written, produced, directed, and starred in any drama even approaching this for message, plot, staging, and just plain class?

CAIAPHAS, "GOOD-GUY" OR "BAD-GUY"?

There is a natural inclination, especially for those of western cultural origin, to assign "good-guy" or "bad-guy" connotations to characters we meet. It occurred to me as I was writing this, that we have been guilty of "judging" Israel's High Priest, Caiaphas, by tabbing him as arch-villain in our Passion drama.

But, since we know that the Divine Presence was indeed dwelling in the Temple after The Crucifixion, let us just pause to consider a "tradition-shaking" implication. This means God accepted Caiaphas as High Priest! (That's right. I said "accepted.")

Now, (after the dust has settled) why would I even suggest such a "revolting" idea?

On the next Day of Atonement, after a few months following The Crucifixion, Caiaphas was required to appear as Israel's High Priest before the Lord (in His form as Shechinah) in the Holy of Holies to plead atonement by confessing and requesting forgiveness of his own sins as well as those of Israel. (See Talmud MISHNAH quoted under "The Crimson Strap," Chapter 7.)

If the Lord did not accept Caiaphas after his vile actions at the "trial," He could have struck Caiaphas dead. He certainly wouldn't have to permit Caiaphas to come before Himself at the Divine Presence. There, especially, He would have had "just" reason to strike Caiaphas dead, to show all of Israel His displeasure with their High Priest.

Talmud, Yoma 9a, records that the period of the Second Temple was rife with corruption in that high and Holy office. Further, tractate Pesachim 57a reveals that often men who once became High Priest would continue to hold great prestige even after being deposed! At times there were often several men who held such power and intimidation just through the title of the position. Reading between-the-lines of the Gospel, we see some of this intrigue and injustice in the nepotism and blatant criminal blasphemy of Caiaphas and his father-in-law, Anas. More of this shameful history will be presented in Chapter 7.

But the Lord chose not to deal with Caiaphas and Israel in the way that perhaps you or I would have preferred. Everyone knows the "bad-guy" always gets his just "reward" eventually. (The Lord forgave all of us at The Cross.) If Caiaphas repented after he saw all those weird signals "forty years before the Temple was destroyed," he may even have received salvation. We cannot judge Caiaphas.

If the Lord can forgive King David and Paul (and you and me) and King Nebuchadnezzar (Daniel 4:34–37) and lots of other "bad-guys," then maybe—just maybe—He can also forgive Caiaphas. Let us not hate Caiaphas by judging him; even though we must certainly detest his actions when he was confronted by the Lord Jesus.

Historians record that Caiaphas was deposed from his office as High Priest after The Crucifixion. We can only wonder now—did he see these things as they began to happen "forty years before the Temple was destroyed?" Of course he did. He had to have seen those signs. He was the High Priest. This happened during his "watch."

Did Caiaphas perhaps have second thoughts about that resolute carpenter who would not deny that He was Messiah? After all, didn't these signs begin to appear immediately after that "wretched imposter and blasphemer" was put to death? Was Caiaphas relieved as High Priest perhaps because all these incidents caused him to soften his position against this "Galilean apostasy," which was now gaining strength in Jerusalem, and in all Judea, and in Samaria, etc.? Who can know?

STANDING-TALL, BUT BOWING-LOW

There is a sermon of sorts in the symbolism of the Red Heifer sacrifice that we wish to share with you. Since that sacrifice and the Miphkad Altar figure so prominently in the Shechinah story, it seems fitting that we should present it here.

We are drawn in this theme to the cedar tree and the hyssop plant, used in that sacrifice for the burning. In Jewish tradition, the cedar of Lebanon, stately and tall, is often a symbol of haughtiness, while the hyssop, in contrast, is a symbol of humility. (See reference 16.) These two opposite "pictures" provide a message.

When men or nations begin regarding their own "stature" and "tallness," God usually causes them to be "brought low" in order that they may again become more like the hyssop—lowly, plain, lacking "color" and inconspicuous. These traits are especially regarded as "wicked" in God's eyes when we attribute our "comeliness" and our "sheen" and "image" to our own creation rather than by His Grace and to His Purpose.

When we begin "preening" (individually or as nations) before our peers and then solicit and/or savor men's lauding of our *own* "magnificence," we surely are provoking the Lord to chasten us and to bring us back down to earth.

We must then be reminded that we are ALL a part of His family. ALL are created for His Purpose—and "increased" only through His Hand—certainly not by our *own* puny and ill-guided efforts. When we begin to say, "I AM what I AM because of what I AM!," we are "tempting" God to diminish the increase that He alone has given us.

In the past few decades, as well as throughout the Bible and all of history, there are many examples of "kings" and nations who have been "brought low" as the hyssop. We need not mention names. I am sure you can think of some (nations and "kings") who have been in the headlines as recently as yesterday.

We also must notice that some of these same "kings" and nations have been "brought back" from their lowly estate as the hyssop, to rise again to become "tall and stately" once more. And then, if they do not become too haughty and begin "preening" again, the Lord may permit them to remain "tall," *if* they also regard and obey Him.

God presents some learning examples for us through His messenger, Zephaniah, Chapter 3 (NASB):

His warnings: (Verses 1 & 2)	Woe to her who is rebellious and defiled, The tyrannical city! She heeded no voice; She accepted no instruction. She did not trust in the Lord; She did not draw near to her God.
His "Rod": (Verse 6)	I have cut off nations; Their corner towers are in ruins. I have made their streets desolate, With no one passing by; Their cities are laid waste, Without a man, without an inhabitant.
His Healing: (Verses 11–13)	. . . and you will never again be haughty; On My holy mountain.

> But I will leave among you
> A humble and lowly people,
> And they will take refuge
> In the name of the Lord.
> ... For they shall feed and lie down
> With no one to make them tremble.

Jesus also gave us a similar but brief instruction on this theme:

> For everyone who exalts himself will be humbled, and he who humbles himself will be exalted.
>
> Luke 14:11 (NASB)

Can we possibly comprehend or appreciate the humility of Jesus, who **IS** God, as He approached the Temple where His Divine Presence also dwelt? Here He stood in debate with the doubting Pharisees, who were unaware they were actually scheming to trap the Great "I AM" concerning the Law that *He* had written! No *ordinary* man could have resisted the urge to quip, "Shall I ask My Father to come out and convince you?"

Learning from these examples, we should pray that He would give us strength to "stand tall" like the mighty cedar—resisting the worldly "winds" of temptation, "modern change," conformity, and "lusts." We should "stand tall" in our faith against these worldly rages in order that we demonstrate (witness) our strength in our Lord before "the world."

Further, we should pray that He would show us how to remain humble as the lowly hyssop concerning our "increase" brought about by His Heavenly "winds" of Wisdom, Grace, and Strength. Pray also that we would not become a "haughty" cedar, showing pride before the eyes of men. Pray we remember that before God we are merely hyssops. HE is the Cedar.

Our best example is the Lord Jesus. He is our tall and stately Cedar; although His stance is as the hyssop. Only Jesus is worthy to stand tall. He is justified to haughtiness, but He is not.

* * * Jesus bows at *our* feet that we may worship *Him*. * * *

THE CHARACTER OF GOD

This story of Shechinah illustrates the character of God. We see Him saddened by the disobedience of His children. We share His sorrow as we hear Him weep and rebuke them as He withdraws from His earthly palace. The Lord is saddened at leaving and, with "human" emotions, He returns for one-last-look before leaving His house. He is depressed, but at the same time He is firm and resolved to correct these "naughty children." Yet, He is also patient and caring in that He doesn't just condemn them and rush off. He stays to rebuke and to plead with them for 3 $^1/_2$ years—trying to keep them from certain disaster.

Finally, however, after giving them adequate time to repent, He departs using a subtle gesture involving locale (Olivet Summit) to show them that He will return for them after He goes "back to His Place." This single incident shows the "human" qualities of the Lord, which are often seen in the Scriptures, but which we seldom have seen from any other historical source.

Truly, this is a love story, another like so many stories in the Bible, that demonstrates God's love for His People and for the rest of us. It all begins with our response to His "courting" of our favors, our acceptance and use of his "gifts," but at first without our commitment to a "betrothal." Then, our fickle hearts turn away from Him after being attracted to other "lovers." This rejection does not deter Him, however; for He continues to "pursue" us (His "bride") and forgives our perfidy. Finally—a happy ending! We surrender to Him "unconditionally" and are reunited with Him.

Jesus said it best, when Phillip asked about God's character:

> ... he that hath seen me hath seen the Father. . . . (John 14:9)

6 Prophecies Relating to This Event

Several **popular and** Scripturally sound teachings of prophecy are impacted by the Shechinah event and other related facts in this story. This discussion addresses some new thoughts that should be considered. Again, you are invited (encouraged!) to think of other prophetical relevance that we have not discussed.

More "Heifers" for the Unclean

Much of this story has touched upon the Ashes of the Red Heifer and the Miphkad Altar because of archaeological interests and other factors that are fundamental to the Shechinah Withdrawal Event, as well as being of great importance relative to The Crucifixion. These facts also are of vital importance in prophecy and should be included in this segment of our study.

A key prophecy relating to the "Last Days" is given in Daniel 9:27. The "prince that shall come" (Antichrist) "shall cause the sacrifice and the oblation to cease" exactly three and one half years (one half "week") before Messiah arrives. It is obvious then, Israel surely must resume the Temple sacrifices at some time before the sacrifices are halted.

BUT—The sacrifices cannot be offered unless and until the ashes of the Red Heifer are recovered. (Huh??? Why is that?) The Law requires that the Temple, the priests, and all articles used in those offerings must be purified by sprinkling of those ashes from the burnt Red Heifer mixed with "living water." (Numbers, Chapter 19)

Furthermore, the ashes of that first heifer, burnt by Moses and Eleazar in the Sinai, mixed with the ashes from all heifers offered since that time are the only ashes that are acceptable under the Law. A commandment from the Lord (Numbers 19:10) and from the Law (Talmud, Parah 3:5) instructs that those first ashes are "for a statute forever." In other words, they cannot just burn a new heifer. The original ashes as mixed with all the others must be found and recovered and used "as a purification for sin."

For all of the reasons stated in Scripture and in the Law then, the sacrifice of the Red Heifer is the single most important sacrifice of all the Jewish sacrifices, without question. No ashes, no priests, no Tabernacle, no Temple, no sacrifices!—no fulfillment of prophecy! We know *that* cannot be! So then, "It's not to worry!" Those ashes *will* be found! There can be *no* doubt!

It is a tragic irony that the Red Heifer is the least known and the least understood of all the Jewish sacrifices while it is without question the most important. So, is anybody trying to find these ashes? Again, it's not-to-worry! A joint Jewish and Christian archaeological team is close to recovering the ashes after an exciting search of about twenty years.

Through a "stroke-of-luck" (more like a miracle!) directions and detailed instructions for locating the ashes were found several years ago. (Why does nobody ever tell us about such things?!) Some try, but many people (especially the conservative Christian media) seem not to want anyone to hear such things—especially you. They seem to fear that you might become too "excited" and/or—worse yet—you might even become too anxious and eager for Messiah to arrive (or return!). Have you ever noticed that most preachers avoid mentioning the return of Jesus as a reality that we could experience in the very near future? Perhaps they have good intentions in not wanting you to become too hopeful for His soon return and then to suffer disappointment if He delays for a time. (But I think we can handle it.) We must be patient and pray for these folks. Maybe they are not ready yet.

One search team, headed by Texan minister/archaeologist Vendyl M. Jones and formerly the late Chief Rabbi of Israel, Shlomo Goren, is expected to reach the precious urn (Kalal) containing the ashes sometime in the very near future. Then we can get on with the remaining fulfillments of all prophecies leading up to the return of the Lord Jesus! However, we must take note here that the ashes and fulfillments of prophecies discussed here have absolutely nothing to do with the next fulfillment; i.e., the taking away or "rapture" of The Church.

Another reason for urgency toward finding the Red Heifer ashes (and Miphkad Altar) is that the Jews are almost certain to run out of ashes unless they burn at least one new Red Heifer during the coming seven years of The Tribulation. Many scholars of prophecy teach that the battle of Gog and Magog, the Russian invasion of Israel, will occur early during the Tribulation and perhaps soon after Antichrist is revealed. (This is not the battle of Armageddon.)

The key to this subtlety concerning an early need for more ashes is given by the prophet Ezekiel. Briefly, the armies of Gog will be so badly mauled that only one sixth of their number will survive in defeat "upon the mountains of Israel" (Ez. 39:2). Then comes the cause for nearing depletion of the ashes. "Yea, all the people of the Land (Israel) shall bury them." (Ez. 39:11)

Yes! There will be so many dead among the invaders from Russia and her allies that seven months will be required for the Israelites to bury the dead in order "that they may cleanse the Land." (Ez. 39:12) This means all those Jews who bury the dead must be purified afterwards by those ashes if they are to return to "cleanness" under the Law. Over one million Israelis burying dead enemy soldiers is going to require an awesome quantity of ashes. According to the prophecy then, all or most of Israel will have returned to living under the Law at that time. A tendency towards that condition can be seen today in Israel's political strata.

Ancient Judaism was not so blind concerning Ezekiel's prophecy (Chapters 38 & 39) of the invasion of Israel when this great army from the North comes "to take a spoil" in the latter days. Rodkinson's Talmud,[24] in Pesachim tractate, records a statement written in about 200 A.D. by Rabbi Johanan ben Nappaha, in which he says the time of that war will be just before the coming of Messiah and "will be the worst period for the Israelites to pass through."

Worse than the Holocaust? Sadly, yes. Jesus says the Earth will be in such turmoil, if He were to delay beyond His timely arrival, there would be nobody remaining to greet Him.

> And except that the Lord had shortened those days, no flesh should be saved; but for the elect's sake, whom He hath chosen, He hath shortened the days."
>
> Mark 13:20

His "elect" will survive that "time of Jacob's trouble," having been "elected" to greet Him at His coming and to "look upon Me whom they have pierced."

It is interesting that the Jewish tradition of the Talmud, Sukkah 2a, discloses that Judaism considers the Messianic age as that same time which Evangelical Christians call the Kingdom Age or the Millennium, etc.

Along this same trend, "at the end of days" another Talmudic commentary reveals a traditional view of things "of the future world." Tractate Berakoth 17a says the future world is not like this world. In the next world there will be no eating, no drinking, no propagation, no business, no jealousy, no hatred, no competition. But, the righteous will sit with their crowns on their heads feasting on the brightness of the Divine Presence. This observation is taken concerning Exodus 24:11.

So, we see that in some ways the Jewish Believers are not so far different from Christians in some of their interpretations of Scripture. Surely the basic difference exists only in the *Personal* identity of that *One* whose (pierced) feet shall stand that Day on the Mount of Olives.

THE CLOSED DOOR POLICY

One of the key archaeological interests in this study has been the immense Eastern Gate (Nicanor's Gate). Its halting expanse of gleaming, golden-hued bronze dominated the front of the Temple complex and shielded the front of the H'ekhal from direct view. This same gate is very prominent in prophecies of "the End Times" as well:

> Then He brought me back by the way of the gate of the outward sanctuary which looketh toward the east; and it was shut.
>
> Then said the Lord unto me; "This gate shall be shut, it shall not be opened, and no man shall enter in by it; because the Lord, the God of Israel, hath entered in by it, therefore it shall be shut.
>
> It is for the Prince; the Prince, He shall sit in it to eat bread before the Lord; He shall enter by way of the porch of that gate, and shall go out by the way of the same."
>
> Ezekiel 44:1–3

We encounter a curious situation here concerning Jewish interpretation of this prophecy of the gate that "shall be shut." That is, "the gate of the outward sanctuary which looketh toward the east." Almost anyone would reason that Ezekiel is referring to the mammoth east gate (Nicanor's Gate) because everything he has been describing (measuring) for the previous two chapters and beyond this passage has been "outside the House"—in the courts and walls. Moreover, he has referred to the intricate arrangement of folding doors, located behind the Veil at the entrance, as "doors" and not as "gates." (Ezekiel 41:2)

Ezekiel was given these measurements in "the five and twentieth year of our captivity"; several years before the Second Temple was built by Zerubbabel. The Jews were following the measurements and "ordinances" directed through that prophet as they rebuilt the Temple. The Rabbis did not consider any difference between the "Millennial Temple" and this rebuilt (Second) Temple. They thought they were building the Temple for Messiah, the Prince.

They expected this to be the Temple from which "living waters" would flow from the "Water Gate" on the "right side" of the House. They followed all the cubit measurements for the House, the courts, the chambers, the gates. All of the Lord's "ordinances" for the priests and the sacrifices were instituted "to the letter." And yes, they "shut the gate" as they believed the Lord had instructed—but they shut the wrong gate at the wrong time!

The Jews of the first century were expecting the Messiah to come and rest His feet on Olivet and bring victory over Israel's oppressors and enemies. They expected Olivet to "cleave in the midst thereof" and the living waters would cause the little desert village of En Gedi to be a commercial fishing center! (Ezekiel 47:10) Have you ever been to En Gedi?

They were expecting a victorious, conquering Messiah to sit in that Gate. They were not looking for—nor did they welcome—this Nazarene carpenter who surrounded Himself with the likes of commercial fishermen, tax collectors, prostitutes . . . lepers!

Nevertheless, imagine now the frustrating, puzzling, "pained!" choice the Rabbinical "lawyers" faced. Some of the vision of the Temple was instruction for building the Second Temple and some of it was prophecy of things that were to happen to the rebuilt (Second) Temple and even to the Millennial Temple in days to come. Close inspection of this Scripture while following the Temple descriptions recorded by Josephus, Talmud, etc., reveals that the Jews were "religiously" dedicated to compliance with Ezekiel's specifications. Nevertheless, the Jews of the Second Temple encountered considerable difficulty in separating "instruction" from "prophecy" in Ezekiel's message. Put yourself in their position.

Their reasoning must have been something like this:

- If this is prophecy that has been fulfilled sometime in the past, then it means if the Lord had already "entered through it," just when could He have done that?—The Second Temple had not yet been built when Ezekiel wrote in the "five and twentieth year" of our captivity.

- Or, if this is a prophecy not yet fulfilled, then He will shut the gate whenever He does "enter through it."

- But, on the other hand, if He is instructing us to keep Nicanor's Gate shut, how can we do that? In the words of the Prophet himself, that gate must be opened on the eve of each Sabbath, on each new moon, and on each Feast Day. (Ezekiel 46:1) The High Priest must peer carefully through that gate from Olivet summit when he sprinkles the heifer's blood "directly before the Tabernacle seven times." He must therefore be saying the "doors" at the front of the H'ekhal must remain closed. Yea! That's it!

- The opposing "lawyers" counter: "Rubbish! We cannot close the entrance to the H'ekhal!—that the doors 'shall not be opened.' The High Priest must enter there to plead for our atonement on the day of Yom Kippur. He must enter through those doors and walk along the north wall of the Holy Place carrying the Censer and the Blood into the Holy of Holies. How can the doors remain shut?!"

- Then, one attorney who was well-practiced in the delicate jurisprudence of compromise, offered a brilliant codicil to the parties favoring the closed doors at the H'ekhal entrance. He suggested, "Let us keep the doors on the south closed in perpetuity; however, we shall grant easement to the High Priest for entry on Yom Kippur on the appointed day through the north doors. In this way, we will remain in compliance with the principal overgoverning statute by maintaining closed doors in keeping with the 'in-contestarium' statute from the Lord's solemn instruction; which at the same time, will satisfy all of the pursuant clauses in participle with the aforementioned ancillary statutes; namely, the incinerated Offering of the Red Heifer attendant with and pertaining to the ministrations stipulated in adherence by the High Priest on Yom Kippur."

This is how they seem to have settled the matter. The southern doors ("gates") were shut, but the priest was permitted entry through the north doors on the Day of Atonement. This way everybody was happy—everybody except the Lord, that is. The Rabbis did not want to accept this idea that the Lord would shut Nicanor's Gate as punishment for their iniquities and transgressions.

The Lord Jesus "entered in" by Nicanor's Gate to make his sacrifices, thus fulfilling that portion of prophecy. And we *now* know for certain this was a prophecy and not an instruction. Forty years later the "closure" was fulfilled, when Nicanor's magnificent doors were crushed, burned, and melted by rampaging Roman soldiers.

Now, at this point some may argue, as no doubt some rabbis countered, "But Ezekiel 43:4 says the Divine Presence *entered* the Temple by that gate 'whose prospect is toward the east' and the prophecy was thereby fulfilled when He 'entered in.' So, we must see that it remains shut.—It is a commandment from the Lord thy God."

Others would amend that by saying Ezekiel 43:4 refers to the return of the Glory to the Millennial Temple or possibly even the "New Jerusalem" and the prophecy of Ezekiel 44:2 was therefore fulfilled when Jesus "entered in." With these latter Rabbis I must agree, because the Temple Ezekiel discussed here has "waters" rushing from under the "right" side of the threshold.

How do we know Ezekiel is speaking of a much later Temple? Just a few verses later, Ezekiel 43:7, the Lord says:

> ... where I will dwell in the midst of the children of Israel forever. . . .

That latter promise has not yet reached fulfillment, because Israel has not yet reached the Messiannic Age.

We maintain therefore that Jesus fulfilled the "entering in" portion of Ezekiel 44:2. Then, the return of the Glory to the Millennial Temple or possibly the New Jerusalem (Heaven) will (someday) satisfy Ezekiel 43:4.

Yes, it is complex and difficult to follow. Although, it is much easier if one has 20/20 hindsight. The Rabbis could not figure out how the Lord was going to "pull this off." Sadly then, the Rabbis interpreted the Scripture into a "Law" to make this a "statute" instead of recognizing that it was a prophecy.

The prophecy continues by saying in Ezekiel 44:2 that "The Lord, the God of Israel hath entered in by it"; and in verse 3, " . . . He shall enter by the way of the porch of that gate, and shall go out by the way of the same." Here is a very subtle legal problem. Nobody was permitted to leave the Temple by exiting through the East Gate; because in so doing, one would turn his back on the Holy House. Remember in Ezekiel's vision (Ez. 8:16–17) the displeasure of the

Lord against the priests who worshipped the sun with their backs to the Temple? There was only One who could turn His back on the Holy House while deliberately ignoring and departing from His former dwelling. (He certainly was seen to do just that on the Feast of Pentecost, 66 A.D.)

In dedication to "legal perfection," however, it must be observed that at least one exception was made for exiting through this gate. The High Priest and his entourage left the Temple by the way of that gate when escorting the Red Heifer to the Mount of Olives. (Middoth 1:3) Nevertheless, it can be expected that all, except the Heifer, were required to walk backwards, facing the Temple, until they reached a "respectable" distance from the Holy House.

Jesus entered by "the porch" of Nicanor's Gate, with all other devout Jews, to bring ritual sacrifice for a burnt offering on the Altar in the Court of Israelites. As an obedient and "ordinary" citizen, Jesus exited the court at either the south or west gate just like the other Israelites had done for fifteen centuries—ever since the Tabernacle.

In 66 A.D. on the Feast Day of Weeks, the Pentecost, the East Gate was opened in keeping with the Law, and the Lord, the God of Israel (as Shechinah), "went out by way of the same" gate He (as Jesus) hath entered in. The prophecy was fulfilled, exactly as Ezekiel had foretold. Ezekiel omitted one important detail. The Lord entered through the East Gate traveling incognito as a Galilean carpenter come to present His burnt offering before God. Most would agree that it would have been difficult for first-century Judaism to have understood this.

And so, the Gate was shut. Not by Suleiman in the sixteenth century, but by the Roman soldiers as they burned and sacked Jerusalem and the Temple after the siege in 70 A.D. So, it was written; and so it came to pass.

Fulfilling the Feasts

Many scholars and teachers of end-time prophecy have taught (and not with casual reasoning) that Jesus has fulfilled the first four of the seven Feasts of Jevhovah so far, with each in its chronological order and on the exact day of each feast. The last feast fulfilled is considered to have been the Shavuot (Pentecost) and—most believe—the next to be fulfilled will be the Feast of Trumpets (Rosh Hashanah.)

It would seem that the departure of the Divine Presence from the

Temple on Pentecost in 66 A.D. would be another major fulfillment. There also may be prophetic significance in the fact that this occurred exactly thirty-six years (6×6) after Pentecost 30 A.D., which we recognize as the beginning of the Church Age. (Later in this chapter we shall explain some of the significance of the number "six.")

Although Chanukah is not one of the seven Feasts of Jehovah, the likelihood of the Shechinah Ascension occurring during that season may also figure into this puzzle in some way. But this sequence certainly is disruptive to the order that has been taught (and accepted) with such popularity. Perhaps an explanation is needed.

Before discussing fulfillment of these feasts, strictly a Christian interpretation, we should identify the significance of each feast from the traditional Judaic perspective.

Pesach (Passover)
Celebrating the sparing of Israel's firstborn in Egypt when the blood of the Passover Lamb was smeared on the doorposts to turn away the Angel of Death. The lamb is to be slain on the evening of the fourteenth day of the month, Nisan.

Hag Hamatzah (Unleavened Bread)
In memory of the haste in departure of the children of Israel from Pharoah's tyranny.—They could not wait for their bread to rise. After sunset, as the fifteenth of Nisan begins, the Passover Lamb is eaten at the meal (Seder). Talmud (Pesahim 119b) instructs that one who eats the Seder must finish the meal with the taste of the Paschal Lamb and the unleavened bread in his mouth. Since fermentation is ritually "unclean," no yeast or leavened bread is permitted for seven days.

First Fruits
Thanking the Lord for the first harvest of Spring, especially the barley harvest. This feast begins on the first day of the week (Sunday) following the next Sabbath; that is, the first Sunday after the fifteenth of Nisan.

Shavuot (Weeks or Pentecost)
Celebrates the spectacular events that occurred at Mount Sinai, when Moses was given the Law, by observing those forty-nine days

as "counting the omer" (a measure of grain). This period connects between the barley harvest (First Fruits) and the beginning of the wheat harvest (Shavuot). Shavuot is the fiftieth day after First Fruits and is therefore also on a Sunday, seven Sundays after First Fruits.

ROSH HASHANAH (NEW YEAR)
Jewish interpretations of Rosh Hashanah are varied and numerous. Brief discussion would hardly be adequate to describe some of the deep (and hidden) meanings involved. Briefly, however, according to Rosh Hashanah tractate, the teaching concerns:

— Rosh Hashanah is the first day of the month, Tishri, and the beginning of the Jewish New Year.

— The beginning of Creation.

— Coronation of the King of Kings.

— The first of ten days of repentance.

— A reminder of the destruction of the Temple.

— Sounding of the shofar makes one tremble before God.

— A recalling of fear of the coming Day of Judgment.

— To awaken a yearning for the future gathering of Israel's dispersed returning to the Land—as we have shown prophetically.

— To recall faith in the future resurrection of the dead.

During the Second Temple period and since that time, Jewish teaching is mixed on the concept of life after death. Nevertheless, those who do teach of a resurrection seem to have looked forward only to life in Messiah's Kingdom on Earth during the Messianic Age to come. Some say those who go to punishment in Gehenna (Hell) will suffer eternally, but others teach that punishment will be for a limited time. (See Shabbath tractate 33b and then see Daniel 12:2.) The Lord says that "some will go to *everlasting* shame and contempt." (His Words.)

The ten days between Rosh Hashanah and Yom Kippur are known as "the Days of Awe" and constitute the most Holy season of Jewish observance. The thirty days preceding Rosh Hashanah consist of the month, Elul. This entire forty day season is known as the season of Tshuvah, meaning a return to the Lord and/ or repentance. (The Hebrew word *tshuvah*, which means "repent," also means "return.")

YOM KIPPUR (DAY OF ATONEMENT)
This most Holy Jewish festival occurs on the 10th day of Tishri and is a day of deep introspect, prayer and repentance by observant, worshipful Jews. Rabbis caution that repentance can atone only for offenses against God. Trespasses against a fellow human must be atoned by reconciliation with the person who has been wronged. (Yoma 85b.)

SUKKAH (OR SUKKOTH, BOOTHS, FEAST OF TABERNACLES)
A commemoration of the Israelite's life in the Sinai desert enroute to their Promised Land. (They dwelled in huts or "booths.") This is also a celebration of the Autumn harvest—sort of a Jewish Thanksgiving.

Christian interpretation of the Jewish feasts is of course in the Messianic context and is therefore understandably greatly different from the Jewish view. We should note here that *all* of these feasts so far have been fulfilled to Jewish participants on these Jewish occasions.

Mentioned earlier, each of the first four feasts has been fulfilled on the exact day and in the exact order as they were commanded to Moses. These were fulfilled to the Jews exclusively, as follows:

Passover Celebrates the sparing of Israel's first born.	The Crucifixion—(The Lamb of God was slain to defeat the angel of death.)
Unleavened Bread No leaven (fermentation) or any type of ritually "unclean dough," representing impurity or sin, is permitted in the Jewish home during the coming seven days. (See introduction to tractate Pesahim and tractate Rosh Hashanah 3b.)	The body of Jesus lay in the tomb. (The sinless, "unleavened" body rests.)
First Fruits Celebrating the first fruits of the spring harvest.	The Resurrection—(Jesus was the first of those to be resurrected from the dead. He now lives in a resurrected, incorruptible, eternal body. That first "harvest.")
Pentecost Celebrating Moses' receiving the Ten Commandments.	The Holy Spirit, as tongues of flame, descended to the disciples. (They received their "commandments.")

Feasts of Jehovah remaining to be fulfilled will continue in the following order and on the occasions described: (Note: Purim and Chanukah are not Feasts of Jehovah.)

Trumpets (Rosh Hashanah) Celebrates the New Year.	The "great trumpet will sound" and all Jewish people will be "gathered up" to Jerusalem to prepare for their "New Year" with the Lord, the inauguration of the Messianic Age.
Atonement (Yom Kippur)	Messiah will arrive at Olivet summit. (Jews will be atoning when

All Jews and the nation atone for the sins of the past year.	"they look upon Me whom they have pierced.")
Sukkoth (Tabernacles) Celebrates Israel's exodus wherein they shared their Tabernacle with their Lord.	Messiah will begin His reign over His Promised Kingdom as Son of David. (All nations will come to "Tabernacle" with the Lord.)

It is important to note, however, that the first Christians were Jews and that no Gentile Christians were yet "in the fold" with Jesus' disciples at the time of the Crucifixion and the Resurrection. Neither were any Gentiles present fifty days later at Pentecost. This "no-Gentiles" policy is even more specifically reflected in Exodus 12:48 in the Lord's commandment that no "uncircumcized person" (Gentile) shall eat at the Passover meal (Seder).

For these reasons a theory could be formulated to suggest that the next feast to be fulfilled, Rosh Hashanah (Feast of Trumpets), also will be fulfilled to the Jews rather than to Gentile Christians at the Rapture of the Church. This theory would continue with the prophetic indication that all Jewish people remaining alive on Earth at the end of the Tribulation will be translated bodily to Jerusalem "from the four corners of the Earth" when "the great trumpet sounds."

This theory is based on a promise from God to Israel in Isaiah 43:5 and 6, (KJV):

> Fear not: for I am with thee: I will bring thy seed from the east, and gather thee from the west; I will say to the north, Give up; and to the south, Keep not back: Bring my sons from afar and my daughters from the ends of the earth.

Also, the prophet Jeremiah has delivered this same Promise:

> And I will gather the remnant of my flock out of all countries whither I have driven them, and will bring them again to their folds; and they shall be fruitful and increase.
>
> And I will set up shepherds over them which shall feed them.
>
> and they shall fear no more, nor be dismayed, neither shall they be lacking, saith the Lord.

Jeremiah 23:3,4 (KJV)

Now, listen again to the Word from our messenger, Isaiah:

> And it will come about in that day, that the Lord will start His threshing from the flowing stream of the Euphrates to the brook of Egypt; and you will be gathered up one by one, O sons of Israel.
>
> It will come about also in that day that a great trumpet will be blown; and those who were perishing in the land of Assyria and who were scattered in the land of Egypt will come and worship the Lord in the holy mountain at Jerusalem.
>
> Isaiah 27:12, 13 (NASB)

The "great trumpet" will sound "that day" and "those scattered" will be "gathered up" and brought to Jerusalem "one by one."

The references to "Assyria" and "Egypt" are not to be interpreted literally, simply because "that day" was far in the future and may still be. "Assyria" and "Egypt" instead were used here to denote far and distant lands in terms of the known world of Isaiah's time.

At this point some prophecy students will say: "But Israel has already returned to the Land—in 1948. Is he saying they are going to return again?" Not at all.—The miraculous rebirth of the *nation of Israel* in 1948 was the fulfillment of the prophecy in Chapter 37 of Ezekiel; whereas, in this prophecy we are speaking of the return of all *people of Israel* to the Land. This includes *all Jews*, living or dead. Yes, the Lord says that He will gather them up, one-by-one, on that Day—Rosh Hashanah—Judgment Day! (This is *not* The Great White Throne Judgment. That *Final* Judgment occurs about one thousand years later.)

The prophet Daniel also describes this exciting deliverance of his people, Israel:

> And at that time shall Michael stand up, the great prince which standeth for the children of thy people: and there shall be a time of trouble, such as never was since there was a nation *even* to that same time: and at that time thy people shall be delivered, every one that shall be written in the book.
>
> And many of them that sleep in the dust of the earth shall awake, some to everlasting life, and some to shame *and* everlasting contempt.
>
> Daniel 12:1–2

Michael is the name that certain occult religions have assigned to Jesus. Perhaps they were influenced by this verse. However, Michael is the angel who protects Israel and he will especially protect Israel during this "time of trouble." Nevertheless, he is *not* Messiah and he is *not* Jesus.—Michael is an angel.

Some Christian theologians have even taught that Michael the "protector" is he who will also deliver Israel. Again, Michael will only *protect* until Messiah, Son of David—*The Deliverer*—arrives at Olivet summit. But ten days before that—on Rosh Hashanah—many of them that sleep, and who are written in The Book of Life shall awaken to *everlasting* life. And some, from "that other book," will awaken to *everlasting* shame and contempt. This is why the "intermediates" need to repent and pray toward having their names entered into the right "book." This is also why those who are already *delivered* need to pray and give thanks that they are already in the right "book." That is what we call "Blessed Assurance!" The choice is ours: To be "In The Book" or to have "an unlisted number."

All of this will occur ten days *before* that reunion at Olivet summit, which they have been awaiting so eagerly (and poignantly) for all these centuries. Messiah wants them to be prepared and waiting for Him across the valley in The Old City of Yerushalayim when He alights on the Mount of Olives. He will not wait to "roust" them out of their graves on Yom Kippur, because that mountain is going to "cleave in the midst thereof." It would not be a very gentle or appropriate way to awaken His Elect, many of whom have "slept" on that Holy Mountain for centuries, just so they can be there to behold Him and greet Him when Messiah comes at last.

This "gathering" obviously has not yet been fulfilled because, for example, today there are still more Jewish people in the United States than there are in Israel. This Promise, in fact, is given about two dozen times in the Old Testament. Does anybody think the Lord was making this Promise to people other than His Chosen? He said: "O sons of Israel."

The prophet Joel, in his graphic and dramatic descriptions of "that great and terrible Day of the Lord," adds another Promise concerning this remnant body of Jewish survivors.

> ... when the Lord gives the word there shall yet be survivors on Mount Zion and in Jerusalem a remnant whom the Lord will call.
>
> From Joel 2:32 (NEB)

Prophecy reveals that on Rosh Hashanah, the "Feast of Trumpets" (1 Tishri, the first day of the seventh Jewish month, Tishri), 1,250 days after Antichrist halts the sacrifices by committing "the abomination of desolation" in the Temple, *all* Jewish survivors of that terrible seven years of tribulation will be carried supernaturally to Jerusalem; just as Phillip was "caught-up" unto Azotus (Acts 8:39, 40).

It will probably take the next ten days for them to "get-their-feet-on-the-ground," so to speak, after their fantastic "ride" to Jerusalem from Johannesburg, Poughkeepsie, Buenos Aires, Munich, Sydney, or wherever they might be among "the four corners of the Earth" on That Day. They will then be alert, anxious, and ready for the next ten days, discussing and encouraging each other for what is about to happen on 10 Tishri.

There they will be "encompassed by armies" from all nations of the world. Nevertheless, in faith they will "minister" to each other, prepared to make atonement as they "look upon Me whom they have pierced" on the Day of Atonement, Yom Kippur (10 Tishri). He will then arrive at Olivet summit *with* Shechinah, in Power and great Glory on the clouds, to rescue Israel's surviving remnant from the armies of "the world." (Ezekiel 43:2; Matthew 24:30; Revelation 19:19–21)

Then, They Will See Their Conquering—(Pierced)—Messiah!!!

Still not convinced?—Well, the Lord Jesus said:

> But in those days, after that tribulation, the sun shall be darkened, and the moon shall not give her light, and the stars of Heaven shall fall and the powers that are in Heaven shall be shaken.
>
> And then they shall see the Son of Man coming in clouds with great power and glory.
>
> And then shall He send his angels, and shall gather together His elect from the four winds, from the uttermost part of the earth to the uttermost part of Heaven.
>
> Mark 13:24–27

Perceivably, some Jewish readers might take exception to these words of doom since they are quoted from the New Testament—a wholly Christian source. However, as is frequently the case throughout the New Testament, Jesus is quoting *all* of these prophecies from the *Jewish Bible*, the Tenach or what Christian Gentiles call the Old Testament. These can be summarized in detail as follows:

New Testament Reference	Old Testament Sources
Mark 13:24–	Joel 2:10, 3:15, Isaiah 13:10
Mark 13:25–	Isaiah 34:4
Mark 13:26–	Daniel 7:13
Mark 13:27–	Deuteronomy 30:3, Zechariah 2:6

Primarily, we offer this comparison to demonstrate that most of the New Testament prophecies of End Time events (as well as the life stories of Jesus) have their origins from Old Testament prophecies. Indeed, if all Bible prophecies were detailed in this manner, they would comprise a fair sized book. Here, Jesus has described the days of the Tribulation, "The Time of Jacob's Trouble." Talmudic Rabbis *and* conservative Christians agree that it will be the most terrible period in Earth's history—the worst that *ever* has been or *ever* will be. These things will "come to pass" immediately before the arrival of Messiah (Son of David) to rescue a then beleaguered Israel from destruction. Jewish agreement with this interpretation of prophecy is stated in Talmud, Sanhedrin 97a.

Thus it appears that the Earth is going to be in great turmoil on "that day" and everyone on Earth will be in a state of panic and desperation. (They will think "the world" is-coming-to-an-end . . . and it IS!) . . . That is, the world as we know it will be ending. They will behold an amazing spectacle of "lights" in the heavens surrounding this one "Super-Light."

Next, every Jewish man, woman, and child on Earth will be gathered up and translated to Jerusalem for protection from a world gone mad. These are the Jewish people "elected" to survive the Tribulation and who will be "gathered" to Jerusalem to greet Him when He arrives at the Mount of Olives.

But Jesus is going to make the world "sweat it out" for about ten days before He arrives at the Mount of Olives, accompanied by whom??

Why, it's the Glory, the Divine Presence, Shechinah. (And, oh yes!—the Church, will also arrive with Him). That "Super-Light" is really comprised of three "lights," remember?

1. The Father (as Shechinah, His visible Presence)

2. The Son, Jesus (the Bridegroom)

3. The Holy Spirit, which at this time will be "lighting-up" all Saints (the Bride) like a Chanukah bush!—because He dwells in us.

The whole world will be watching, terrified and in wonder at what is happening. During those ten days the world will go absolutely mad. There will be "gnashing of teeth" and "men's-hearts-will-be-failing-them-for-fear." (Matt. 25:30; Luke 21:26) They will be able to observe the "light-show" very well because the sun will be blotted out at that time.

During those ten days the last armies of the Age will be marshaled and readied in the valley of Megiddo. There they shall prepare for their own grisly destiny in the Valley of Jehoshaphat at the east wall of the City of God, Jerusalem, on Yom Kippur—10 Tishri. His feet will then stand on Olivet.

Five days later the Kingdom Age will begin when all will come to "tabernacle" (gather) with the Lord in Jerusalem on the Feast of Tabernacles (Booths) on 15 Tishri. Thereupon, all seven Feasts of Jehovah will have been fulfilled—fulfilled to the Jews—in a Jewish context. These fulfillments have not been made to Gentiles, except as we, "the Church," are identified within our relationship to Messiah and the Jews.

Daniel 9:27 predicts the desolation of the Temple by the Antichrist. Since the Evil One will defile the Temple 1,260 days before the Lord returns, then, counting back from 10 Tishri, that date becomes near 14 Nisan (Passover) if some Jewish calendar "leap-months" are included within those $3^1/2$ years. Still, I do not have any explanation to offer as to what fulfillment the Shechinah Event may have presented other than for Ezekiel's prophecy.

Many sincere and learned prophecy scholars have taught that the next feast, Rosh Hashanah or the Feast of Trumpets, will be fulfilled when Jesus comes to "gather up" all believers at what is known as "the rapture of the Church." Nevertheless, since all of the first four feasts were fulfilled only to Jews, I believe the remaining three will also be fulfilled exclusively to the Jews. Another reason for eliminating Rosh Hashanah as a time for the rapture is that Jesus said He will come at such time that "ye think not." (Luke 12:40, Matthew 24:44) In other words, the rapture will come as a "thief in the night"—a surprise. He wants Christians to be expectant and alert for His coming, but does not want all of us to be standing over at the Mount of Olives on each Rosh Hashanah waiting for Him to arrive. Jesus wants Christians to live every day in such a way that they would be prepared and expect that He might arrive to take them unto Himself at any time.

Finally, it is my belief that all Bible-believing Jewish people who survive until seven years later, at the end of the "Great Tribulation," will know the exact date of His Coming at Olivet. They will know the exact date because by that time they will have become convinced that the New Testament and the Old Testament are both speaking of the same One who will stand at the Mount of Olives. Both of these Scriptural works state, in several places, that Messiah shall arrive three and one-half years after the Evil One defiles the Holy Place and proclaims himself as God. They will believe and know He will arrive exactly 1,260 days (or 42 months or $3^{1}/_{2}$ years) after Antichrist commits this "abomination of desolation." They will know when he is coming and they will be ready. (Dan. 9:27; Rev. 11:2–3)

Jewish tradition has always observed those ten days between Rosh Hashanah and the Day of Atonement (the High Holy Days) as a time of preparation, a time to alert themselves to a consciousness of their behavior toward other men and their relationships with God. Since Rosh Hashanah is regarded as "The Day of Judgment," a time for repentance and renewal prayers is in order. The High Holy Days are sometimes specified as "the Days of Awe" (Yamim Nora'im). Midrash Rabbah of Psalms teaches that Psalm 27 refers to the Days of Awe being from Rosh Hashanah until Yom Kippur.

A deeper and more spiritual background for the High Holy Days is stated in tractate Rosh Hashanah 16b. The narrator, Rabbi Kruspedai, says that three books are opened in Heaven each New Year: one for the thoroughly righteous, one for the wicked, and one for the "intermediate." He continues by saying that names of those in each category are inscribed in either the Book of Life or the Book of Death, as appropriate to one's behavior—*except the "intermediate!"* The doom of the intermediate is "suspended" during those ten days from Rosh Hashanah until Yom Kippur. During those days, then, if one is not quite confident as to which "book" will have his name inscribed, he is advised to pray and repent earnestly during the time. Many modern Jews of the most conservative observant groups continue this practice today.

During these ten days, for example, the prescribed Jewish greeting becomes, "May you be sealed until the day of redemption." This introspection then prepares them for their atonement on the Day. In the same way, those Jews who will be translated to Jerusalem when "the great trumpet" sounds will have the same interval in which they will contemplate the imminent arrival of Messiah on the Day of Atonement.

During the Kingdom Age that follows, Messiah Jesus will rule the world from Jerusalem. All true believers will return with Him to the Mount of Olives.

So, there we are with the Prince of Peace in our glorified bodies ready for one thousand years of Perfect Peace on Earth. It would hardly seem that He would not have us work during this period. He certainly does not need man's insignificant efforts to assist Him, but He has always wanted us to work. Of course, it does not matter to us because men will cheerfully do Jesus' bidding.

Jeremiah gave a hint about this work in Chapter 23, verse 4: "And I will set up shepherds over them (Israel) which shall feed them...." Yes, we saints of the Lord's Purpose will be assigned as shepherds, to teach ("feed") the survivors of the Tribulation. We will teach them like no Sunday School teachers they ever saw. By that time Jesus will have trained us to teach His flock what they would not (or could not) hear from Him "at the time of their visitation."

Thus, we begin to understand now why it is important for people to love and respect and learn about how Jesus can be seen in Judaic tradition and in the Old Testament.

WHEN DID THOSE "TWO DAYS" START?

Another popular concept in prophecy relates to the "two days" of "smiting" against Israel after the Lord said, "I will go back to My place." (Hosea 5:15 and 6:1-3) A question emerges concerning the Lord's return after the "two days." Popular teaching has been: "Of course, the 'two days' is to be counted from when the Lord Jesus returned 'to His Place' in 30 A.D." Now, we must also ask the question: "But, what about the Lord's returning to His Place in 69 A.D.?"

Some believers, nevertheless, are somewhat justifiably excited by this; although, we should not try setting up a "time-schedule" for the Lord's return based on this or any other prophecy.

The prophecy that brings this focus is as follows:

Come, let us return to the Lord.

He has torn us to pieces, but he will heal us;

He has injured us

But he will bind up our wounds.

After two days he will revive us;

On the third day he will restore us,

That we may live in his presence.

Let us acknowledge the Lord;

Let us press on to acknowledge him.

As surely as the sun rises, he will appear;

He will come to us like the winter rains,

Like the spring rains that water the earth."

Hosea 6:1–3 (NIV)

It is understandable at the present time in history why this specific prophecy should be exciting for all who believe. The Lord has said He will punish "naughty" Israel, but He will heal them, raise them up after "two days"; i.e., after He goes back to His place. After the two days (two thousand years, prophetically) they (Israel) will live in His presence during the Kingdom Age, in His 1,000 year earthly reign. As surely as the sun rises, Messiah will come after the Tribulation, that final seven years of Israel's "refining as silver" (The time of Jacob's trouble, the "week" of temptation, etc.). His arrival and subsequent restoration of this parched planet at that time will certainly be welcome as "the winter rains."

It is interesting to note another interpretation of prophecy that is derived not so much from Scripture as it is taken from what should be called "tradition." It is therefore not to be taken very seriously; although, this prophecy may have been "inspired" by Hosea's prophecy of the "two days."

The so-called Apostolic Father, Barnabas, is credited with having written an "epistle" or letter that included this prophetical observation. It should be pointed out that Barnabas was certainly not a valid Apostle nor was any of his work Canonized as Scripture. Nevertheless, he was a righteous man despite some human failings and was well known as a companion of the Apostle Paul.

Barnabas noted the following "time table" concerning prophecies of "The Time of the End":

- There were two thousand years or two "days" from the time of Adam until the time of Abraham.

- There were two thousand more years (two more "days") from the time of Abraham until the time of Jesus Christ.

- There will be two thousand more years (two more "days") from the time of Jesus' first visitation until the time of His return.

This prophetic vein continues (although not from Barnabas) with the observation that six "days" are given unto man on Earth. "Six" is the number of "man" in the context of Scriptural numerology. Man was created on the sixth day, etc., etc. Then, the seventh "day" shall be the Lord's Day, a day of rest and peace, which is of course the one thousand year Millennial reign of Christ on Earth. (Revelation 20:4)

Earlier we mentioned that Barnabas may have been influenced by Jewish traditional interpretation in having made this somewhat profound observation. The latter portion of this discussion can be traced back to Jewish tradition on this subject as recorded in Talmud, Rosh Hashanah 31a. Here it is stated that the world is to last six thousand years. Then, at this point the Rabbis seem to be confused about how many "days" are to follow those six. One Rabbi says the world shall be "desolate" for one thousand years. Another says it will be desolate for two thousand, as he then refers to the verses from Hosea, which we have discussed.

Now, we with our 20/20 hindsight, would say the latter Rabbinical interpretation is the more accurate, although, the "desolation" has been determined upon Israel rather than to the world. This same Rabbi evidently had been reading the "Fine Print" in his Tenach also; because he goes on to quote: " . . . as it says, 'After two days He will revive us.' "

A tragic Rabbinical note is recorded in tractate Sanhedrin 97a, which also teaches that the world is to last six thousand years. In the first two thousand there was "desolation"; i.e., there was no Torah. In the second two thousand years the Torah is said to have "flourished." Then it is stated that the third period of two thousand years was the Messianic Era—meaning Messiah, Son of David, *was* to have arrived at the *beginning* of that interval, at the dawn of what we call "the first century." Some call that time C.E. ("Common Era") and others call that time A.D. (Anno Domini). But, . . . no matter.—It was THE time!!!

Then, in remorse, the narrator says the delay "is due to our sins." (They *were* expecting Him then, as now!) Another rabbi states in Talmud Sanhedrin 97b, "all the predestined dates (for redemption; i.e., through Messiah, Son of David) have passed." He is telling Jewish people that God had announced through the Prophet (Daniel 9.24–26) the *exact* date when their Redeemer would come. And, since God is not a liar and since that date has passed, . . . there can be only one conclusion—He *was* already here! However, as we have shown from Hosea 6:2, after "two days" He will revive them and they will live in His sight for ever.

It should be clear to all of us at this point that none of us can agree on what these prophecies reveal as to the "day" of His coming. Despite our "20 / 20" advantage, it appears that Christians cannot reach agreement on this concept of prophecy much more than our Jewish brethren at this time. We shall all agree later, but we certainly cannot agree right now about when "later" is to be.

If nothing else, these kinds of observations should be another gentle cautioning against our temptation, at the present time, to "set dates" for the Lord to arrive at the Mount of Olives. My favorite anecdote on this sort of temptation is based on something the distinguished novelist, Mr. Alex Haley, once commented upon. In the closing epilogue of the ABC television epic, "Roots," Mr. Haley recalled his grandmother's feelings concerning the slaves' impatient hopes for freedom as she rocked with him on their old porch swing. "De Lawd don' always do things jess 'wen folks thinks He should, but He always dooze 'em RIGHT ON TIME."

Olivet, a Holy Mountain

A prophecy observation of my own inspiration may be of interest here, especially since it is nearly certain that Jesus was crucified on the Mount of Olives.[12, 25] In fact, the Mount of Olives should probably be considered one of the most Holy places on Earth; perhaps second only to the Kodesh Ha-Kodashim (Holy of Holies) on Mount Zion at the Temple site. Mount Zion is, of course, frequently called Mount Moriah. In fact, II Chronicles 3:1 refers to the Temple Mount as Moriah, thereby leading us moderns to assume that to be the place where Isaac was offered. The Moriah-connection (if you will) then, is carried back to a traditional belief that Abraham's obedient approach to the sacrifice of Isaac was on Mount Zion as "Mount Moriah." As we have seen, traditional "thought" is extremely difficult to dissuade from our minds, especially after hundreds of years of such "thinking."

However, the popular name of that particular mountain is of man's choice, not from God, necessarily. From Genesis 22:2, " . . . get thee into the land of Moriah; and offer him there for a burnt offering upon one of the mountains which I will tell thee of." God didn't tell us which mountain. He told Abraham. We have a subtle clue, however, because in verses 3 and 4 we are told that Abraham "went unto that place" and that "he saw the place even from afar off!" —"Afar off?"—Yes, the Mount of Olives can be seen even from "afar off," but Mount Zion can not be seen from a distance because Olivet looks down upon Zion! In fact, Zion is the lowest peak in the area, whereas Olivet is by far the highest peak.

We demonstrated in Chapter 5 that the Red Heifer sacrifice was the most important of all the Jewish sacrifices. Considering all of the important happenings that have occurred and will yet occur on the Mount of Olives, this is most likely the mountain on which Isaac, as a "type" of Christ and of the Red Heifer, was offered. (Why, Isaac may even have had red hair!) That offering of Isaac may even have taken place at the site of the Miphkad Altar, which may also have been the place of that greatest sacrifice, ever! (Also see Professor Martin's analysis.[12, 25])

But, of course the story doesn't end here, because Isaac asked: " . . . 'but, where is the lamb for a burnt offering?' And Abraham said, 'My son, God will provide Himself a lamb for a burnt offering' . . . " (Genesis 22:7, 8)

Since the Hebrew language has no punctuation, as we know it, can it be that this last sentence has a very profound meaning, which is lost by the absences of subtly intended Hebrew punctuation? It may be that this sentence should read:

> My son, God will provide Himself,
> a lamb for a burnt offering. . . .

For that is exactly what God, the Father, did at that same mountain about 2,000 years later. God provided His own and only Son, our Lord Jesus, as a "lamb for a burnt offering." Thus, when we place that last phrase in apposition, the meaning is profound indeed. The Lord did not merely supply the sacrifice "Himself"; rather, He supplied "Himself" as the sacrifice.

Punctuation does not appear in *any* manuscripts from earlier than the ninth century, and those are found only in Latin manuscripts. It is significant to note, therefore, that all translations from Greek, Hebrew, and Aramaic, where punctuation produces an influence on the meaning of the text, have interpretations based merely on *human* authority. The commas we have added to this verse then give it a different meaning, although we possess no greater and no lesser "authority" than that of the King James translators. It is left to our readers to decide for themselves which version they prefer.

Further detailed study of Scripture, however, provides a clearer identification of "Mount Moriah." Genesis 22:13, 14 says that Abraham looked behind himself and saw a ram caught by its horns in a thicket. Abraham may then have gone across this valley to take the ram and offer it there on what later became the Temple Mount. Verse 14 says Abraham built an altar, named the spot, and that the place is still known as Mount Moriah, to this day. Notice, the ram was sacrificed at Mount Moriah, but the lamb that God provided (Himself) was offered at the Mount of Olives—the same place where Isaac was offered.

Yes, the Temple Mount is also the place where, one thousand years later, rams and goats were offered at the Temple Altar and it is still known as Mount Moriah to this day. But, that place cannot be seen "afar off," whereas, we know from Verse 4 that the place where Isaac was offered had to be higher than the surrounding peaks. The topographic features and placements of the Temple Mount (Moriah) and the Mount of Olives are consistent with Scripture as well as Talmudic Law and tradition concerning the Temple sacrifices and the Red Heifer sacrifice. There were distinct and separate locations for the "ordinary" sacrifices at the Temple—on the Temple Mount (Moriah)—and for the most Holy "burned" sacrifices at Olivet summit; e.g., the Red Heifer, the Atonement Goat, and a few other most sacred offerings.

As a result of studies involved with this work, I am moved to make the following speculations:

I believe the offering of Isaac, the burning of the Red Heifers, and the Crucifixion of Jesus of Nazareth all took place at (or near) the

Miphkad Altar site on the Mount of Olives. The Lord provided Himself as a lamb for a burnt offering. He sacrificed His son in our stead and withheld the "blade" of judgment.

I further speculate that the Ascension of Jesus of Nazareth, the Ascension of the Divine Presence (Shechinah), and the return of Shechinah with Jesus Christ as King of Kings will all have taken place at a single location on the summit of the Mount of Olives.

The Divine Number

Notice in both sequences just discussed that there are three fulfillments. There seems to be a somewhat obvious prophetic pattern here, which punctuates the authority and the Glory of the Trinity. With some help from Mr. Clarence Larkin's priceless storehouse of truth,[17] we see the importance of the pattern described:

- Three is the "Divine Number" because it appears so often in connection with Holy personages, events or things.

- Father, Son, and Holy Spirit (The Trinity of God.)

- Body, Soul, Spirit (The Trinity of man).

- God appeared on Earth in three forms: as "fire," as "cloud," and as man.

- The three great feasts: Passover, Pentecost, Tabernacles. (All Jewish men are commanded to participate).

- Three pieces of matzah are served at the Seder (Passover meal).

- Israel has been brought back to The Land three times.

- The three temptations of Jesus.

- Peter's three denials of the Lord.

- Jesus asked three times: "Lovest thou me, Peter?"

- Jesus commanded three times: "Feed my lambs (Sheep)."

- Jesus was annointed three times with perfumed oil.

- Three crosses at Calvary.

- Three "days" are associated with the restoration of Israel and with the

Resurrection of Jesus and with Jonah's deliverance. ("Three" different personages raised on "three" different occasions.)

- Three "veils" in the Temple.

- Man, woman, child (The trinity of marriage, birth, family.)

- Day, month, year (The trinity of time).

- Land, sea, sky (The trinity of Earth).

- Red, blue, yellow (The trinity of color).

- Solid, liquid, gas (The trinity of matter).

- Animal, vegetable, mineral (The trinity of Creation).

The Master of the Universe places considerable importance with the number "three." One cannot prove these speculations, but they nevertheless are interesting.

Also, there is the trinity of dimension: length, width, height. One might ask, "What about the fourth dimension, relativity, the speed-of-light, etc.?"

It is my view that there will be no fourth dimension under the control of man; i.e., where man would actually control "time." Time is a part of Eternity. Time and Eternity belong only to God.

What If Israel Had Repented?

Before closing our subject of prophecy, we should address an important eschatological question: "What would have happened if Israel had repented and returned to the Lord in 69 A.D.?" We can only speculate on the events to follow, but we know for certain that all prophecy would have been fulfilled. Somehow, God would have brought on the Antichrist, the wars, the famines, etc., and would have "refined" Israel. Then, they would have been purified to accept "the one whom they had pierced" when He arrived in power and glory at the Mount of Olives. The "Church Age" would have been of very brief duration and the Kingdom Age would have had a much earlier beginning than we shall witness. Nevertheless, it would ALL have "come to pass" at that time, had Israel returned unto Him who had Promised that He would then return unto them.

But, we modern Gentile Christians would never have been born. Our potential ancestors would have been annihilated in the final wars. Without The Crucifixion and later failure of first-century Judaism to recognize their Messiah, it would all have ended right then and there.

However, Jesus came to save that which was lost. Yes! That was Gentiles! We had no way to come to the Lord except as proselytes through Judaism. The Lord wants all of humanity to be heirs in His Kingdom. (John 10:16) He had a far better plan for reaching Gentiles and washing away their sins—by offering His Son as "the lamb for a burnt offering"—on one of the mountains "in the land of Moriah."

He permitted their "blindness" in order that we might "see!" We both wait for the same One to touch His feet on that Holy Mountain, Olivet.

Tucked-away obscurely in the Index of "The Works of Josephus"[2] under "prophecy" is the following note:

> Prophecies could not agree to the events,
> if the world were governed by chance.

7 "Signs and Wonders"

I **never cease** to wonder at the fact that Israelites always have expected the Lord to "give them a sign." And God has been very responsive and accommodating to His Chosen People in that regard. No other people in history have ever been given so many "signs," including the ultimate sign—God Himself dwelling in their midst—as "fire"—as "cloud"—and as man. God may sometimes ask, "What do I have to do for these people?" Well, He does know what to do, and He will do it, in His time.

It is interesting to observe that no other nation (or people) have ever had personal visitations from God Almighty Himself. Only Israel. He appeared to them as a "fire" and as a "cloud" during the Exodus. He dwelt in the Temple as this same "fire" or "cloud," to which they refer as Shechinah (or Divine Presence). Nobody said it better than the Lord Himself in Deuteronomy 4 (NASB):

> 4:7, for what great nation is there that has a god so near to it as the Lord our God whenever we call on Him?

> 4:33, Has any people heard the voice of God speaking from the midst of the fire, as you have heard it, and survived?

4:34, Or has a god tried to go to take for himself a nation from within another nation by trials, by signs and wonders and by war and by a mighty hand and by an outstretched arm and by great terrors, as the Lord did for you in Egypt before your eyes?

4:35, To you it was shown that you might know that the Lord He is God; there is no other besides Him.

4:36, Out of the heavens He let you hear His voice to discipline you; and on earth He let you see His great fire, and you heard His words from the midst of the fire.

4:37, Because He loved your fathers, therefore He chose their descendants after them. And He personally brought you from Egypt by His great power,

4:38, driving out from before you nations greater and mightier than you, to bring you in and give you their land for an inheritance, as it is today.

4:39, Know therefore today, and take it to your heart, that the Lord, He is God in Heaven above and on earth below; there is no other.

After hearing these pronouncements of His great love for this People, how can anyone say the Lord has not maintained His Promises to Israel today? And, as He says, has He shown His great fire to any other nation? Or has Almighty God Himself ever spoken in person to any other nation?

SIGNS OF THE JEWELS
Among the many little known or seldom discussed "signs" is one that Josephus[2] describes, Antiq., 3/214–218, which was given to Israel via the jewels that adorned the shoulders of the robe worn by the High Priest. The accounts given by Josephus, as well as the accompanying commentary by the translator, are quite detailed and I hesitate to repeat all of them here. Briefly, therefore, one of the jewels, a sardonyx on the priest's right shoulder, shone when God was present at one of their sacrifices. Brilliant rays darted from this gem and could be seen even at a great distance.

A concealed and delicate "picture" is suggested in this sign of the sardonyx. But, just what is a "sardonyx"? The sardonyx is a translucent, quartzlike gem having a reddish brown hue. So, what is so "delicate" or subtle about a reddish brown jewel?

The Red Heifer certainly had a reddish brown coat (and with no more than two odd-colored hairs). Many Christians would agree that the Red Heifer is a "type" or "picture" of Jesus, pure and "without spot or blemish" and offered as a sacrifice "for a purification for sin."

What is not so obvious is a remote document from Roman antiquity which records that Jesus had hair and a beard "the color of wine" or what might be called reddish brown or auburn in color. This description, although unauthenticated, is presented[27] as having been recovered from a document supposedly written by an acquaintance of Pontius Pilate.

It may also be noted that King David, the earthly ancestor of Jesus, is mentioned in Scripture (I Samuel 16:12 and 17:42) as being "ruddy," which is to say "reddish" in his coloring—perhaps hair, skin, or both. So, there may be some "genetic" background in this connection as well as a spiritual picture.

Now that we have seen Jesus reflected in the Red Heifer, could He also have been represented in the sign of the sardonyx? This really appears to have too much credence to be just a coincidence. It was a "sign" to the Jews, but to Christians it is a "picture" of the One who was giving the signs. One wonders if modern Christians can continue to ignore these Jewish "signs."

Josephus indicates another sign from this source, " . . . still more wonderful than this . . ." took place before Israel was to go into battle. Here God declared prior to the battle whether Israel would be victorious; causing all twelve of the stones, known as the "Urim and Thummim," which were inserted into the High Priest's breastplate, to give off a "super-brilliance" such that all of Israel's army could see this encouraging sign.

The commentary by Mr. Whiston is quite interesting. He states that apparently King Saul was the first to become slack in consulting this "oracle," but that King David consulted this sign frequently and complied with God's recommendations with appreciation. (So, why shouldn't we be impressed by David's military victories?) But none of David's successors ever consulted God through this Divine Revelation.

Then, after the return from Babylon, this "sign" returned, was consulted by "some" of the kings over the years, until the death of one of the most beloved of all High Priests, John Hyrcanus. (See reference 12.) Josephus says this sign ceased to come forth about 200 years before his writing, perhaps about 100 B.C. Further comment hardly seems necessary.

SIGNS ABOVE THE CITY

Josephus was really "into signs." Again, just before the departure of the Glory from the Temple, he describes: "Thus, there was a star resembling a sword, which stood over the city, and a comet, that continued a whole year." (See Appendix A.)

Now, what does a sword resemble, especially when the blade is in a vertical position with the hand-guard at the uppermost? Of course this description also resembles a cross, a patibulum fastened to a tree, a "sign" that, a few centuries later, became one of the best known emblems of the Christian faith.

Josephus doesn't stop here. Just a few days after the Glory of the Lord departed from the Holy of Holies, another strange "sign" appeared over Jerusalem: "On the 21st of Iyar, just before sunset, chariots and troops of soldiers in their armour were seen running among the clouds, and surrounding of cities." Many similar incidents were reported during the 1967 "Six Day" Arab / Israeli War.

A SIGN TO BE SEEN, BUT NOT HEARD

Earlier, in Chapter 4, we discussed the mysterious opening of the huge brass (or bronze) gate, Nicanor's Gate, east of the sanctuary. This miracle was described in detail that is typical of the reporting expertise of Flavius Josephus. However, Josephus either neglected to inform us or was unaware of the most spectacular facet of this miracle of the gate.

Talmud, Yoma 39b, observes that whenever this mammoth gate was opened or closed, the noise of its "turning hinges" could be heard at a distance of eight Sabbath "limits." A "limit" was a Sabbath Day's journey or two thousand cubits. Thus, the gate noise could be heard from a distance of more than four miles.

This gate must have been bronze rather than brass as described by Josephus,[2] since brass had been invented by the Romans only a few years earlier in 15 B.C. and bronze had been in use since about 3500 B.C. Talmud, Yoma 38a, describes Nicanor's gates as Corinthian bronze, a more refined bronze having a brilliant golden hue, as opposed to the duller ordinary bronze. Nevertheless, both of these metals have good resonance properties and would have high friction coefficients against the iron hinge supports. These qualities would have contributed strongly toward creating the vibration or "hummmm" tone that could be heard at a distance of eight Sabbath limits—almost as far as Bethlehem.

The noise was apparently produced by resonant vibration of the heavy brass gate structure caused by friction of its "turning hinges." They did not have effective lubricants in those days. Josephus says twenty men were needed to open or close this gate "with difficulty." The sound of its opening on the eves of Sabbath, on New Moons, and on the Holy days would herald such occasions to much of surrounding Judea.

The fact the gate opened "of its own accord" would seem to be of sufficient stature alone to rate as a "miracle." The Lord, however, was only content to open it so quietly that the guards had to run upstairs and TELL their captain the gate had opened. Under "normal" conditions, the captain and all of Jerusalem would have been shaken out-of-the-sack at midnight by its great noise. (And they wanted a sign!!)

Since the gate was finished in brilliant Corinthian bronze, it shone with a dazzling, blinding reflection in the early morning sun. As the sun rose above the Mount of Olives the magnificent splendor of the Temple blazed forth with an unforgettable scene. This golden bronze gate, the white marble buildings, and walls gave the Temple a glory unmatched by any other architectural marvel before or since that time. (Other mysteries concerning Nicanor's Gate are described in the Talmud.)

A TIME OF THE SIGNS

I am certainly no authority on Josephus, nor even a scholar of any note. I must, however, respect these declarations from this marvelous reporter because he was there on the scene! It appears that many strange events were taking place just prior to and during this first century Divine Judgment on Jerusalem. Josephus (and many others) were apparently impressed sufficiently that they documented these events in considerable detail—to be noticed later by those who would look. At least one noted and brilliant scholar, Joseph Scaliger, had the highest praise for Josephus as an historian. (See Appendix C.)

As mentioned earlier in the main story of this work, my own speculation is that the departure of the Divine Presence from the

Mount of Olives summit may have taken place during Chanukah, which is, ironically, the Festival of Lights. This event occurred forty years after Jesus, the Light of the World, was "put out."

This speculation that the departure occurred at Chanukah should not, however, appear to be purely a guess; because the estimation is based on extending $3^1/2$ years beyond Pentecost, the time of the Shechinah withdrawal from the Temple. Since Pentecost is generally near June and Chanukah is near December, a half year after June, then it is logical to estimate such a pattern. It does seem peculiar, however, that the Midrash commentary, otherwise very detailed, makes no mention of the date or that feast. With a better understanding of the first century Jewish calendar, leap years, leap months, etc., perhaps some scholar will elaborate or improve our understanding of the date for that final ascent from Olivet summit.

A WOE IN THE DARKNESS

At the Crucifixion it is well known that the sun was darkened from the sixth hour until the ninth hour when Jesus gave up the Ghost. (Luke 23:44) Whether this was truly caused by a solar eclipse or by dense cloud cover cannot be determined conclusively from Scripture alone. Some recent scholars of the twentieth century have proposed that a solar eclipse did in fact occur at Jerusalem in 30 A.D. on the 14th day of Nisan (Passover eve) from about 12 noon until 3 P.M. These conclusions are based on analyses performed by "back-calculating" from astronomical data, using modern computer technology to solve the complex orbital mechanics problem that must be addressed.

Some of those same orbital analyses add that a lunar eclipse also was experienced at that same Passover in Jerusalem. This dual eclipse must have been regarded by Judeans as a "sign." Scripture makes mention only of darkening the sun between noon and the hour of His death. However, the Jewish tradition and culture of that day considered an eclipse of the sun or the moon as a harbinger of doom.

Talmud, Sukkah 29a, notes that an eclipse of the sun is a bad omen for the world. Further detailed disclosure states if the sun is eclipsed in the east, a bad omen is seen for the nations to the east. If the sun is in the west during the darkening, it bodes ill future for nations to the west. But, if the sun is darkened while it is "in the midst of heaven" (i.e., at midday), the woe will befall the entire world. Matthew 27:45 says there was "darkness over all the land" from the sixth to the ninth hour; i.e., noon to 3 P.M., while the sun was "in the midst of heaven."

Even more depth of meaning is seen in Jewish superstition regarding a lunar eclipse, which was taken as an extremely ill omen for Israel. Among the reasons believed to cause Israel to deserve such an omen are:

- On account of "those who perpetrate forgeries"—as in the case of the "forged" charge of sedition, the claim of "kingship," etc., against Jesus.

- On account of "those who give false witness"—as for those lying witnesses at the "trials" of Jesus.

- On account of "those who cut down good trees, even though they are their own"—as was "The Branch" who was cut down by His own who received Him not!

- On account of "cutting down a fruit tree" (even if He was their own)—as Jesus was the First Fruit of The Resurrection.

The Gemara of Sukkah 29a goes on to add that when Israel fulfills the Lord's will, they need not fear all these omens. Reference is made to Jeremiah 10:2:

> Thus saith the Lord; learn not the way of the heathen, and be not dismayed at the signs of heaven, for the heathen are dismayed at them.

The idolaters and heathen of the nations will be dismayed by such signs, but Israel will not be dismayed, Talmud says. How sad it is that Israel was dismayed by these omens, because she did not remain in the Lord's will, failing to see His victory at the empty tomb three days after these "signs."

If a dual eclipse did occur, just picture yourself a Judean on that day. The City drew mysteriously dark at midday, without a cloud in the sky (presumably). This dark "hour" occurred as the Romans were crucifying, along with two thieves, the gentle Galilean teacher, so beloved by many of the common folk and who caused such a stir as He rode into the City astride a donkey the other day. Several of the Pharisees were very distraught, because many of the people had proclaimed Him Messiah, the Lord's Annointed. The Pharisees were openly hostile to Him, but who would have thought it would come to this? They have crucified Him! And now the City and all around is in darkness. I wonder... has there been a terrible mistake?

That was bad enough to warn the populace of the Lord's displeasure, but then that night they were expecting their usual and astronomically prompt full moon of the Passover. On the Jewish calendar, received from the Great "I AM," the fourteenth day of the month was a full moon. They were all expecting that full moon to rise, glistening, over the top of the Mount of Olives. But all that came up was darkness. Nothing! Empty! So, now this! No moon on the Passover! Something is wrong! ("Do you suppose He was Messiah?!" they whisper, "Is this another sign?!")

Those at Jerusalem on that Passover had to be frightened, regardless of whether they believed Jesus was Messiah. Seeing these signs had to be a moving experience. What would you have thought? What would you have felt?

It would appear that the Lord tried to speak to Israel through "the sons of Aaron" for a full generation by giving "signs" through Jesus, the Temple, and sacrifices. Then, having been spurned by the priesthood, it seems He "took his case to the People" by speaking to them in Person from the "fire" and the "cloud" on the Mount of Olives for $3^1/_2$ years; perhaps the same duration as Jesus' ministry.

Some observations can be made here on the subject of dates and "years" used in this historical study:

> (1) It is not clear, after two millennia, what type of "year" was being used by any given historian at any given time.
> (2) The intricacies of the Judaic calendar, leap-years, leap-months, etc., are extremely difficult to apply with dates prior to the calendar revisions by Hillel II, about the fourth century A.D.
> (3) Synchronizing dates between the presently revised Judaic calendar and the Gregorian (sixteenth century) calendar leaves room for an amount of error that could be of significance. The revision by Pope Gregory XIII in 1582 was, after all, a fairly "recent" date in comparison with the time of the first four centuries.

It has already been shown by Professor Martin[17] and others that the birth of Jesus was probably on Rosh Hashanah about 3 B.C. relative to our Gregorian calendar. Thus, it is hoped that more precise dating for the Shechinah Event can be established by more informed and talented scholars using application of astronomy, orbital mechanics and/or more precise historical documentation.

The "Sign" of the Disappearing Signs

Several wondrous supernatural events, which are reported by Talmud, Yoma 39, occurred in the Temple during the forty years in which Simeon The Righteous served as High Priest, about 300 B.C. These events occurred regularly during that period. Then, after his death, these signs would only appear occasionally and, when they did show, a "good omen" was interpreted.

This strange sequence would seem to indicate the Lord was "speaking" to Israel through all this and saying there was something admirable in this man. Removal of the constancy of these events after Simeon's passing told the Jews they were doing something wrong, because the priest who followed Simeon (John Hyrcanus) was also apparently in the Lord's praise.

This man, Simeon The Righteous, lived around the time of Alexander the Great and was respected and proclaimed throughout the civilized world of that day. Jewish historians record (Talmud, Yoma 69a) that during a Jewish revolt, upon meeting Simeon at Antipatris, Alexander dismounted from his carriage and bowed before this beloved sage in deep respect. Judging by the supernatural signs beginning in the Temple during his time, Simeon must certainly have been high in the Lord's favor as well.

So far, no definite evidence has surfaced to explain why these signs appeared during the office of Simeon. It would be interesting to study that era of Judaism to find why the Lord might have given Israel this "reward." The giving of these signs from the Lord would seem almost as if He were commending them. It would be interesting also to find whether there is any correlation of the later sporadic signs with any particular merit on the part of Israel or her priests at those times when the signs did occasionally appear after Simeon's time.

History is somewhat obscure regarding early (350–300 B.C.) Greek rule of Palestine. However, the Gentile conquerors of that period seemed to delegate actual administration and civil control of the Jewish citizenry to the High Priest and the Council of Elders. Their oppressors comprehended and appreciated the benefits of ruling a disciplined society already conformed to a rigid system of law, likely even more effective than their own. Then, reading between the lines, it appears that some of these periods were more pleasing to the Lord than other periods, depending to a large extent upon the integrity and obedience of the High Priest.

This period began a decline in Jewish tradition and obedience under the worldly influences of the "advanced" Grecian society and under leadership of some corrupt "shepherds." Israel's failures under these decadent High Priests can be understood through a maxim that is reputedly quoted from a Prussian general:

> A regiment can be only as good as its sergeants;
> but it will always be as bad as its colonel.

This principle applies also to nations, free or servile, just as it applies to Judaism or the Church. Through these signs, the Lord may have been trying to encourage Israel when they had chosen a good "colonel" and to chastise them when they had a poor one.

The so-called minor prophets relate some of Jewish history up until about 400 B.C. (Malachi). No Biblical entries were given between 400 B.C. and 164 B.C. Then, our awareness of Jewish history is again restored in the Apochrypha as we reach the time of the Maccabean Revolt, 164 B.C. Grecian Hellenistic rule under Antiochus III brought a tighter rein on the Judeans than previous masters had drawn. When his heir and successor, Antiochus IV Epiphanes, humiliated and oppressed the Jews (and the Temple) to a new low, they had finally had enough, and once more, they called upon their Lord. During the revolt that followed, the Lord answered them by the "Miracle of Lights," which has inspired the season of Chanukah, and was definitely a positive indication from Shechinah that "YHWH" was pleased with their resolve and renewed faith.

From the history we have sketched for the High Priests, it can be seen that Judaism had again reached a despicable state by the time of Jesus. But, the Lord still did not give up on His "naughty children." He didn't give up on them then and He didn't give up on them in 70 A.D.—Even though we Christians have treated Jews as if He had rejected them. But, He did "go back to His place" for a time.

An obscure passage in Yoma 9a indicates that Simeon The Righteous was High Priest for forty years and was succeeded by John Hyrcanus who remained for eighty years. These two most beloved patriarchs had by far the longest tenures of all the priests in that office during the times of both Temples. The discussion continues by pointing out that Solomon's Temple had a total of eighteen High Priests in a period of four hundred and ten years. In comparison, over three hundred High Priests served during the four hundred and twenty years of the Second Temple. Other than Simeon and John Hyrcanus, all but two of them served less than one year. At the last, including the time of Caiaphas, the office was purchased from Roman officials.

After The Crucifixion, these supernatural signs *never* again appeared in the Temple. (They were "no more forever," as He says in Exodus 14:13). The Rabbis and Talmud lament this loss as they describe each sign as it appeared under Simeon, then occassionally appeared, then completely voided during the "forty years before the Temple was destroyed." One thought that may have been going through Jewish minds at that time was: "Titus destroyed the Temple 70 A.D. Seventy minus forty! Hey! 30 A.D. . . . That Nazarene! Could he have been Messiah?"

However, some of the Judeans at that time perhaps also recognized, through absence of these signs, that something was wrong. Examine these signs now as we describe their detail and possible meanings to Judeans after 30 A.D.

"Drawing the Lots"

On the Day of Atonement, two unblemished male goats ("he-goats") were brought into the Temple from across The Heifer's Gangway. Then, both goats were brought before the High Priest, one goat on his left and one to his right. Two "lots" were placed in a golden urn (kalpei), Yoma 4:1. According to some sources, they were black and white "pebbles," but they could be made of any material (Yoma 37a). One of these lots bore the inscription: "For the Lord"; on the other was written: "For Azazel"; i.e., "scapegoat." (It is interesting here to note that the ritual of the "black-ball," a rejecting vote as cast against a prospective member of a fraternal organization, has very ancient "roots.") The urn was then shaken and the High Priest would reach into the urn, grasping one of the lot pieces in each hand. Then came a supernatural "sign."

During the time of Simeon The Righteous (about 300 B.C.), the lot "For the Lord" always came up in the High Priest's right hand. However, after that time the lot "For the Lord" would come up "now in the left hand or now in the right," purely at random. If the Lord's lot came up in the right hand, this was considered "a good omen."

Then, of course, the goat on the side facing the priest's hand holding the lot "For the Lord" was slain and given as the burnt offering for the atonement of Israel's sin. But the other goat, the

Azazel or "scapegoat," was set free to roam in the wilderness after being led out of the City across the Azazel Bridge (Scapegoat's Gangway—Figure 6). A priest was selected to follow this spared goat, representing a renewed and now penitent Israel, to see that no harm came to him and that he adjusted to his new environment and freedom.

From this we find that the term "scapegoat" is used incorrectly as a figure of speech to denote someone who has been punished, in a sacrificial way, for having committed a crime that was also committed by others who are not being punished. In this ancient Jewish ritual, from which the term is borrowed, quite the opposite is true.

After the Crucifixion, 30 A.D., the lot piece "For the Lord" *never* came up in the priest's right hand, indicative of a very bad omen.

"THE CRIMSON STRAP"

Another supernatural sign concerning the Azazel was perhaps the most spectacular of all of these that we shall discuss. Each end of a "strap" (or strip) of crimson cloth was tied to the scapegoat's horns, thus hanging under his throat, to represent symbolically the severed throat of the Lord's goat, which was to be slain and its blood to be sprinkled on the Altar of Sacrifice. The situation is discussed in the Gemara of Yoma 39a.

The importance of this sign existed in the fact that Jewish "tradition" said (although, God never said this) Israel's sins were only turned from "scarlet" to "snow-white" when the Azazel goat reached the wilderness. During the time of Simeon, that crimson strap was tied to one of the Temple doors when Azazel was led out. (Yoma 68b) Consistently, the strap then turned white and after a few hours it was determined, that, yes, Israel's sins had been washed, as promised. (They simply would not trust Him. They still had to have a "sign.")

Then after Simeon, when this sign was no longer "reliable," they devised an elaborate system to determine when the promise was manifest, just in case the strap did not turn white that time. Guards were stationed with "towels" (probably white) along the Azazel departure route (Sketch 6) at distances where each guard could be seen by each other guard at the stations before and after his own station. In this way, when the Scapegoat reached the wilderness, they relayed a signal back to the Temple by waving the white "towel." Then they considered their sins had been forgiven by the Holy One.

Again, after The Crucifixion, the crimson strap *never* turned white as in previous years. Truly a startling supernatural "sign" to the priests. This was very disturbing to the Jews because from the Talmud it is said, "If it became white, it signified that the Holy One, blessed be He, had forgiven Israel's sin." (Isaiah 1:18) This verse has a profound meaning here where it says " . . . though your sins be as scarlet, they shall be as white as snow. . . ." But, they still didn't make any connection of this "sign" with that fateful day at Passover "forty years before the Temple was destroyed."

Further drama of this occasion is drawn from the Mishnah of this text, describing some of the movements and speech of the High Priest on the Day of Atonement. Again, from Yoma 4:2,

> MISHNAH. He bound a thread of crimson wool on the head of the he-goat which was to be sent away. And (meantime) he placed it (at the gate) whence it was to be sent away; and the he-goat that was to be slaughtered, at the place of the slaughtering. He came to his bullock a second time, pressed his two hands upon it and made confession. And thus he would say: "O Lord, I have dealt wrongfully, I have transgressed, I have sinned before thee, I and my house, and the children of Aaron, thy Holy people. O Lord, pray forgive the wrong doings, the transgressions and the sins, which I have committed, transgressed and sinned before thee, I and my house, and the children of Aaron, thy Holy people. As it is written in the Torah of Moses, thy servant: "For on this day atonement be made for you; from all thy sins shall be clean before the Lord." And they responded: "Blessed be the name of His glorious Kingdom for ever and ever."

One must not scoff or ridicule this Jewish ritual. How unlike His "ways" are man's ways. Men, Jewish or Christian, still have much difficulty in the discernment of "works" from "Faith." The Lord accomplished all the "work" that was needed for cleansing our sins, "forty years before the Temple was destroyed." All we need is Faith to believe He will do as He promised.

THE TWO "HE-GOATS"

The connection of the Atonement goats with the sacrificial death of Jesus does not end here, however. The Roman Procurator, Pontius Pilate, actually took a "type" role of the High Priest as he had Jesus and Barabbas before him. Both men had the Hebrew given name "Y'shua." The name "Barabbas," as stated in the New Testament, was actually derived from the Aramaic form of this young man's name. His "full" Hebrew name was Y'shua ben Abbah, meaning "Y'shua, Son of the High Father." But the New Testament translators used an Anglicized version of the Aramaic form of this name, which was "Jesu bar Abbas." The translators may also have wisely called him "Barabbas" and dropped the given name (Jesus) in order to avoid confusion of his name with that of Jesus of Nazareth.

Whereas, the other young man, whose Hebrew name was Y'shua ben Yusef, was of course the true "Son of the High Father," JESUS of Nazareth. Thus, Pilate "drew the lot" by leaving the choice to the assembled crowd as to which "Y'shua" would be spared as the Scapegoat? (All say, "Barabbas"); and which "Y'shua" would be "For the Lord?" (Jesus.) Knowing all these things, and knowing how thoroughly Jesus fulfilled the Law, we can develop the following speculations:

— Both Jesus and Barabbas were probably brought into Jerusalem by way of "The Heifer's Gangway" Bridge, which was near the place of His betrayal and "capture," Gethsemane. (See Sketch 6.)

— Jesus of Nazareth was probably standing on Pilate's right and Barabbas on his left when Pilate asked the crowd to decide the "lot" of each man.

— Barabbas was probably adorned in some way with a "crimson" sash, neckerchief, hat, or other article as he was released.

— Barabbas was probably escorted out of the City via the Azazel Bridge ("Scapegoat Gangway").

— Barabbas probably left that same scarlet (or crimson) article tied to a Temple door or gate after being released to be led out of the city and into the "wilderness." It later turned mysteriously white after a few hours, " . . . because the Holy One, Blessed be He, had forgiven (all) sin."

— Somebody probably was sent to keep Barabbas under surveillance for a few days to insure that he behaved himself; at least until all the "fuss" about this Nazarene "troublemaker" blew over.

Thus, an interesting picture of "types" appears relative to the Atonement goats, very closely paralleling the Jewish Laws and the rituals concerning that Holy Day. In these ways, Jesus fulfilled the Law concerning Yom Kippur, the Day of Atonement. All must be fulfilled!

An appropriate but poignant footnote is given in Yoma 63b concerning the he-goat to be sacrificed "For the Lord." The Rabbis had ruled that casting of lots was necessary because the lot determines what is "fit for the Lord"; i.e., whose time has come. How tragic it is that the Jews did not recognize their Atonement "he-goat" who was truly "For the Lord"; though surely, His time had come!

"The Westernmost Candle"

A very meaningful sign appeared during the time of Simeon concerning the candlestick (Menorah) in the Holy Place. The seven candles were positioned along the south wall of the Holy Place; the western-most candle being nearest the Holy of Holies. (See Sketch 8.) All seven candles were cleaned each evening and filled to the same level with oil. The westernmost candle was lighted first and the other six were lighted from the flame of the western candle. And yet, during Simeon's priesthood, the westernmost candle always was still burning each evening after all six remaining candles had long been consumed!

Then, after Simeon's passing, the western candle would sometimes continue burning after the others—and sometimes not. Finally, during the "forty years before the Temple was destroyed," the western candle *never* outlasted the others. Was the Lord trying to tell them something?

Talmud states (Shabbath 22b) this miracle was taken as a sign that Shechinah rested over Israel. Thus, it was well understood that when that miracle ceased, this was recognized as a warning that Shechinah was going to depart. As we have shown, about forty years later (69 A.D.) the Lord did indeed depart into Heaven from Olivet summit.

"The Logs for the Altar"

By the "Law," only two logs were used for the burnt offerings on the Altar of Sacrifice. The fire was ignited in the morning and could not be rekindled until the next morning and no more logs could be added during the day's burning. During Simeon's time the two logs were sufficient to last for a full day of Temple sacrifices. However, the Talmud is clear that after 30 A.D., this miracle also ceased to be manifested at the Temple.

"The Breads"

Talmud describes this miracle in somewhat cryptic fashion and only the main theme of this story is clear. It is stated as follows: " . . . an 'omer,' the two breads and the shewbread. Each priest got a piece the size of an olive, ate it, and was satisfied, some leaving something over. There was a curse on the breads 'from that time on' so that each priest received a piece the size of a bean." The implication is that after "that time" the priests were no longer satisfied from having eaten a piece the size of an olive. The discussion of the "curse," etc., is not clear at this writing.

"THE H'EKHAL DOORS"
It is also stated that during this same "forty years before the Temple was destroyed," doors of the H'ekhal would open by themselves. It can be observed in the Temple plan details, Sketch 7, there were many "chambers" and "gates" within the walls of the H'ekhal, which had doors to contribute to some occasions that must have been a little "spooky" for the Temple custodians, guards, and priests.

HOW THE JEWS REGARDED THE SIGNS
As we now look back on the tragic disappearance of all these Temple signs, it's almost as if the Lord were saying: "You have ignored the meaning of all the 'signs' I have given to you; including the 'burnt offering' of My only Son here on this Holy mountain, Olivet. Now, I give you one last 'sign' as I speak to you in Person on the mountain. If you still will not heed this sign, repent, and return to Me, I will go back to My Place." But, they did not.

Jewish people, as well as the rest of us, have ignored and / or have been shielded from this story. Nevertheless, it would be interesting to hear what worshipful Jews would find from this Event as a meaning for their people.

This occurred at a terrible time for Judeans. They were intent upon survival and most of these events happened very rapidly, during much pressure from the Romans. Maybe they were so confused, frightened, and harassed, they didn't know what to do, think, or feel. However, we know from the historians and from Scripture that the siege of Jerusalem and burning of the Temple left them with wounded hearts that can only be healed by Messiah.

It is a bitter irony that they wait for Messiah, and yet, He waits also for them.

> Behold, I stand at the door, and knock: If any man hear My voice, and open the door, I will come in to him, and will sup with him, and he with Me.
>
> Revelation 3:20

For Christians, there are some deep meanings that can be derived from some Jewish impressions received at this time. First, a summary statement in Yoma 39, which yields some of the pathos and alarm felt through all of this.

> Our Rabbis taught: During the last forty years before the destruction of the Temple, the lot ("For the Lord") did not come up in the right hand; nor did the crimson color strap become white; nor did the western-most light shine; and the doors of the H'ekhal would open by themselves until Rabbi Johanan ben Zakkai rebuked them, saying: "H'ekhal, H'ekhal, why wilt thou be alarmer thyself?" (i.e., Predict thine own destruction.) "I know about thee that thou wilt be destroyed for Zechariah ben Ido has already prophesied concerning thee." (i.e., concerning this significant omen of the destruction of the Temple.) "Open thy doors, O Lebanon, that the fire may devour thy cedars."
>
> (Zechariah 11:1)

Note:
According to Judaic historians, Rabbi Johanan ben Zakkai was the most honored and prestigious Jewish sage of the first century. Thus, the Temple priests knew desolation of the Temple was imminent. They must have prepared replicas and then secreted the most precious Temple articles to desert caves. An exciting archaeological search is currently seeking these items.

The Judeans of the First century, as well as twentieth century Jewish people, have been taught that Shechinah has accompanied Israel into exile. From Midrash Rabbah, Exodus 23:5, "Whence do we know that the Shechinah accompanied Israel in exile? Because it says, 'For your sake I was sent to Babylon.' ... and Moses said: (Lev. 26:44) 'and yet for all that, when they are in the land of their enemies, I will not reject them.'" Again from Midrash Leviticus 26:44: "I cannot abandon them, for I am the Lord their God."

Encyclopedia Judaica points out that although the presence of God is everywhere, the Shechinah rests permanently on Israel rather than on the Gentiles, because Israel is a people chosen and sanctified by God to be carriers of His will to the world. (See Exodus 33:16.) *Judaica* also mentions concerning Shechinah: "... which dwelt in the Temple, and was seen by the prophets in their visions, and which disappeared with the destruction of the Temple...."

Earlier, in Chapter 2, we referenced yet another traditional Jewish view on Shechinah's movements from tractate Rosh Hashanah 31a. Here it is said: "The Divine Presence tarried for Israel in the wilderness six months in the hope that they would repent. When [it saw that] they did not repent, it said, let their soul expire, as it says, 'But the eyes of the wicked shall fail and they shall have no way to flee and their hope shall be the expiry of the soul.' " (From Job 11:20)

From these comments, it appears that Jewish authorities are mixed in their opinions, as to the present disposition of Shechinah. We can note, however, Hosea said that He (God) was going to "return to His Place" and the Midrash has documented that Shechinah did depart into Heaven indeed, saying those very words, likely during Chanukah, 69 A.D.

Rabbi Akiba (first century) wept as he expressed his grief at the departure of Shechinah from the Temple. His lament is recorded in the Talmud, Sanhedrin 65b: " . . . he who fasts that the pure spirit [the Divine Presence] may rest upon him—how much more should his desire be fulfilled! But alas! our sins have driven it away from us, as it is written,

> But your iniquities have separated between you and your God. . . .
>
> (from Isaiah 59:2)

Thus it is seen again that deep grief and mourning accompanied this Event as the most devout Jews looked back and contemplated the Scriptures, the circumstances and the signs given to them just prior to this period. It is significant that Rabbi Akiba is credited as the most published of the Talmudic writers of the first century. He wrote at a time when all these events were still fresh in memory of those on the scene at this tragic sequence of events.

We should pause to note here that many of those first-century Christians were of the Priests and Pharisees. Many perhaps came to know Jesus as their Lord and Savior as a result of being closely involved with the Temple and having seen these signs. These fortunate and wise saints "made the connection." During those "forty years" they saw these things happen, recognized the error that had been made, told their friends, and . . . the "Church" was on its way to Glory!

So, we have reviewed here just a few of the "signs" given to the first-century Jews immediately following their rejection of and the Gentiles' indifference to the most endearing "sign" God has yet sent to man. Jesus declared (Luke 11:29) that these were a "wicked generation," continually asking for "signs." We can see that they had been given what should have been more than enough signs, but they still didn't "see" because they were blinded by their disbelief, by "tradition," and/or were being misled by their Rabbis.

Hear now, as the Lord admonished young King Solomon about what would happen to Israel if they did not continue keeping their part of the Covenant, from I Kings 9:6–9 (NASB):

> 9:6 But if you or your sons shall indeed turn away from following Me, and shall not keep My commandments and My statutes which I have set before you and shall go and serve other gods and worship them.
>
> 9:7 Then I will cut off Israel from the land which I have given them, and the house which I have consecrated for My name, I will cast out of My sight. So Israel will become a proverb and a byword among all peoples.
>
> 9:8 And this house will become a heap of ruins; everyone who passes by will be astonished and hiss and say, "Why has the Lord done thus to this land and to this house?"
>
> 9:9 And they will say, "Because they forsook the Lord their God, who brought their fathers out of the land of Egypt and adopted other gods and worshiped them and served them, therefore the Lord has brought all this adversity on them."

The Lord would say (again) to Israel today:

Deuteronomy Chapter 4:7, 8, 27–40

I Kings 9:3–9

Ezekiel 37

Hosea 5:15; 6:1–3

God has certainly held up His Chosen People as a "learning" example to us Gentiles as "a proverb and a byword." The same destiny falls to our "kings" and peoples, as has befallen the Jewish rulers and people, when we go astray and / or turn our backs on the Lord.

Isaiah said it well:

> "He has blinded their eyes
>
> and deadened their hearts,
>
> so they can neither see with their eyes,
>
> nor understand with their hearts,
>
> nor turn—and I would heal them.
>
> As quoted by John 12:40 (NIV)
>
> (from Isaiah 6:10)

This "stiff-necked" attitude of Israel was portrayed eloquently by the farmer, Tevyeh, in one of the early scenes of the musical, *Fiddler on the Roof.* In his description of the Jewish "position," he proudly said it was ... TRADITION!

Is "The World" Learning?

Just as Israel was given "signs," Gentiles are also being given "signs." Gentiles are being given "Latter Day signs."

— Are Christians ignoring the "sign" of tremendously increased occurrences of major earthquakes and volcanic eruptions? Major quakes occur all over the world "in diverse places." (Matthew 24:7)

— Are Christians ignoring the "signs" from the recent increase in devastating famines ... starving literally millions of people? (Mark 13:8)

— Are Christians also unaware of the "sign," showing many times more wars, rebellions, military aggression, riots of all sorts than have ever occurred simultaneously during all the history of the Earth? Our newest "high-tech" news-media can't even keep up with all the "wars" and "rumors of wars." (Matthew 24:6)

— Are Christians ignoring the "sign" given to all mankind by the recent strange and alarming (not to mention "deadly") increase of incurable, highly contagious diseases and viruses? New disease ("pestilences") such as AIDS and Herpes Simplex are appearing in greater numbers than ever before. (Luke 21:11)

— Are Christians ignoring the "sign" consisting of Earth's relentless temperature increase which is producing "weird" weather, raising sea levels, causing the increased drought, depletion of rainforests, etc.? The world's leading scientists admit they are powerless to halt, retard, or reverse this trend which, if it continues, will produce the "greenhouse effect" which sheltered man from the sun before The Great Flood. (This vapor shield protected men from the sun's radiation; perhaps explaining why men at that time lived to be about 1000 years old.) This is a condition which will exist again on Earth during Christ's Millennial reign. How far can we be from "that day?" (Isaiah 65:20, 22)

— In these times especially, we should take note of Jesus' words from the unique translation given for Luke 21:9–11 in the Lamsa Bible.[8] Among the signs he describes as appearing just before His return are: "wars and revolutions," "great earthquakes in different places," "famines and plagues," and He says, "the winters will be severe." Perhaps the Lord is saying, "Signs? You want signs? Children, I'm giving you signs!"

"Indeed God speaks once, or twice,

yet no one notices it."

Job 33:14 (NASB)

But, He is giving us lots of "signs" in the meantime (especially for those of us who are just a bit "near-sighted"). Not to "scare" us, though. For He said, " . . . when you see these things, you will know that your redemption draweth nigh." (From Luke 21:28) We are instructed, also: " . . . wherefore comfort ye one another with these words." (From I Thess. 4:18)

Those who are not familiar with the Promises of God may ask: "How can you say 'comfort' when all those horrible times are going to come upon the Earth? What kind of 'redemption' is that?"

The "GOOD NEWS" is:

The Lord wishes that all men should fear not. The Lord says if you will truly repent of your sins and if you will accept eternal salvation, paid-for by the life blood of the Lord Jesus Christ, and offered as a free gift through His Grace (You do not EARN it), then you will not be on this Earth "when those things come to pass." You will be taken up "in the twinkling of an eye" to be forever with the Lord, before these things "come to pass."

If you believe that Jesus is your only "burnt offering" and believe that He conquered death by rising from the tomb after three days, then, you have a "confirmed reservation" to dwell forever with Him.

Don't take my word for it. Please read:

    Luke 21:36

    I Corinthians 15:51–57

    I Thessalonians 4:16–18

    Revelation 3:10

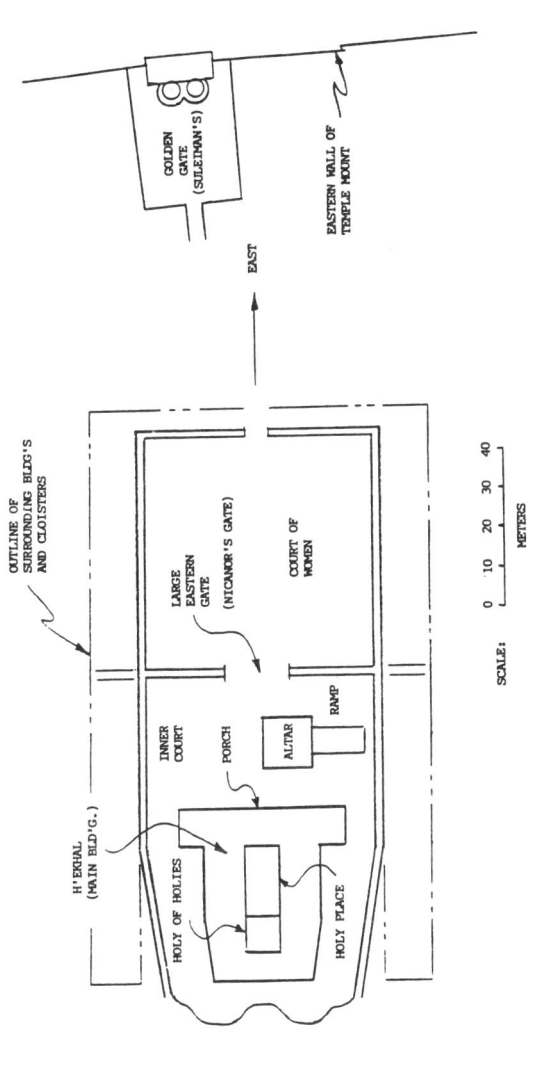

Sketch 1 - Plan of the Second Temple as detailed by Dr. A.S. Kaufman in Biblical Archaeology Review, Mar/Apr -- 1983, (p. 51) "Where the Ancient Temple of Jerusalem Stood." Printed with permission.

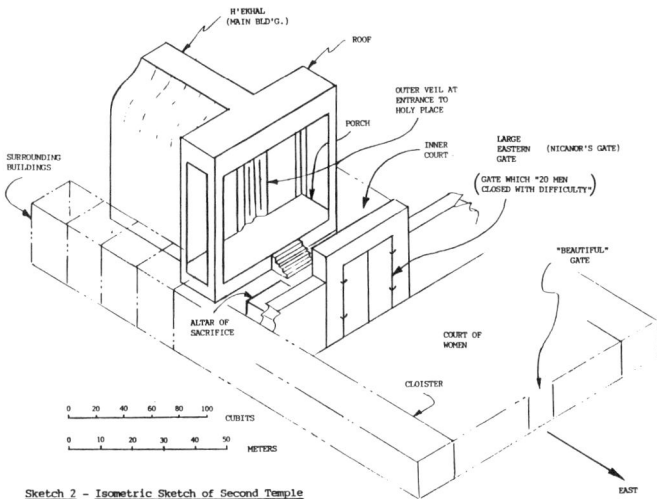

Sketch 2 - Isometric Sketch of Second Temple

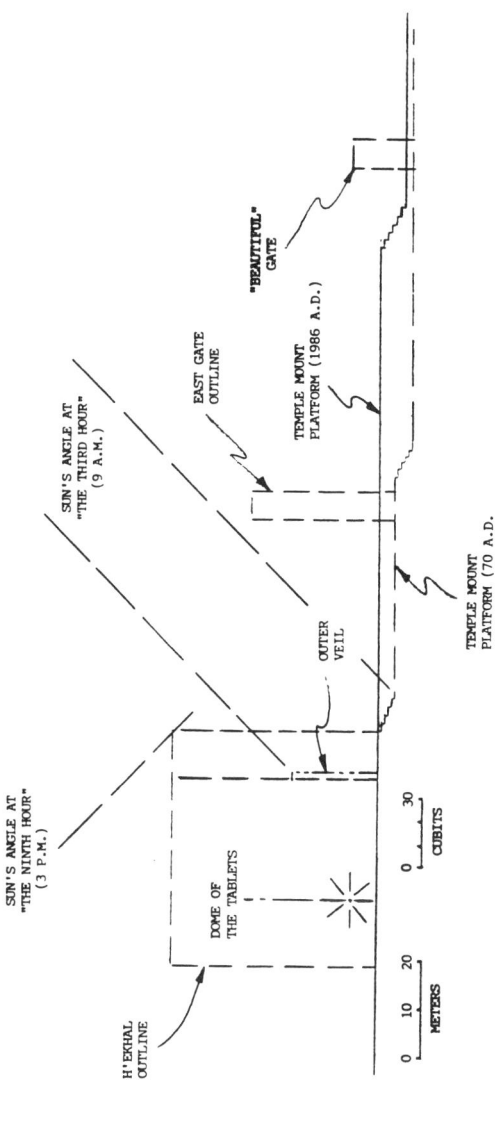

Sketch 3 - Detailed Elevation of Second Temple

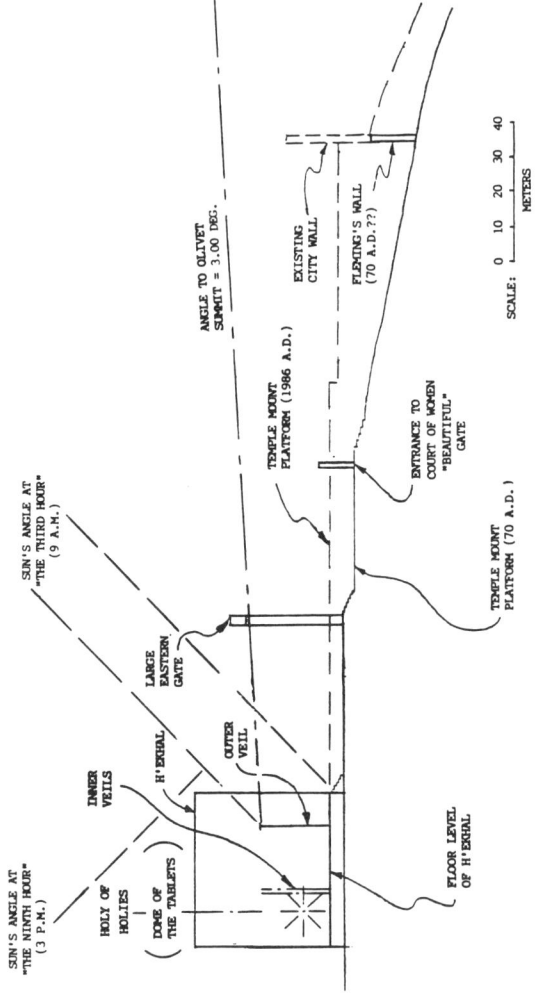

Sketch 4 - Elevation Profile of Temple and Temple Mount

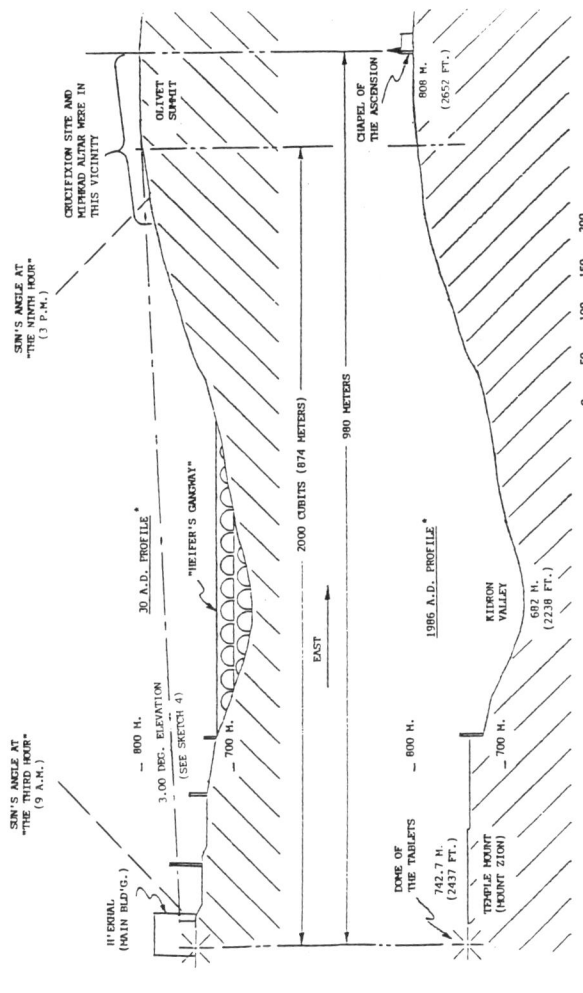

Sketch 5 - Elevation* Profile of Temple Mount, Kidron Valley and Mount of Olives

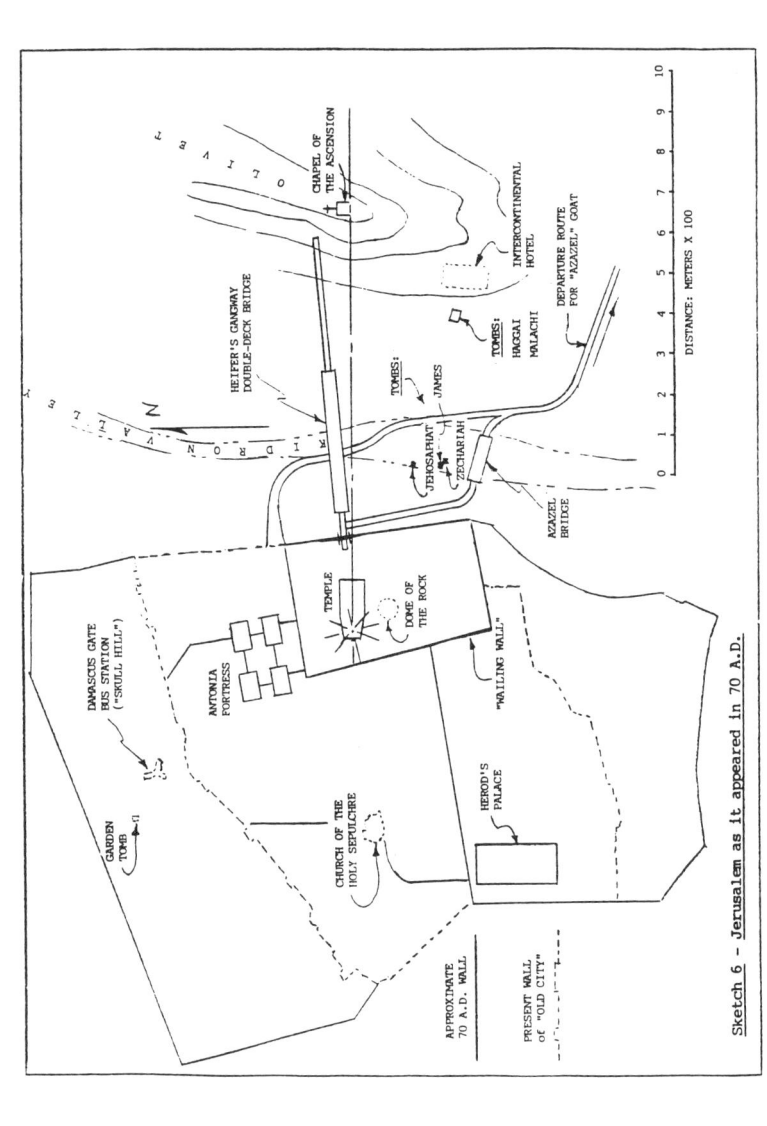

Sketch 6 - Jerusalem as it appeared in 70 A.D.

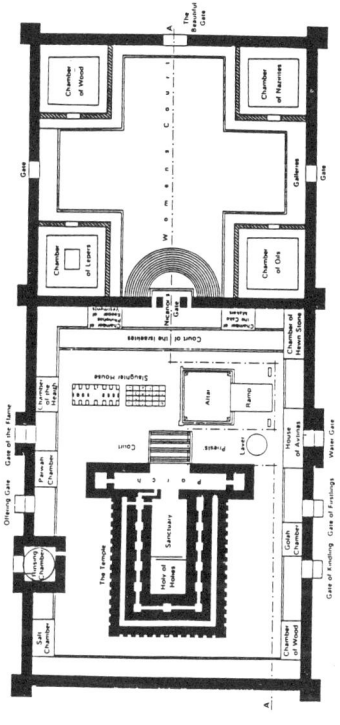
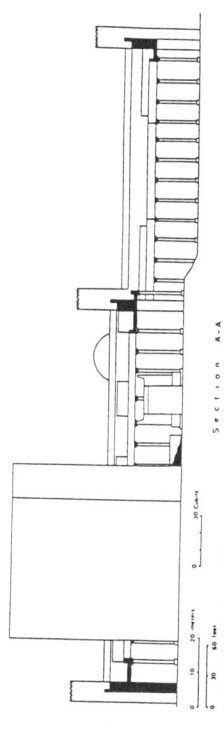

Suggested restoration of the Second Temple, according to Mishnah *Middot* and Josephus, *Jewish Antiquities*. Based on *Atlas of Israel*, Jerusalem, 1970. (Printed with permission, ENCYCLOPEDIA JUDAICA - Keter Publishing House Jerusalem Ltd.)

Sketch 7 - Detail of the Second Temple

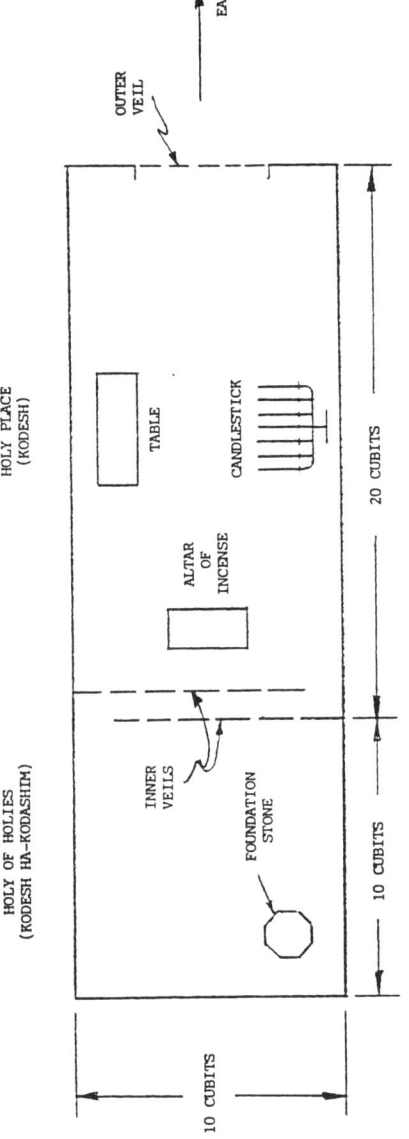

Sketch 8 - The Sanctuary of the Second Temple

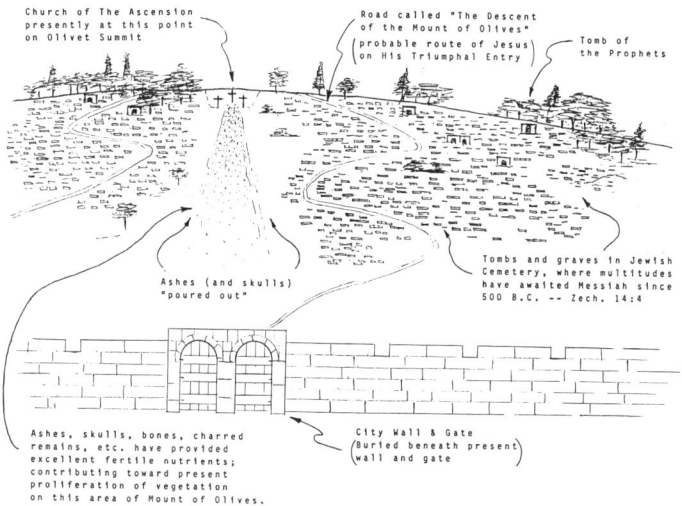

Sketch 9 -- Mount of Olives as viewed from the Temple on the day of The Crucifixion.

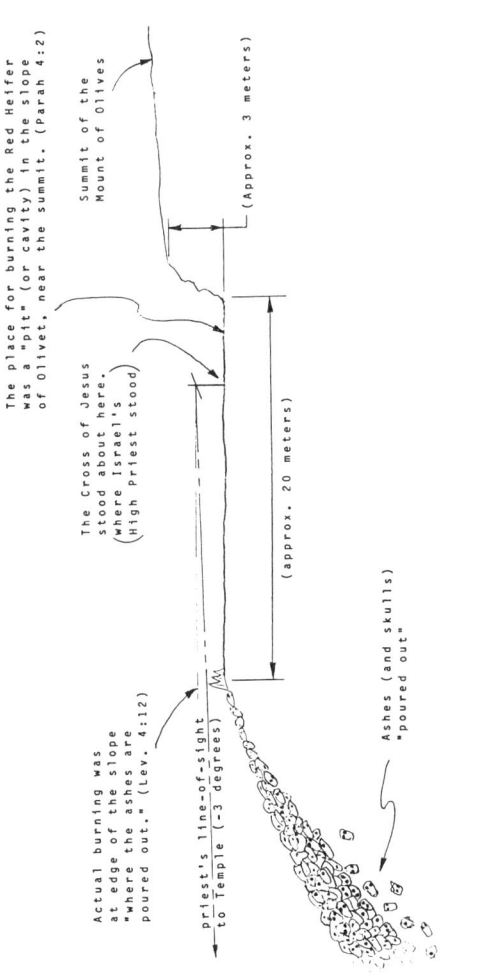

Sketch 10 -- Detail of the "pit" or "cavity" in the face of the Mount of Olives.

8 The Controversy

Telling this story to Jewish friends and to fellow Christians, I have occasionally met some obvious lack of enthusiasm from each side. In fact, I have encountered indifference, resistance, ridicule, suspicion, doubt, and yes, even hostility. But this is to be expected when an "unknown" person tries to bring out hard evidence in the face of 1,900 years of prejudice and suspicion between Judaism and Christianity. This task becomes even more difficult because these negative views are backed-up by some very "stiff-necked" teaching from some of the most beloved and well-intentioned "patriarchs" of both sides.

Many readers understandably will feel some of the same skepticism, fears, doubts, accusations, "Yeah—but's," etc. We must therefore identify these factors to prepare the foundation for debate of these points and in order to stimulate thinking on both sides. Those who would support this account need to be aware of these points as well.

THE ACCUSATIONS

For most people, never having heard of this event before, I know one doubting thought they must have:

If this story is really genuine, why have we never heard of this before now in any Christian or Jewish teaching? Why are we hearing it only now?

I do not know why we have not been told this story. Nevertheless, I have only uncovered a lot of hitherto "unknown" facts that have been chronicled by ancient historians (presented in Appendices A and B) and have been sitting in our libraries, more or less ignored by our scholars for all these years. It has turned out to be certainly a very beautiful and yet a very sad story.

One local Rabbi said recently: "It is all a mistake. The Midrash translation is in gross error." This was especially amusing because, unknown to the Rabbi, this translation was given by a member of his own congregation who speaks, reads, and writes Hebrew with much greater skill than this Rabbi himself. (The Rabbi was "squirming.") Those who will take time to read this passage from a published English translation of the Midrash[13] will soon discover that my Jewish friend's version is almost verbatim with the published English text and is, in fact, a much more beautiful and a much more heart-appealing translation.

The Soncino[13] English translation, however, has one particular variation that we should discuss. That source translates the Hebrew word "shalom" as "peace" instead of "good-bye" or "farewell." This oversight or variation overlooks (whether intentionally or not) the principal theme or essence of the occasion. Of course, most Gentiles already know "shalom" means "peace" or "good-bye" or even a friendly greeting. The word "shalom" can have a few different meanings, depending on its context in usage. Its use here should be obvious.

Nevertheless, reading from the Hebrew Midrash, my translator felt the emotion, pathos, and drama of this Holy Event. He translated "shalom" as "good-bye" (my precious vessel) "good-bye" (my Temple), etc. The quotation from Rabbi Akha (Appendix B) makes it obvious the Divine Presence was leaving His "palace," His "precious vessel," etc.—making "good-bye" most appropriate in this drama. Somehow, "O' the peace of my precious home," etc., just does not come across with what the Lord should be feeling and is feeling about His People and His Temple.

The indifferent make no accusation. It's much worse! They just say: "So what? What does this mean to me as a Christian? I see no salvation message here—nor any life-application of the Gospel of Jesus. That's just Jewish theology. It doesn't strengthen *my* faith.

The Jews are lost. Sorry, but this story just doesn't do anything for me . . . etc., etc."

This is usually the same reaction I get from those same Christians when I try to share with them Biblical archaeology discoveries or End Time events showing in the world today. These I pity most of all. They are just not "turned-on" by this sort of news. They do not realize that even though such is surely not needed for their salvation, there are many unsaved who may be reached if only they could learn these things. Many of us are like Thomas, needing to "see the print of the nails" and to "put our hand in His side" in order to believe.

One pastor I spoke with recently had the impression that the Midrash had occult contents. The Midrash is certainly not cannonized as Scripture, and I suppose there is certainly some material in those writings that could be challenged. Nevertheless, it seems unfair to reject all Midrashic text on the principle that some portions are undesirable. Further, one could expect the Rabbinical authorities made fairly stringent review of Midrashic text before it was accepted and passed down through all these centuries.

Unless we find contradicting Scripture, I am prepared therefore to give the Midrash Rabbis benefit of the doubt as far as this story is concerned. We certainly should hold no doubt, since a major prophet (Ezekiel) said this was going to happen. Another source also recorded the event (Josephus) and the Gospel of Jesus Christ (Matthew) declares literally that Shechinah (the Father, "I AM") was present in the Second Temple. (But here I am getting into the "debate" already!) One simply cannot discount all of the Midrash, even if there may be some occult influence in other portions of that text.

Some clergymen say all this is merely "extra-Biblical-trivia" and is of no spiritual importance. It seems to me, if for no other reason, an eyewitness account that documents fulfillment of Ezekiel's prophecy should rank as a Biblical event, which can hardly be dismissed as trivia. And yet, the most "popular" accusation has been made that no record of this event is stated in Scripture. Again, not only is there Scripture that says it was going to happen, but also there is Gospel and a statement from the Apostle Paul that literally says Shechinah (Divine Presence) was there at the time.

The actual Withdrawal Event is not mentioned in the New Testament simply because the last books (except The Revelation) were written just before 66 A.D.—before the event. It is likely those writers only knew of the Withdrawal afterward, since none of them remained in Judea after James ("the Just"), brother of Jesus, was martyred (62 A.D.). They were obedient by preaching the Gospel "unto the uttermost part of the earth." John's Revelation, although admittedly written much later (96 A.D.), dealt only with future events.

We cannot know why God chose to withhold this truth from His Word. Nevertheless, we can no longer ignore such a Glorious Event just because we are embarrassed to find out about it at this late date or only because some just do not want to hear it!

Also, we have plenty of other non-Scriptural Judean eyewitnesses whom one would expect to be the very last persons to admit (and even record) this incident. I believe such "circumstantial" evidence would certainly bring a "conviction" in a fair court!

We must not forget to list the understandable but unjustified Jewish accusation that Josephus was a traitor to the Jewish cause at the siege. Those who would so accuse should read the speech (more like a sermon) Josephus delivered at the Jerusalem wall to plead with his countrymen to surrender. (Reference 2, Wars, 5/348–419) Titus, the Roman commander, did not want all the bloodshed and certain destruction of that beautiful city that a siege would surely bring about.

For this reason mostly, I suppose, even modern Jewish people do not hold Josephus in esteem as a "Jew," although perhaps they recognize him as an historian. Those who object to the position of Josephus at that wall should read his speech and then read the messages delivered by Jeremiah some six hundred years earlier. (Jeremiah 7 and 21) They have very similar themes. Josephus must have read and believed *The Works of Jeremiah*. Read more about a scholar's evaluation of Josephus in Appendix C.

One "accusation" is that Ezekiel (Chapters 10 and 11) "saw" the Glory withdraw in 586 B.C. This is absurd, since Ezekiel clearly states (Ezek. 8:1–3) he was given this as a vision while he was physically in Babylon, sitting in his house, with a group of the elders of Judah seated before him. (Again, more "squirming.")

A seemingly legitimate criticism might contend that if the Glory had been in the Temple as late as 167 B.C., Antiochus Epiphanes would have been struck dead before he could have sacrificed a sow on the altar. This argument is of course based on "assumed" entry of Antiochus into the Kodesh Ha-Kodashim. However, since the Altar of Sacrifice was outside the H'ekhal, it was not necessary for Antiochus to have actually confronted Shechinah and he therefore was spared.

Roman conqueror Pompey even entered the Holy of Holies about 62 A.D., but was spared, perhaps, because he was respectful of the Temple and because he immediately urged the Israelites to resume their religious practices. The Romans did not admire "backsliders," even within the religions of vanquished nations. Titus entered the forbidden chamber in 70 A.D., but of course, the Presence had withdrawn from the Temple just three and one-half years earlier.

Another accusation persists when some people are confronted with any sort of "Biblical" information. In defense, they instantly dig in their heels by saying: "But how do we know that's true? There are so many 'interpretations,' so many language changes over the years, so many 'contradictions,' etc., etc." (And so many excuses for disbelief!)

THE RESISTANCE

The second category of criticism is so-named because, although most of these are sincere Believers, they do not want to believe this story. Why not? I can only surmise it is because they have been brought up on what has lately been termed "Replacement Theology."[4] This is the popular Christian concept that Christians are now God's Chosen and He is, for now at least, finished with those "naughty disobedient" Jews. The fact that this story (let alone the Bible and recorded history!) says the Glory was in the Temple at the time of Jesus and forty years afterward really disturbs some Christians.

Ironically, however, most Jews also "resist" because it is obvious from this story that Shechinah had some sort of "connection" with Jesus of Nazareth. So, here we have a story that is documented by Jewish records, but which the Jewish people "must" resist. The Jews therefore have preferred to keep it quiet. Then, also it is resisted by Christians because they have overlooked, ignored, or doubted this event and have all along been taught something entirely different. Now they do not seem to want to hear the real story.

— Jewish people are embarrassed to be shown, from their historians (and from Scripture!) that . . . YES!!! Jesus "probably" is Messiah.

— Christians are embarrassed to be shown, again from Jewish historians, that we have been either ignoring or teaching in error concerning the visible Divine Presence during the time of Jesus.

So, it is no wonder that I have been getting "flack" from both sides. NOBODY enjoys hearing what he doesn't want to hear! What we have here is some very human behavior.

But why cannot Christians, at least, overcome their human "phobia?" This story certainly underlines the fact that Jesus is Messiah and that "I and my Father are One." It takes nothing away from Jesus; in fact, it brings new meaning to the Gospel in addition to documenting the fulfillment of Ezekiel's prophecy. How could believing Christians resist, doubt, ignore, or delay such a beautiful story about our Lord, which demonstrates (historically) the close relationship of the Son to the Father?

Much as I dislike stereotyped "labels," my own religious position label would fit most closely as a conservative / fundamental / evangelical, "born-again" Christian. The most bitter and "stiff-necked" criticism of this story has come from "traditionalist" brethren of that same label. Liberal Christian contacts have been inclined more to politely doubt my claim, smile and simply say, "No thank you."

Conservatives have given more of a "hardball" type of response. Most have just totally ignored any request for review, examination, or discussion. They respond with deafening silence. That is the most cruel, most humiliating, most insulting, and yet most impotent of arguments. Some of my more compassionate conservative brothers use an accusation borrowed from the Gospel and from Paul's epistles. These accuse me of "straining at a gnat" and some caution me against becoming "puffed up with knowledge." (I Corinthians 4:6)

Jesus scolded the Talmudic scholars (lawyers) against "straining at the gnat" (Matt. 23:24), but it is obvious to any who would examine the Talmud that His advice went unheeded. This story, although quite intricate in many ways, has been shown to be that complex by the Lord's own design—not entirely by man's choice. He went to a lot of trouble to make this Event happen as it did, as indicated by Scripture, by the Law, and by historical records. It is an affront to the Lord to belittle or ignore this Event. Those who would dismiss this as "gnat-straining" or "puffing-up" need to be wary and watch for the truth. Jesus said He would fulfill "every jot and tittle." He also Promised that the truth would make us free, but not if we remain complacently mired down in the quicksand of tradition.

Some "resisters" say they don't accept Josephus and the Midrash as reliable sources. This is mindful of that well-known resistance put up by unbelievers who say they don't believe the Bible, but admit they have never read it.

But the chief resistance gets back to the problem some Christians have with the thought of God's Presence remaining in despicable

Herod's Temple after Jesus had said it would be "desolate" and even called it a "den of thieves." They take this to be a claim that God then accepted both Christ-rejecting Judaism and Christ-glorifying Christianity by remaining "under the same roof with those devils after what they did." They just cannot accept the fact that God gave the Jews another full generation of years to repent and return unto Himself. He did not just go out through the torn Veil and slam-the-door on the Jews when Jesus gave up the ghost. We have been assuming such and it is difficult to change, but the real story is far more beautiful, far more Christ-glorifying, and far more God-glorifying.

Much of anti-Semitism and what I call patronizing of Judaism stems from the Gentiles' "gut-reaction," which faults the Jews for the Crucifixion. Condemnation of the Jewish people for the death of Jesus Christ makes about as much sense as blaming the citizens of Dallas, Texas for the assassination of President John F. Kennedy. They did not cause it to happen. They simply did not prevent it. They could not have prevented it!

One type of "squirming" is the frequent use of Bible verses to prove "assumptions." Keep in mind that the latest writings of the New Testament, except The Revelation, were written about 66 A.D. in places far from Jerusalem and just prior to this tragic event. Some enjoy a particular "zeal" in quoting verses that were written a few years previous to this event, a thousand miles distant, and are obviously being taken out of context concerning Shechinah. And yet, these "resisters" stand with unblushing ignorance and disbelief, attempting to discredit historical records from those on the scene, at the time. A "favorite" of this sort is from II Corinthians 4:6 (NASB). Paul writes from Ephesus, circa 57 A.D.:

> ... knowledge of the glory of God in the face of Jesus Christ.

This is certainly speaking of the glory of God, which certainly is shown in the face of Jesus Christ, but it is certainly not speaking of the "cloud"—the "fire"—the Shechinah. Shechinah was an extraordinary visible Presence of the "I AM." But, He appeared only to the Israelites—perhaps only to the High Priest, after 970 B.C. when Solomon's Temple was completed—and until He departed the Temple and "removed hence" to Olivet summit in 66 A.D. This remains a fact that is very difficult for some Gentiles to accept; nevertheless, it was His Promise to the Jews in Deuteronomy 4:33 (NASB):

Has any people heard the voice of God speaking from the midst of the fire, as you have heard it, and survived?

But the Jews (and Gentiles) seem to have forgotten or ignored these words. They also have overlooked verse 30:

> When you are in distress and all these things have come upon you, in the latter days, you will return to the Lord your God and listen to His voice.

Finally, some Christians who resist this story are apparently disturbed, albeit mistakenly, by anything that might be construed as overshadowing The Resurrection of Jesus Christ. Heaven forbid! Rather, The Resurrection and Ascension of the Lord Jesus Christ is Punctuated—Magnified—Glorified—even more greatly by this event on the part of the Father, "I AM." Let us not forget, either, that the Father IS first and sovereign within the Trinity. Jesus always prayed to His Father before He did anything. Jesus also always gave His Father the Glory and credit for anything He (Jesus) did.

We should therefore take delight from and see glory in the action of the Father in having ascended from that same locale (Olivet Summit) forty years after His Son, Jesus. I surely don't believe Jesus would have "pouted" because His Father had the last "Word"—nor should we.

Some Missing Pieces

An "accusation" or doubt that deserves answer is the absence of certain details from Scripture or even from the usually detailed reporting by Flavius Josephus. Such answer can be provided only by speculation based on "assumptions," a little imagination, and simple logic using available history and of course, Scripture. Realizing I have shown scant mercy toward traditional criticism for having founded its stand principally on "assumption," I will likely feel a merciless response from "traditionalists." We cannot know why these pieces of this puzzle have been kept from us; however, if we are moved to try, then we must start somewhere.

Typical of these kinds of missing pieces are:

Why didn't Josephus and the Rabbis of the Midrash report the "great noise" of Nicanor's Gate? Why didn't Josephus or the Rabbis report that this gate opened silently, if that were the case? Why did the guards need to tell their captain the gate had opened, if it did not open silently—"of its own accord?" My only certain answer to these questions is simply, "I don't know."

However, there are several things for which we have some confidence as "fact" because they seem to be supported by Scripture, by the writings of Josephus and/or by plausible reasoning:

— Each bronze "door" of Nicanor's Gate was about 60 ft. by 23 ft.

— The gate must have been very heavy and had great friction, because it "had been with difficulty shut by twenty men" and effective lubricants were not available to ease its friction.

— The conditions described would, from an engineering sense, indicate a possibility that such a gate would make a "great noise" when pivoted on "its turning hinges."

— The noise was sufficiently "great" to be heard at a distance of more than four miles—almost as far as Bethlehem.

— Both Scripture and the Rabbinical reporters of Talmud verify that this gate was normally opened only on the eve of the each Sabbath, on New Moons (first day of the month), and on Feast Days.

On the basis of the information listed then, it has been assumed that the gate opened silently "at about the sixth hour of the night." Reasoning for the assumption follows:

— Midnight was not the normal time for opening the gate.

— Midnight was not the Sabbath eve, even if that day had been on a Sabbath, because for the Jews each day begins at sundown.

— The date was the eighth day of the month (Nisan) and not a New Moon, which occurs on the first day.

— For the aforementioned reasons, nobody was expecting to hear the gate being opened, especially the captain who was probably asleep in his quarters. He had forty guards under his command. He did not remain awake throughout all three watches. This was delegated to lower ranking officers of the guards who commanded each shift or "watch."

Yet, for all the reasoning and data outlined here, it has been assumed that the gate must have opened silently at this Holy occasion because the guards ran to tell their captain the gate had opened. Under normal conditions, the captain would have been awakened by the "great noise of its turning hinges" and he would have jumped out of his bunk and raced out shouting something like, "Why in blazes are they opening the East Gate?! What's going on out there?!" But, no. The guards instead ran to tell their captain they had seen the gate open.

It has been assumed then, nobody heard the gate—not even the townsfolk in Jerusalem a few hundred meters west of the gate. It is assumed again, Josephus would perhaps have included the midnight rousing of The City, if they had heard this. I cannot explain these voids of explanation. Perhaps some scholar can provide these answers.

Another question, even more obvious, concerns the omission of the details of that sight, which was beheld by the centurion and his squad at The Cross. Here we need to remember that all of those "stalwarts of the Faith" (the twelve) scattered like flushed quail even before Jesus was "lifted-up"—even at His capture and arrest. Mark literally "barely" escaped! (Mark 14:50–52) Yes, all except one! John was the only one of "the twelve" who is known to have been at The Cross.

Some might say that since John was the only disciple at The Cross, and since he did not say the centurion had seen the torn Veil, then it must have been the earthquake that "terrified" the soldiers. None of the other three Gospel writers was at The Cross, yet all three wrote of the torn Veil as seen by the centurion. Why didn't John write of this, especially since he was the only one of the disciples at Golgotha?

We just don't have all these answers; nevertheless, examining carefully and literally the words of the Apostle, in John 19:27 we find:

> Then saith He (Jesus) to the disciple, "Behold thy mother!" And from that hour that disciple took her unto his own home.

This verse is given early in John's narrative of The Crucifixion. Then, continuing, in verse 28:

> After this, Jesus knowing that all things were now accomplished, that the Scripture might be fulfilled, saith, "I thirst."

Then, in verse 29, they gave Him the "spunge." Summarizing then, while John was at The Cross, they gave Jesus the sponge just before the ninth hour when He departed, just after he had instructed "the disciple whom Jesus loved" to take their mother home. John, a sensitive and compassionate man, probably saw a nod or eye-cast from Jesus that expressed silently: "John, if you are the one whom I love, please take 'our' mother away from this. I prefer that she not be here at the end."

At that, John obediently and immediately "from that hour" removed gently to take Mary home. John was not present at the end nor, to our knowledge, was any other disciple. In his narration, John did not choose to say the Glory shone through the torn Veil nor did he mention "those things that were done." (John reported only what he saw.)

The other three Gospel writers didn't see this, but all three say the centurion SAW "those things." Somebody perhaps told them about the centurion's witness, but maybe they did not know the centurion saw Almighty God. Although, neither do they tell us of any other event that was so terrifying that it might inspire this sudden Roman evangelical response. (Maybe they thought nobody would believe their story!)

It may be significant that Mark and Luke reported only the torn Veil. No mention of the quakes, the graves, or any other of "those things." This can be taken to imply that the other "Things that were done" were unimportant. So, what was so important about the Veil being "rent in twain from the top to the bottom?" Mark says this was sufficiently impressive that the centurion said, "Truly, this man was the Son of God." Yet, neither Luke nor Mark says anything about the centurion being "terrified." (Only Matthew.) They just say the Veil was torn and this convinced the centurion that Jesus was the Son of God. But, we do know why the centurion was so impressed, even though Mark did not present any rationale for the centurion's remark. (See Matthew 27:51–54; Mark 15:38–39; Luke 23:45–47, and John 19:30–36.)

I don't know why the writers of the Gospel omitted such details, but those historical and Scriptural details that are available provide the answers we have offered. Although some of the pieces of these puzzles are missing, we can see the picture assembled, except for a few details that the Lord has preferred to cloak in mystery for a time. Notice: "Three" writers said the centurion saw the torn Veil.

It has been said that Jews search Scripture to discover "why?"; while Christians search Scripture to discover "how?" Those philosophical positions remain intact considering everything we have encountered in this story.

YOU SHALL KNOW THE **TRUTH!**
Extracting the truth by unfastening all the buttons, buckles, zippers, snaps, etc., holding in place the cloak of prim, comfortable, convenient, respectable, "traditional" teaching can be compared to dealing with constipation. It may require taking some "untasty" medicine, perhaps even an enema—may cause some discomfort (struggling, even!)—may even take some time—and we may have some "awkward" moments as we "hasten" to unfasten all those zippers, buttons, etc., when we finally begin to realize and accept the TRUTH. But, when we finally release all that "blockage" of tradition that has been holding back the "freedom" that accompanies the truth, we are going to feel a lot better. And, as the Essenes of the West Gate discovered, despite our holding back, we will eventually have to "come forth"—perhaps not without some pain and embarrassment.

Again, the Bible provides added meaning (and rich blessings) when we know the Shechinah still resided in the Temple during the time of Jesus and when we accept literally those things described by the New Testament writers, instead of just accepting "traditional" teaching without question. As Professor Martin noted, the local Jewish "tourist-guides" of the fourth century really "did a number on us" when they showed Helena, Emperor Constantine's mother, several alleged Christian "Holy Places," which were actually revered Jewish sites, tombs, etc., or nothing at all. Many of our most popular sites were identified to Helena by those ancient "rip off artists" and some actually by Constantine himself, through his idolatrous divinations and "visions."[25]

For reasons we might never know, Christian scholars at that time must have overlooked Chapter 27 of Matthew, or else they could never have been so completely hoaxed. And after all, who was going to argue with this brand-new Christian, Emperor Constantine? Even Bishop Eusebius eventually had to bow to this concept from his Emperor's "Divine Revelation." And so, for all these years, we have followed this tradition (although, more recently a more "modern" and more "accurate" location has been proclaimed by Britain's hero of Khartoum, General Charles Gordon.)

One year before his death at Khartoum, the distinguished general toured Jerusalem, observing what appeared to be the image of a skull on a cliff of clay northwest of the Old City, near the present Damascus Gate Bus Station. Gordon fondly but blindly concluded, "This must be Calvary!" Although General Gordon was not an archaeologist, he *was* a treasured national hero, even before Khartoum—and, it is very unwise to contradict war heroes (or *any* generals *or* emperors for that matter!) concerning religion or warfare or anything else.

Understandably, General Gordon could not have known that area had been the site of the city latrines during the first century. Sadly also, the general did not possess thorough Biblical awareness of the centurion's line-of-sight to The Veil, as related by Matthew. No evidence has surfaced to indicate that Gordon was misled by "tourist guides." Just as many of us might be tempted to do, he evidently misled himself by eagerly and fondly seeking what he *wanted* to see, rather than by seeking the Truth.

A few decades later, some Christians discovered an empty tomb a short distance from "Gordon's Calvary," perhaps having been similarly inspired by romantic but blind enthusiasm. This popular and revered Christian pilgrim stop has been named "The Garden Tomb." In these fashions, Christians tragically for many years have been misled concerning authenticity of these Holy sites. Nevertheless, they continue to cling to these traditional spots with a most tenacious romantic fervor that surely will not easily give way to the Truth, no matter the facts. Tradition is powerfully soothing and addictive.

Even so, lest we be derelict in this effort, we still need to determine why the Jewish survivors at Jerusalem would seek deliberately to deceive Christian pilgrims. They demonstrated what is perhaps the ultimate *chutzpah* by doing this in the face of the mighty Emperor, Constantine!

The answer to this query appears obvious when we stop to consider the fact that the Jews of the third and fourth centuries were even then eagerly awaiting their Messiah and the restoration of their Temple. (We must never forget that this situation exists with may Jewish Faithful today as well.) When and if the Temple were restored and the burnt offerings, the Red Heifer burnings, etc., were resumed, *the Jews would certainly not have wanted Christians or anybody else erecting shrines, conducting tours, gawking around, and tramping over the graves in the vicinity of their Miphkad Altar at Olivet summit*! So, the Jews grasped these naive, wide-eyed Christians by the nose and led them precisely in the opposite direction from the true location—to the west side of The City, rather than eastward to Olivet.

It well may be also that this is one of the reasons why the Lord has permitted delay of publication of this book for several years. Consider this: If Christians were suddenly to awaken to the fact that The Crucifixion occurred at Olivet summit, and if the Jews were to resume Temple sacrifices at Olivet, just imagine what would be the reaction of Judaism and Islam. To say the least, it would be an "explosive" situation.

All this should at least in part explain why we and our theologians and scholars have been so inaccurate during all these centuries in our location of the place of The Crucifixion. (After all, God has "permitted" our ignorance for His Holy Purpose.) From what we have developed in our study, the evidence points undeniably to Olivet summit for that most Holy site.

This was a piece of very cleverly contrived "disinformation" that was perhaps originally intended as a cruel joke on some very powerful but very gullible Christian Gentiles. (They were telling them what they wanted to hear!) And so, for many generations afterward we have continued to be "duped" by those rascals—partly because we have followed traditional teaching instead of studying and believing the literal wording of the Scriptures to obtain and verify the truth.

Nevertheless, we must agree from the findings of this study that tradition has been very accurate in its disclosure of the Place of the Ascension. As always, Satan again has managed to delude and confuse us by "salting" his lies with just a "dash" of truth. That Prince of Darkness surely knows how eagerly we mortals are willing to reach out and grasp those things we want to hear.

It is apparent that Gospel writers omitted (and / or were not "commissioned" to reveal) several details of the Law that are very important and relevant toward more thorough understanding of certain contexts in the Gospel. It seems the Lord inspired them to write their stories and to just drop these details, as if to say, "Why, everyone knows that!"

Typical of such a void in our Judaic awareness is our Biblical misunderstanding concerning "the veil." The Bible (Exodus 26:35) instructs only that a veil of red, blue, and purple shall separate the Holy of Holies from the Holy Place. Then, in verse 37 it says, "... thou shalt make an hanging for the door of the tent, of blue, and purple, and scarlet. ..."

Confusion for us Gentiles arises from the fact that the Jews deviated a bit from the Biblical instructions pertaining to The Tabernacle given in Exodus. Solomon's Temple had two cedar partitions separating the two Holy chambers of the H'ekhal and had a veil before the outer partition and "an hanging" before the Temple entrance doors. In the Second Temple, however, the cedar partitions were replaced by two veils. And, as in the Tabernacle and in Solomon's

Temple, they provided "an hanging, of blue, and purple, and scarlet" for the door.

Then, adding to our confusion, they called this outer "hanging" a veil, also. (Thus, three "veils," OK?) Josephus referred to this outer veil as a huge Babylonian curtain. This outstanding historian also was unaware that two veils divided the H'ekhal. Now, since the Gospel writers were Jewish, they also referred to this outer curtain as a veil or our translators used the word "vail" to describe that "hanging" or "curtain." After all, in ancient languages such as Hebrew and Aramaic, which have far less vocabulary choice for words than is available in, say, English; the words "veil" and "curtain" or "hanging" can have virtually the same meaning.

Evidence of this multiplicity of terms concerning "the veil" can be cited in the Talmud. Tractate Hullin 90b describes it as the "curtain" that graced the entrance to the Temple. This passage further states that the curtain was one handbreadth thick, woven twice each year, and had to be immersed by three hundred priests, etc. Tractate Shekalim 8:4–5 describes the "veil" as one handbreath thick, woven twice each year, etc. Both tractates mention the eighty-two damsels.

It appears that the translators of the New Testament used the word "veil" instead of "curtain" when they described "the rending of the vail." The centurion could have seen the outer "curtain," under the proper conditions, but he could not have seen either of the two veils inside the Temple.

Nevertheless, once again it has been shown that what some would call Biblical "confusion" or "contradiction" is not the result of error or failure in the Scriptures. Rather, it is because of man's failure to "do his homework!" We have cut ourselves off from Jewish Law and tradition and anything "Jewish" in order to avoid having our Christianity become corrupted by Judaism. Ironically, however, this persistence in ignorance has hidden much of the "beauty" of Christ that is cast throughout The Talmud and Midrash. Hidden just because we would not do our homework.

Now, having encountered a few such details from the Talmud in this work, the following thought comes to mind: Any Jewish scholar who is knowledgeable in Judaic Law and tradition must sometimes regard parts of our Christian teaching with a certain amount of humor. He might be justified to have that thought when he observes how misinformed and how uniformed we are about the very roots of our faith. (We have not done our "homework!")

At the same time, we Christians are so smug with our 20/20 hindsight, as we observe sympathetically, but impatiently, "How could they have been so blind?" Jews must also be saying, "How can they be so naive?!"

So much of our "traditional" teaching has overlooked these details of Judaic Law and history, which are so important to Christian knowledge. Gentiles descended from Ham and Japheth are supposed to "dwell in the tents of Shem;" i.e., "learn" from Shem (Genesis 9:27). Shem was the eldest of Noah's sons and is the ancestor of all "Semitic" peoples, including the Israelites. God's Word is further glorified by these "jewels" from its Judaic roots.

9 The Debate

Now that we have discussed most of the doubts and "fears" that cause the critics to "accuse" and/or "resist," these issues can be debated.

EZEKIEL'S PROPHECY OF THE GLORY WITHDRAWAL
Scholars calculate that Ezekiel was carried off to Babylon about 597 B.C. and was given this particular vision about 591 B.C.—about five years before Solomon's Temple was destroyed. Some critics of this account would insist that Ezekiel "saw" the Glory of the Lord withdraw from the Temple before the Babylonian destruction (586 B.C.). This point is then used to counter any claim that the Glory was ever residing in the Second Temple. These have assumed Shechinah never returned. This is the first of two popular, traditional "myths" concerning the Shechinah that we shall disprove.

This position proposes that Ezekiel was translated or "raptured" to Jerusalem from Babylon to witness the departure of the Shechinah Glory. Even if the prophet had been raptured to Jerusalem, it is not reasonable to suppose that he was the sole observer of this Glorious Event. If, in fact, he "saw" the departure, why did no others see it? Why is there no 586 B.C. record of that remarkable, dramatic occasion? Supporters of this theory have no plausible explanation for these voids. They are simply teaching as they have been taught, by tradition!

These would suggest that blinding "fire" or that imposing "cloud" would have just passed over all the Temple guards, priests, townspeople, etc., and just moved over to Olivet without even a soul present to behold this scene. We are left to believe nobody in Jerusalem even looked up to see their Lord. They all just went on about their business. When one stops to think about such a suggestion, it is ludicrous.

These should be reminded that Ezekiel was very specific about times and places of his visions—and this was a vision; although some of our most beloved and knowledgeable teachers insist Ezekiel was translated to Jerusalem. Ezekiel clearly states, beginning in Ez. 8:3, this entire dissertation was a "vision." He also indicates he was not physically in Jerusalem when he "saw" these events, "in the visions of God," but that he was in his house in Babylon seated before a group of elders (Ez. 8:1–4). True, he does say he was taken up "by a lock of mine head," but that he was brought to Jerusalem "in the visions of God."

Ezekiel even says his vision of the rebuilt Temple (Ez. 43:3) was given in the same way (Ez. 9:5) as this vision. As mentioned, this prophet was meticulous about dates. He records that the vision, which extends from Chapter 8 through Chapter 11, was given "in the sixth year of our captivity." The date he records for his vision "given in the same way" for the future Temple, to be rebuilt upon Israel's return to The Land, is "the five and twentieth year of our captivity"—about fifty-two years before Zerubbabel began construction. Definitely a vision of the future.

Then, closing in verse 11:24, he explains: " . . . So the vision that I had seen went up from me." The literal Word of God says there was no "rapture." Ezekiel saw this only as a vision.

Clearly, any insistence that Ezekiel was raptured, or even physically on the scene when Shechinah withdrew, is based "purely" on assumptions, which contradict literal translations of Scripture and are boldy opposed to documented historians' dating and timing of the event. Josephus notes the date as "before the Jews' rebellion," i.e., 66 A.D. Talmud, Rosh Hashanah 31a, dates departure of Shechinah as before the destruction of the Temple.

Some sympathy can be offered toward the misunderstanding, which results by assuming Ezekiel "reported" this event rather than "predicted" it. This prophecy is yet another example of the "prophetic-perfect-tense" that is frequently used by the Prophets to emphasize importance of certain prophecies. In this style they actually wrote in the past tense in order to establish that the prophecy was so certain that it could already be considered to have happened! Ezekiel's prophecy of the Shechinah departure is just such a prophecy. Let us not be confused and therefore miss the truth and the importance of this glorious event.

Some would say that no Scripture ever described the Glory withdrawing from the Second Temple and that only Ezekiel describes it (before Solomon's Temple was destroyed—586 B.C.) and therefore that prophecy applies only to Solomon's Temple.

Ezekiel did not indicate when the prophecy was to be fulfilled. Claiming this applies only to Solomon's Temple, just because the vision was given before Solomon's Temple was destroyed, is simply another unfounded assumption. This assumption, even if it were correct, includes the implied proviso that a prophecy can be fulfilled only once. Most beginner Bible students soon learn that many prophecies have been or will have been fulfilled more than once.

Literally, Ezekiel's vision says only that the Glory would (someday) withdraw from the Temple and sit down upon the mountain east of the City (Jerusalem) and would (someday) return to the Temple from the mountain (Ezekiel 43:2). Strangely, Ezekiel makes no announcement that Shechinah will "rest" on the mountain for three and one-half years nor that He will ascend into Heaven. Hosea 5:15 declares that God will "go back to His Place." The Midrash Rabbis confirmed that He did in fact do just that—because "they" would not repent, despite the fact that Scripture does not fill in all the details concerning His delay at the Mount of Olives and His Ascension afterward.

The favorite evasion of some "squirmers" seems to be an insistence that all prophecy and Biblical knowledge must be verified by Scripture—no secular records accepted. (They believe this ploy will cause me to "squirm," also.)

There are scores of prophecies that have been, and are today being fulfilled without Scriptural "verification." Many of these do not appear in Scripture simply because they were fulfilled after the last books of the Bible had been written. Some prophecies, however, have even been fulfilled during the Biblical period and still are not documented by Scripture. Let's take just one example as an illustration. Ezekiel (26:14) said Tyre would be "like the top of a rock." And it is—Alexander (The Great) saw to it. The Bible doesn't need to say it happened! All Believers could rest assured it would happen—some day. (Not when or how it would happen.) Jesus alluded to that fulfillment in Matthew 11:21 and Luke 10:13, but He did not describe those "mighty works which were done" in Tyre. And they were done and yet, this is documented and described only in secular records circa 300 B.C., and by what we see of ancient Tyre today.

A more recent example of non-Scriptural fulfillment documentation is the rebirth of the nation, Israel. Ezekiel (Chapter 37) issued the Lord's Promise 2,500 years ago that He would "make them one nation" (Ezek, 37:22). Although no mention of Israel's rebirth appears in Scripture, you can see for yourself that He has made them "one nation" as Promised—beginning as of May 1948. (How many times had we heard that old spiritual ballad about "'dem dry bones?" And we didn't even know that was from Ezekiel's prophecy!)

However, the best example is Jesus' prophecy that the Temple would be destroyed, " . . . There shall not be left here one stone upon another, . . ." (Matt. 24:2). Since the last books of the New Testament were certainly written *before* the destruction, no Scripture reports that fulfillment. And yet, the world surely believes the Temple *was* destroyed and in the manner and on the date as described by Josephus and the Rabbis of Talmud and Midrash—the *same* historians who recorded the Shechinah Withdrawal.

Whose "House"?

Another form of Scriptural opposition claims Shechinah could not have returned to the Second Temple because Scripture does not describe such an event (as was given for Solomon's Temple, II Chron. 5:13–14).

We do not witness prophetic fulfillment by what the Bible doesn't say about these events. We have just shown that the Bible doesn't tell everything. Just because the Bible does not say Shechinah returned doesn't mean He didn't return. The remote Aramaic Lamsa Bible includes a Promise that has been omitted from our more popular ("conventional") Western Bibles. Lamsa[8] translates Ezra 6:12 "And the god whose name we have found there, *there shall he dwell*," in describing the Lord's dwelling in His rebuilt Temple after the return from Babylon.

Scripture makes no mention of the return of the "cloud" to the Second Temple. However, as we read Nehemiah 8, 9, and 10, it is difficult to believe our Merciful and Loving Father would continue to punish and "turn His face away" from these worshipers after they had repented, confessed, rejoiced, and praised and convenanted with Him so fervently and sincerely on that occasion. Nehemiah 12:43 says their rejoicing at Jerusalem "was heard even afar off." (How could He resist?)

Additional Scriptural evidence of this return through the Promise of prophecy exists in God's message through the prophet Haggai. In Chapter I, verse 4 (paraphrasing): Upon their return from Babylon, He tells Haggai to ask Zerubbabel and the People: "Is it right for you to build houses for yourselves, but then to permit My House to remain as a heap of rubble?" Then, in verse 8 the Lord declares: "Go up to Mt. Zion and bring wood and build My House and I will take pleasure in it and I will be glorified."

Next, in Chapter 2, verses 3 and 4, the Lord says: "Even though this House you have been building is not nearly as magnificent as was My first House, be strong! For I am with you!"; and in verse 7 He says, " . . . 'the desire of all nations' shall come and I will fill this House with glory," and in verse 9 He says: "The glory of this latter House shall eventually be greater than that of My former House . . ."

More of the emotion and empathy toward His People can be seen from God's Word as translated from the Hebrew Bible (Tenach) in rendition of Haggai 2:3–5 following:

> 2:3 Which among you of the remnant who saw this Temple in its first glory, and what you see (as the Temple) now, is almost as if it were nothing in your eyes.

> 2:4 And now be strong Zerubbabel, said the Lord, be strong Joshua ben-Jehotzadak the High Priest, be strong all the people of the land, said the Lord, and serve (to build) because I am with you, said the Lord of Hosts.

> 2:5 That covenant which I made with you when you left Egypt and My Spirit stand in your midst, do not fear.

The foregoing verses seem to convey the Lord's unconditional Promise to Zerubbabel and the People concerning the Second Temple:

> Be strong!

> Build My House!

I am with you!

My Spirit stands in your midst!

Fear not!

Many would agree that the Lord makes it sound as though He intends to occupy this House as soon as it is built.

Now does anyone believe that the Lord would so exhort and encourage the Israelites to build that "latter House," which would be greater than the first House, and which He will "fill with glory," and that He would rescind His Promise to them?

Some scholars have claimed that five things from Solomon's Temple were missing from the Second Temple, and that one of these was Shechinah. This belief was probably inspired by an entry in Yoma 21b, in which Rabbi Samuel ben Inia said that the First Temple *differed* from the Second temple in five things. He was apparently defending against critics who were questioning the Lord's Promise in Haggai 1:8, in which God said He would "take pleasure in it (the Temple) and be glorified."

Referring to those startling supernatural signs in the Temple, the Rabbi concludes by saying, "I will tell you.—They *were* present, but they were not as helpful as before." He is saying Shechinah was in the Second Temple, but He was not as "helpful" concerning the lot in the right hand, the crimson strap, the westernmost light, the logs, etc., described in Chapter 7. In fact, we presented evidence from Talmud that declares all of those signs disappeared *completely* "forty years before the Temple was destroyed," as they say.

Critical opponents of this account will no doubt point to my enthusiasm for the Withdrawal as being inconsistent with my apparent reticence concerning the claimed return of Shechinah to the Second Temple. "Why did nobody witness and 'document' *that* occasion? Was it not Glorious enough? Did the Lord 'sneak' back into the Temple?"

OK—You got me on that one. I do not know why we have no Scriptural description of His return such as we were given when the Glory "cloud" filled the Sanctuary at the dedication of Solomon's Temple. (I Kings 8:10) Nevertheless, it should be agreed that His Glorious Withdrawal from the Temple was a much more dramatic event than His apparent return to residence after Babylon. Maybe the Divine Presence did not return until the time of Simeon the Righteous, as evidenced by appearance of the signs discussed in

Chapter 7 earlier. That period, 300 B.C., was after His Promise to Zerubbabel and after the last prophet of the Old Testament; i.e., Malachi in 400 B.C.

However, as discussed earlier, it is difficult to understand why the Lord would not have responded to the fervent prayers and rejoicing described in Nehemiah 12:43. As the prophet said: " . . . for God had made them rejoice with great joy so that the joy of Jerusalem was heard even afar off." Nehemiah's description of that jubilant occasion indicates a new-found sincerity and praise among the returned nation after the captivity. (Still, no mention of Shechinah.)

True, we don't know when His glory returned. But it must have been some time before "The Desire of All Nations" (Messiah) arrived because, as we shall soon demonstrate, "The Desire of All Nations" Himself declared that His Father indeed dwelled in that House during His time on this Earth.

Some critics may counter this interpretation of Haggai 2:9 by claiming that the reference is to return of our Lord and His glory to the Millennial Temple ("latter" house). Such a claim will not stand, however, because the Lord clearly states that *this* House will be filled with His glory. Yes, He will also fill that Millennial "latter House" with His glory, but identification as a "present" House is further verified in that He is encouraging Zerubbabel to take heart and to continue building this (present) house. The New International Version emphasizes this by the translation of Haggai 2:9 as " . . . this present house . . ." instead of "this latter house."

The Father (Shechinah) filled that House with His physical (?), visible Presence and Jesus filled it figuratively with His Glory as Messiah. It was the Lord's Promise to Zerubbabel that it would be filled with Glory. How can we deny that which the Lord had Promised?

Did you notice? This is another of those Messianic prophecies that we can lovingly and gently point out to Jewish friends to indicate that Messiah must surely have been in the Second Temple. Haggai 2:7 says: " . . . the desire of all nations shall come and I will fill this House with glory. . . ." As suggested earlier, maybe His Glory returned to the Holy House during the time of Simeon the Righteous. Then Jesus, The Desire of All Nations, did surely come and, as we have shown in this story, His Father (Shechinah) filled that House literally with His Glory up until Pentecost of 66 A.D.

Some would "spiritualize" this verse, claiming Jesus fulfilled that prophecy when He filled that House with His Glory. First of all, the

"House" is the H'ekhal, the main building of the Temple, the dwelling place of God (as the Divine Presence). Some teachers, including perhaps some New Testament translators, frequently gloss over references to "the Temple" as anything within the Temple court complex. Entering the "Temple" does not necessarily include entering the "Holy House," the H'ekhal. Jesus, son of David from the tribe of Judah and not a Levite, was not a priest. Only priests were permitted to enter the Holy House.

Please let us not be careless with the facts by treating such details as trivial. They were important to the Jews. God gave them these details. Jesus was a Jew. He thought they were important, also. Jesus didn't need to enter the H'ekhal to display His Glory. Besides, He would never have violated His Father's Law by doing so. Jesus displayed His Glory by His healings, teaching, forgiveness, and ultimately by His Glorious death and Resurrection and Ascension.

The statements about "shaking" the nations, heavens, earth, etc., in verses 6 and 7 may be both figurative and literal. The appearance of Jesus, as "The Desire of All Nations," has caused considerable "shaking." Then of course there will be literal shaking (earthquakes) before He returns to build His Temple in the Kingdom. So, there may be a dual fulfillment of these prophecies, although they may not be stated chronologically in Haggai's text.

But hear now this convincing prophecy from Zechariah 1:16,

> Therefore thus saith the Lord; I am returned to Jerusalem with mercies: My house shall be built in it, saith the Lord of hosts, . . .

Nevertheless, it is strange that no prophet seems to have recorded the actual return of Shechinah. Similarly, it is strange, too, that we have no Scriptural witness of the adolescent and young manhood years of the Lord Jesus. God, in His Infinite Wisdom, has seen fit to withhold such mystery from us—at least during the Church Age.

In fairness to all theories and positions discussed here, we should focus attention on the prophecy of Ezekiel 43:2

> And, behold, the Glory of the God of Israel came by the way of the east . . .

Critics who claim that Ezekiel saw the Glory withdraw in Ezekiel's Chapter 8–11 need to answer an obvious question: If Ezekiel actually saw the Glory depart in that earlier vision, then in light of Ez. 43:2, why do they claim the Glory never returned? Ezekiel says again, he saw the Glory of God return to the Temple as He "came by the way of the east." So, was Ezekiel translated to Jerusalem again to see this? Probably not—because this vision was given only fourteen years after Solomon's Temple was destroyed. (See Ezek. 40:1.) This return of Shechinah is going to take place in the future when Messiah arrives. An obvious question—with an obvious answer.

Fourteen years after its destruction by King Nebuchadnezzar, "in the five and twentieth year of our captivity," the Temple had not yet been rebuilt. For this reason, nobody saw the Glory return—because only Ezekiel "saw" it—"in the visions of God." However, I must concede that to date I have found no historical record to say anybody saw the return of the Glory to the Second Temple. Record of His Glorious Withdrawal, nevertheless, is available in ample measure, as we have demonstrated.

In Chapter 6 of this work, we pointed to Ezekiel's prophecy of the gate "which shall be shut" as having been fulfilled by the Lord Jesus, who "entered in by it," and by the Lord's Divine Presence, Shechinah, who went "out by the way of the same." (Ez. 44:3) The prophet relates, in the remainder of that chapter, the ordinances that the priests are to follow in the Second Temple. How do we know he is speaking of the rebuilt, Second Temple? Verses 6 and 13 give the Levites (priests) a good "chewing out" for their behavior and "they shall bear their iniquity ... their shame ... and their abominations which they committed." And yet, in verses 14 through 16 and despite their disobedience: "But I will make them keepers of the charge of the House ... and they shall stand before Me to offer unto Me the fat and the blood, saith the Lord God." (Yes, even Caiaphas!)

Very simply, this cannot be referring to the period of the Levites' ministrations in Solomon's Temple, because it had been destroyed thirteen years before this vision was given. Neither can Ezekiel be referring to the Millennial Temple, because the Levites will not be committing any abominations in that Temple. So, this passage is specifying the ordinances they were to follow in the Second Temple, including standing before Him. (Shechinah).

Jewish sages from the Second Temple period give a subtle testimony, saying the Jews considered that "He" resided in the Holy House. The Rabbis' testimony relates a beautiful, yet tragic comforting that mourners and excommunicates could receive from the Divine Presence. Middoth 2:2 says to mourners: "May He who dwells in this House comfort thee." And to excommunicates: "May He who dwells in this House inspire them ("thy colleagues") to befriend thee again." And finally, a third comfort and urging: "May He who dwells in this House inspire thee to listen to the words of thy colleagues that they may befriend thee again."

This last advice is accompanied by an explanation in a footnote. It is noted that excommunication was usually inflicted upon an elder "who would not conform to the majority." The Jews may have had some men who had difficulty matching tradition with what they had read in Scripture and in history and, yes . . . with the truth.

To insist that the Divine Presence was not dwelling in the Lord's Temple (not Herod's!) during the lifetime of Jesus is inconceivable when Scripture never said Shechinah had actually departed or that He did not dwell there, and when secular witnesses say they saw Him "remove hence" in 66 A.D. Just because the Bible does not describe the actual return of the Glory to the Temple, no "proof" is rendered that He did not return. We have just shown His Promise saying that He would return.

As we study the New Testament we need to remember those writings were not composed by WASP Baptist or Presbyterian or Methodist preachers from Middle America, or even from the green and brown countryside of the British Isles. They were written by Jews! It would never have occurred to a Jewish writer to make a finite statement about the Divine Presence being in the Temple! "Of course He is there! Everybody knows that!" That would be like, say, A New York author telling everybody the Statue of Liberty is in New York Harbor. "He must be kidding! Everybody knows that!" (Don't they?)

Notwithstanding their nonchalance concerning the detail of Shechinah's dwelling, not one Jewish Scriptural writer ever said Shechinah was not in the Temple. Still, they stated in two verses of the New Testament that He was in the Temple. Otherwise, they wrote as if to say: "Everybody knows that!" (But do we?) Now do you begin to see what "tradition" has done to our teaching?

Possibly the Divine Presence remained with the Ark of the Covenant when it was removed from the Temple. One of the Apochryphal Books (II Maccabees) states that King Nebuchadnezzar gave the Ark to Jeremiah the Prophet for safekeeping. After all, the Temple was only "shut-down" for a little more than seventy years—hardly even a "jitter" of the sweep-second hand on God's Eternal Timepiece! Besides, the king had heard what happened to the Philistines who captured the Israelites' "golden box." He didn't want any hemorrhoids in *his* secret parts! (I Samuel 5:9)

Again, there are no witnessed records of a 586 B.C. withdrawal (if there was an actual "withdrawal"). It is not "in character" for Almighty God to "sneak" away, "slinking" out the back door, sulking into the night. When He withdrew in 66–69 A.D., He left in a manner that all could see. We actually "obscure" the Glory of God by ignoring this story.

There is a definite "mind-set" among some traditional Christian teachers saying the Glory of the Lord (Shechinah) was not in the Temple during the ministry of Jesus. This "mind-set" is apparently based primarily on the negativism discussed in the preceding debate article. There is "noisy" opposition to any suggestion that the Lord would dwell in "Herod's Temple" . . . built by that disgusting puppet. "The Lord would never permit Himself to be defiled by honoring such a place with His Presence, etc., etc."

Another similar objection points out that Jesus referred to the Temple as "a den of thieves," and said it had become "desolate." The claim is that Jesus would never have referred to the Holy House of the Lord in such terms if the Divine Presence had been dwelling within at that time.

The key evidence, so long overlooked by all of us, is a single verse spoken by the Lord Jesus Himself in Matthew 23:21 (NASB):

> And he who swears by the temple,
> swears both by the temple and by
> Him who dwells within it.

That's right, He said " . . . by Him who dwells within it." Definitely, present tense is used and certainly nobody else dwells within; indicating clearly, once and for all—The Divine Presence was in the Temple during the time of Jesus. Jesus declared it.

There is at least one more Scriptural verse that declares the Glory of the Lord still dwelled in the Temple after Jesus was crucified. Listen carefully now, as the Apostle Paul is expressing his grief that his kinsmen, the Israelites, have not accepted their Messiah. Then, he goes on to say, from Romans 9:4 (NEB):

> . . . They are Israelites: they were made God's sons; theirs is the splendour of the divine presence, theirs the convenants, the law, the temple worship, and the promises.

Paul said: "theirs is the splendour of the Divine Presence"—not "was" (as we have been taught). Some other translations say

"Glory" or "Presence," but in almost all versions, the present tense is used; i.e., "the Glory (or Presence) is theirs."

Luke 24:53 says the Disciples "were continually in the Temple, praising and blessing God...." Now (after The Cross) does anyone really believe these would praise and bless God in the Temple if God (Shechinah) were not present?! Do they think the Disciples were just going through the motions in their worship (as Jews!) after what Jesus had taught them about His Father?

So, if the "squirmers" still want to squirm or if the "doubters" still want to doubt, they will need to "explain away" the Scriptural references offered here. It is my belief that one should assume that God's Word is *first* to be taken literally. That is, He says what He means and He means what He says! Several Scriptural verses say He (Shechinah) was in the Temple right up until the withdrawal as described by the Rabbis and by Josephus. Again, these are: Haggai 2:7—Zechariah 1:16—Mathew 23:21—Romans 9:4

Have you noticed how thoroughly God establishes this fact through His Word in each of our three divisions of Scripture?

But, there is more. The NASB translation of Matthew 23:38 yields:

"Behold, your house is being left to you desolate."

And the little-known and seldom-quoted Lamsa Bible[8] presents this verse as translated directly from the Aramaic of the Peshitta:

"Behold, your house will be left to you desolate."

If the NASB and the Lamsa Bible are actually providing more precise translations, this verse has a much deeper meaning than previously noticed. In saying it is (in-the-process-of being) or (will be) "left to you desolate," Jesus may have alluded to those strange goings-on in the Temple that would begin a few days later and continue for "forty years" until the Temple was destroyed. The Rabbis of the Talmud recognized this later when they said these "signs" meant Shechinah was going to withdraw. However, by that time perhaps few or none of them recalled or knew that Jesus had said this was going to occur. However, Josephus has said: "So these publicly declared, that this signal foreshewed the desolation that was coming upon them." (See Appendix A.)

Further, I believe the Lord would take exception to calling His Holy House, "Herod's Temple." Besides, there were numbers of Kings of Judah who were far more despicable than Herod; and despite their idolatry, sin and disobedience, the Divine Presence remained faithfully in the Holy of Holies right up until the situation was absolutely hopeless—as at Chanukah Season, 69 A.D.

But, what about the "den-of-thieves" remark? Again, the clear answer is in the words of Jesus Himself:

> ... make not my Father's House a house of merchandise.
>
> (John 2:16)

Did you get that?! Jesus thought of the Temple as, "His Father's House." (Note: He did not call it "Herod's Temple!")

Also, in Luke 19:47, just after He had called it "a den of thieves" in verse 46, Jesus taught daily in the Temple. Now, why was it OK for Jesus to be in this "den of thieves," but not OK for His Father, the Divine Presence, the Great "I AM?"

Even after all this, historical record from Josephus has stated, regarding the Temple after the Shechinah Event: "For thou couldst be no longer a fit place for God." (Reference 2, Wars, 5/19.)

We believe it has been shown conclusively, through Scripture and by documented historical records, Shechinah was at Jerusalem until 69 A.D. But, some people are difficult to convince. Some just don't want to believe this story, regardless of any evidence. It is my prayer and hope that my readers will examine the evidence and judge for themselves.

THE RENDING OF THE VEIL

Traditional teaching says the significance of the rending of the Veil exists in that the Temple was then opened to all men. Because of the sin offering of our Savior, man was no longer separated from God. This position is based on the premise that the "Veil" was all that had been separating men from God. Part of this same teaching is sometimes augmented by claiming the Glory of God withdrew from the Temple at that same instant, when Jesus "gave up the Ghost."

I fully agree that the Temple was then opened to man, and it was brought about as a "sign" at the death of Jesus, because He now is our Intercessor at the Throne of God, the Father. Nevertheless, this traditional teaching is based on assumption. The traditional version leads to a very "romantic" doctrine, but it is just not in line with the facts as recorded by historians and Judaic Law, and finally even by the Bible itself. By contrast, when we become aware of these facts, this event becomes even more spectacular, even more glorifying of our Lord Jesus Christ and of His Father than the Gospels ever revealed to us when taken just by themselves.

There were actually three veils; not just the large, thick-braided curtain at the entrance to the Temple main building (H'ekhal). Two additional veils, presumably much thinner, separated the Holy Place from the Holy of Holies. These two were placed in lieu of the two cedar partitions that similarly divided the H'ekhal in Solomon's Temple (I Kings 6:16). Talmud (Yoma 51) explains this was necessary in order that the High Priest would avoid an "affront" to the Lord by approaching Him directly, just striding into His Holy Chamber as maybe one would walk into his neighbor's living room, for example.

These two veils were placed one cubit (about 18 inches) apart, so the High Priest, on the Day of Atonement, would be required to "sidle" along carrying the ash censer between the veils with a sort of sideways "scissor-step." He approached the veils (see Sketch 8) by first traversing along the north wall of the Holy Place, so as to avoid walking past the candlestick (Menorah). He did this so that his immaculate priestly robe would not be "sooted" by the candles.

Next he turned to pass southward across the chamber and behind the Altar of Incense to eventually reach the entrance opening between the veils at the south wall. Now, as described before, he continued by "scissoring" between the veils to finally enter the Holy of Holies at the north wall. He then came before the Divine Presence to plead atonement for Israel's sins.

Thus, we find this romantic notion about the "veil" being "rent in twain" and ending man's separation from God is faulted because of casual knowledge concerning details of the Temple. This is also paradoxial in that most of these same critics who say God was not in the Holy of Holies at the time of Jesus are the same ones who tell us this "veil" separated man from God in a symbolic way.

The traditional story, of course, refers to the huge braided curtain that was drawn across the entrance to the H'ekhal. This is based on the simplistic assumption that the centurion could then just look right into the Judean's Temple when that thick curtain ("veil") across the entry was torn.

One could not just peer into the H'ekhal as if the Veil were like a drapery across an open doorway or portal, for example. More detailed information about the Temple reveals to us from Josephus and the Talmud (Middoth 4:1) that a complex arrangement of four folding doors ("gates") stood just behind the Veil.

Then to be able to "peer" into the H'ekhal, these doors would have to either be collapsed as a result of the earthquake or because they were opened at the time. In Chapter 6 it was noted that only the northern half of these doors was opened and then only on certain occasions. However, even the north doorway would leave an opening only about seven or eight feet wide on that side for the centurion or anyone else at The Cross to be able to see the inside of the House of God after the Veil was torn. Such a narrow opening would have appeared almost as a slit when observed from Olivet summit.

And what about the Holy of Holies? Do they believe God's Divine Presence in the Temple was just arrayed out in the middle of the Temple floor? Or that the Temple was merely "symbolic" of God's Presence? We Gentiles just sometimes have difficulty in accepting that the Jews are God's Chosen People and that He did indeed dwell in their midst, visibly, in a "House" built for Him by those Special People.

But there is much more to this "veil" story. We are going to stand at the Precious feet of our Lord on that Cross, next to the centurion; and we shall "see" as "when he 'saw' all these things that had happened." As we have shown from Scripture, since the Temple faced eastward, and since the Jerusalem cemetery of the Second Temple period was east of the City, the only way the centurion and his squad could have "seen" these things was if they had been standing east of the Temple on the western slope of Olivet. They could not have seen the Veil rent nor the graves opened from any position west of the Temple, such as the Church of the Holy Sepulchre or The Garden Tomb vicinity. (Not unless they had searchlights, mirrors, and binoculars!)

We have shown some evidence in Chapter 5 indicating why the Judeans of the Second Temple period chose Olivet for their cemetery. Further justification for that site exists in Judaic Law. The Jews would just never have buried their dead on the west side of the City, next to the latrines, as Professor Yadin[14] has shown were northwest of the City.

Nevertheless, regardless of the Law and tradition, it should be difficult for any Believer to agree that God the Father would sacrifice His only son just someplace out beyond the "back door" of the Temple! Outrageous thought! They should also have to consider that all of the Jewish sacrifices (which certainly do point to Jesus!) were offered in front (east) of the Temple. In fact the most important

Jewish sacrifice, the Red Heifer, was offered at a point due east and about a Sabbath Day's journey from the Holy of Holies. Now, it just appears logical that God would also "provide Himself, a Lamb for a burnt offering," as that most important of *all* sacrifices . . . East of the Temple! Of course, it is not easy to abolish nineteen centuries of traditional belief—even when hard facts are presented to refute those beliefs.

Painful and disappointing as it is to find that some of our most revered Holyland sites are not authentic, some of this "romantic" tradition (and "tourist" tradition) just does not hold up in the face of truth. And our Lord teaches us always to seek and defend the truth, in all things. This just means we have to "unstiffen" some of our past teaching and look a little deeper.

This happens in the fields of science and engineering all the time. The more we test, the more we learn about "perfecting" theory in order eventually to get theory and test to agree—eventually reaching the truth. We cannot afford to assume we are doing things right just because:

We've always done it that way.

We must be doing something right. Look at our achievements.

You can't argue with success.

Truth finally caught up with NASA management on 28 January 1986. We must look more deeply and do our best continually to correlate Scripture and secular records as they complement each other. (Rightly dividing the Word of God.) We must strive to do as Daniel the Prophet said man would do in the "last days" (Daniel 12:4). We must "run to and fro" through the Scriptures and we will have "increased knowledge" of end-time prophecies as we look at history, science, etc., and compare with fulfilled and unfulfilled prophecy. We who live in the "last days" have a better opportunity to have "increased knowledge" concerning "the end of days." We moderns have the advantage of 20/20 hindsight, as we are able to look back at Scripture, science, history, and archaeology over all those centuries. Thus, we draw ever closer to THE TRUTH.

But, before X-teen millions of my fellow Believers jump all over me—I am certainly not saying the Bible needs to be tested. The TRUTH needs to be tested. We must never close our minds to secular facts, especially when these facts bring new "light" to Scripture;

(even though it may show our traditional interpretation of Scripture to have been in error.)

A Lesson for Us: The Jewish people overlooked their Redeemer because this gentle Galilean didn't fit their traditional interpretations of Messianic prophecy. They were (and still are) taught that Israel was the suffering Messiah. They had been (and still are) expecting the conquering Messiah, not this peasant "misfit!" They have surely been blinded by tradition. So have some of us Gentiles.

What, Then, Did the Centurion See?

He saw the earthquake open the graves of many Old Testament Saints who were buried on that western Olivet slope. Several tombs of those Blessed are, at least "traditionally," located there even to this day. (See Sketch 6.) The tombs of Zechariah, Haggai, and Malachi for example, are well-known tourist sites at the present time.

And yes—he saw the Veil "rent-in-twain." But, how could he determine if the Veil was parted at 3 P.M., "the ninth hour," as he would be squinting into the newly undarkened sun, which was above and behind the Temple? Scripture does not tell us how he was able to see this. Nevertheless, we know for certain that he did see it, because God says he saw it. That is truth. However, common sense tells us that, since the Temple faced eastward, he could not possibly have seen this from any position west of the Temple.

Sound logic also reveals that under normal conditions, he could not have seen that the outer Veil was torn, because it was either in the shade of the H'ekhal portico (150 feet high) or because the sun was possibly still darkened. (See Matthew 27:45 and Luke 23:44.) In either case, under ordinary conditions (sun or no sun), it would have been impossible to see the Veil even from the Mount of Olives at that time.

Further illustration pertaining to visibility of Veil details from the Mount of Olives is provided in Talmud, Shekalim 8:4. It is stated that the Veil, the thick (over three inches) braided curtain across the Temple doorway, was spread out on the cloisters (colonnades) each time a new Veil was produced. This was done twice each year. The Veil was displayed in this manner "so that the people might behold its fair workmanship" from the summit of the Mount of Olives. Otherwise, only the menfolk could see the Veil when they brought their sacrifices into the Court of the Israelites. Remember, the women and girls, underage boys, and of course all lepers were not permitted beyond the Court of Women. This biannual exhibition was likely their only opportunity to see and admire this magnificent Temple furnishing.

At this point some traditionalists have actually come out with the defense:

> Well, the Bible doesn't say they saw the Veil. It only says they saw the earthquake. Maybe somebody told the soldiers afterward about the Veil having been torn.

Now, come on! Next, I suppose if they can wriggle away from this one, they will want us to believe "maybe" the Roman soldiers went over later that evening after "chow" to inspect the damage at the Temple and *that* is when they saw the torn Veil. Stop squirming! Scripture says: "They *saw* the earthquake and those things that were done."

How was the centurion able to see this? And, what was terrifying about an earthquake? A torn curtain? A few open graves? (Those saints appeared in Jerusalem only after The Resurrection.) Roman soldiers terrified by such as this?

The earthquake possibly caused collapse of lintels or other structures supporting all three veils, causing them to part for perhaps just a moment. It was noted earlier that the doors at the front of the H'ekhal also would have to be opened or collapsed by this tremor, as maybe they were. And, oh yes, this now opened the Holy of Holies for man to approach God, but only through His Son. And there was perhaps something truly breathtaking about that "moment."

The centurion saw something very spectacular (yes, frightening and terrifying!), which glorifies Jesus and Almighty God as One in a flash! And that was a flash of brilliant light!

* THE "FIRE"—THE GLORY OF THE LORD! *

Beaming straight through the parted veils from the Holy of Holies! Brighter than the sun, a brilliant shaft of light from the Judeans' Temple across the Kidron now illuminated this Galilean who had just before cried out with a loud voice, "TETELESTAI!" and now was suspended in death on The Cross above the centurion.

What a sight that must have been! What a dramatic event. How much more dynamic and glorifying than the "traditional" scenario. Of course the centurion was terrified.

Furthermore—and this is most important, as we have shown in

our detailed study of the "sight picture" of the veil through the open gate—the centurion would have to be standing at the same spot from which the High Priest must "direct his gaze carefully." Just like the priest, the centurion would not be able to see the Veil even from a few meters away from that precise location on the summit of the Mount of Olives.

Now, we don't know whether any of the other Gospel writers were at Golgotha or not. Nevertheless, even if Matthew, Mark, and some of the others had been "hiding out" somewhere else on Olivet, they could not have seen the Veil. The only ones who could have seen it were standing at The Cross and "directing their gaze carefully" through the East Gate at "the ninth hour." This is just simply a matter of geometry. (Sketches 3, 4 and 5)

Earlier we demonstrated that Jesus willed His own death at the "ninth hour" because He had to maintain His Holy Schedule of fulfilling the Law. There also may be another reason for this timing. The Lord knew where the sun would be at 3 P.M. and He used this condition to enhance the drama of the occasion to those standing at The Cross where they were to see "those things." Jesus wanted those Roman "GI's" to be startled and terrified by that blinding flash coming through the parted veils. The flash had to be much more prominent (and terrifying) coming from the darkened face of the Temple in the afternoon than it would have been had the Veil been in bright sunlight. Therefore, "the ninth hour" was "scheduled" by the Lord in order to achieve this dramatic effect on His executioners and to still permit honoring the Sabbath and fulfilling of the Feasts.

Notice now the beautiful "picture" that has developed:

- Three veils represent the Father, Son, and Holy Spirit.

- Entrance to the Temple (representing Heaven) can be achieved only through the now "torn" outer Veil.

- The torn Veil represents the "broken" body of the Son, Jesus.

- The other two veils were also parted to reveal the Glory of God to be seen by men at the instant of His "payment" for their sins.

- A similar picture is portrayed at the Passover meal (Seder) when the second matzah (Afikoman) is broken and "hidden-away" for a time and later revealed ("found") and enjoyed by all present.

Some traditional teaching contends the Glory of God withdrew from the Temple at the moment Jesus "gave up the ghost" when the "veil was rent in twain." Again, for all this time we have been accepting a very convenient, simplistic, romantic interpretation; but based on assumption—not fact, Biblical or secular. Thus, such assumption results in gross inaccuracy and therefore misses the truth and the blessings that come with it.

This assumption completely ignores the requirement for fulfillment of Ezekiel's prophecy of the Shechinah withdrawal. But, the traditional teaching gets around that problem by very conveniently assuming, again, that Ezekiel 10 and 11 were fulfilled only before Solomon's Temple was destroyed. Although there is no record of such an event concerning Solomon's Temple, there is ample record of His withdrawal from the Second Temple forty years after Jesus was crucified.

10 Will the Real "Chosen People" Please Stand?

Now, we must address another very fundamental debate question: If, as we have been taught all these years (centuries), God was finished with the Jews after they rejected Jesus, then why did His Divine Presence remain in the Temple for another forty years?

Here we have a real "hard-point" for many Christian teachers (who have, in turn, been taught by their teachers), when we challenge the traditional stories we have all been taught. Since we have been taught that the Jews stand in rejection from God because they rejected Jesus as Messiah, the answer to the aforementioned question becomes very perplexing. This is really "the bottom line" for why traditional teaching has such difficulty in accepting a story that claims the Divine Presence remained with Israel until 69 A.D.

Since I am neither a theologian nor a minister, I do not wish to debate on this point with seminary-educated ministers. However, I do wish to surface this argument for all to see. It has been closeted far too long. I wish then, to ask all who are knowledgeable of the Scriptures (pastors, Christian laity, Jewish worshipers, rabbis) to examine facts and Scripture and to answer this question in the light of truth—tradition cast aside.

It seems to me that God did forgive them ("for they knew not") at The Cross. But then, through "signs" in the Temple and through the Disciples via the Holy Spirit, He ministered to Israel for a full generation (forty years) after The Crucifixion. During those forty years many Jews did come to find Jesus as their Messiah, including some of those from the Aaronic priestly orders. (We seem often to forget or ignore the fact that the first "Christians" were "Jews.")

But then, after those forty years, for those who still refused to repent and return to Him, it seems He said:

I will go back to My Place.

Your sacrifices are for naught and your House is desolate.

I am going to punish you—for two days.

I will refine you (in the fire) as silver.

But in "the third day" I will return for you and you will look upon Me whom you pierced and you will mourn for Him as for an only Son.

Then we will spend eternity together in peace and all of your iniquities and transgressions will be removed and forgotten forever and ever.

Jews cannot be saved under the Law unless they repent of their sins. The Law cannot save them from judgment and death for their sins, but it can lead them to repentance if they come to realize that they cannot, by their works, "keep" the Law.

Christians have a similar problem. They cannot be saved from their sins unless they repent—Law or no Law. But, all Christians have that "Blessed Assurance" that if we repent, our sins have been already forgiven because we accept Messiah's payment for our sins. Jews must take a similar route to salvation, but can have no assurance of being acceptable. They can only hope they have pleased Him. Nevertheless, if they love the Lord, they will regret and repent of having offended Him in even the smallest way. Would any deny the same is true for all who would claim to be of Christ's church?

A poignant note on Jewish apprehension concerning their salvation is seen from Talmud, Berakoth 28b, a statement attributed to Rabbi Yohanan ben Zakkai, noted and beloved patriarch discussed in Chapter 7. He is lamenting his fear of death, even though he was considered a very righteous man.

When this beloved sage was on his deathbed, he began to weep as some of his followers gathered to visit. Listen now to his humility and trembling at "meeting his Maker."

They asked, "Lamp of Israel, pillar of the right hand, mighty hammer, wherefore weepest thou?" He replied: "If I were being taken before a human king who is here today and tomorrow in the grave, whose anger with me would not last forever, who would not imprison me forever and who would not put me to an everlasting death, and whom I could persuade with words or could bribe with money, even so I would weep. But, now I am going before the Supreme King of Kings, the Holy One, Blessed be He, who lives and endures forever and ever, whose anger is everlasting, who may imprison me forever and ever, who may put me into an everlasting death, and whom I cannot persuade with words or bribe with money. Nay! When there are two ways before me, one leading to Paradise and the other to Gehinnom (Hell), and I do not know to which I will be taken, shall I not weep?"

Although he was a very righteous man, beloved by the Rabbinate and by the people, Rav ben Zakkai still was not confident that the "Supreme King of Kings" would accept him and take him to Paradise. All of us could learn something from Rav ben Zakkai about humility concerning our own "goodness" and "works" in this world.

We must note here, however, the contrast with the Apostle Paul, who referred to himself with what could be marked as restrained boastfulness, as the Lord's "prisoner." Even as Paul contemplated and awaited the headsman's inevitable sword, from his prison cell he wrote: "It's not to worry!" As comforting to his helper Timothy and to the church they had founded at Phillipi, he said in Phillipians 1:21, " . . . to live *is* Christ, and to die *is* gain."

How different and how ecstatic it is for all of us "prisoners of the Lord" to contemplate our being "imprisoned forever;" with Him who will give us everlasting life; and who has already forgotten His anger at our transgressions; and who perpetually must persuade us to share His infinite riches without asking or expecting even the tiniest insignificant gift or offering from us. We only weep for joy and we know where we are going because we have that Blessed Assurance—merely because we have accepted His most precious gift—Messiah, the Son of God.

Penitent Jewish people who live with righteous intentions and who love the Lord may be "sealed" for Heaven, but—as with Rabbi Yohanan ben Zakkai—they cannot know if they have pleased Him.

Nor can you or I know whether they have pleased Him; just as you or I cannot know whether another is really "saved" or "born again." Only you and God know whether you have really accepted Messiah.

Indeed, Christians can truthfully shout that expression cultivated by the Jewish mamas:

> IT'S NOT TO WORRY!

None of us is qualified to say whether Jewish people, even after 70 A.D., stand in rejection from God. He said He would provoke them to jealousy (Romans 11:11), but I cannot agree that He has rejected them. After all, He has resurrected them as the nation Israel.

In our large "family" of nations, Israel (the Jewish people) may be compared to that one favorite child in some large families. The picture that develops is interesting:

- That one special child is usually somewhat spoiled because he knows he is the father's favorite.

- The father is often more severe in punishment when his favorite disappoints him, even though he seems to let the favorite "get away with more" before he finally administers punishment.

- The father is sometimes more strict with his "laws" for this favorite because he loves this child just a little bit more in a very special way and wants more for him and expects more from him.

- This entire situation is often exasperating to the other children but they are not jealous and they love that favorite child also (sometimes even contributing to spoiling him) because they love their father and they know also how much their father loves that special child.

- The other children know also that their father loves each of them very much as well, but that one special child is still their father's favorite. (The "apple of his eye," etc.)

- He is chosen. They accept this and they love him because they love their father.

Still, some Christians will insist: "But, we are chosen! Don't you believe what Paul says in II Thessalonians 2:13?"

Yes, of course, we are chosen, but the Jewish people are "chosen above all the nations." (Deuteronomy 14:2) We must accept this.—It is the Word of God.

CAN A "JEW" LOVE THE LORD?

Over the years, many well-meaning Christian teachers have sincerely put forth the concept that we Christians (not the Jews) are now God's Chosen People. This concept is what Rev. Vendyl Jones[4] has labeled as "Replacement Theology." There is some indication, though not necessarily a dramatic thrust, from this story of Shechinah that says the Jews are still God's Chosen People and that His everlasting covenant with them is still in effect.

This "replacement" philosophy may have originated from a misunderstanding or misinterpretation of the New Covenant principle introduced by Jeremiah 31:31–34 and as quoted by Paul in his epistle to the Hebrews. Some theologians have taught therefore along the following lines:

— Jeremiah 31:31 says the Lord will make a New Covenant with the Jews.

— That New Covenant is salvation for sinners paid for by the blood of Jesus Christ.

— In rejecting Christ, therefore, they have rejected the New Covenant.

— The first covenant is now obsolete and is no longer valid. (Here they refer to Hebrews 8:13.)

— The Jews, like all others who reject Christ, are therefore lost. There is no more to be said. The Jews are lost.

Please take a closer look now at this idea through the Scripture used as its base, beginning with Jeremiah 31:31,

> Behold, the days come, saith the Lord, that I will make a new covenant with the house of Israel, and with the house of Judah.

Then, verses 33 and 34,

> But this shall be the covenant that I will make with the house of Israel; After those days, saith the Lord I will put My Law in their inward parts, and write it in their hearts; and will be their God, and they shall be My people.
>
> And they (Israel) shall teach no more every man his neighbor, and every man his brother, saying, "Know the Lord!": for they shall *all* know Me, from the least of them unto the greater of them, saith the Lord: for I will forgive their iniquity, and I will remember their sin no more.

Then, just after Paul quotes this passage, he says in Hebrews 8:13 (NASB),

When he said "a new covenant," He has made the first (covenant) obsolete. But whatever is becoming obsolete and growing old is ready to disappear."

It is clear today that God has not yet put His Law "in their inward parts"; nor has He yet written it "in their hearts." Today we know also that "every man his brother" do not yet all know Him. The key phrase here is "after those days." After what "days?" This is to say, after some time He will write His Law in their hearts—some time. He obviously has not done this yet for the Jews; although, he has most certainly done it for Christians, because Christians have already received the New Covenant. We have His Law placed "in our inward parts" and His Law is "written in our hearts." Yes, and He "remembers our sins no more!" We have Blessed Assurance. And remember—the first "Christians" were Jews. But not all. God said all shall know Him when they reach His New Covenant—but not yet.

What about Paul saying the first covenant is obsolete, old, dying? Paul didn't say that. Paul said the first convenant was "becoming" obsolete, and it was "ready to disappear." Here, we need to remember that Paul, as well as all the other New Testament writers, was *certain* that Jesus was going to return in his lifetime. (Barnabus must have come up with this "two-day / two-thousand year theory" much later, after they had become aware that He had "delayed" His return.) This point is extremely important.

Paul just didn't have access to the Lord's time-table (and neither do we!). He didn't realize that "those days" were going to be about two thousand years of what Christians have called "The Church Age." Paul thought the New Covenant was going to begin imminently—as soon as Jesus returned! Paul and the others were expecting Jesus to return at any moment! This is why we read such an urgency—almost panic—in Paul's message to his Jewish brethren, especially. Paul truly believed that first covenant was "becoming obsolete" and "was ready to disappear." And that is true today as well. Time is short. We just don't know what "time" it is.

When Messiah arrives at Olivet summit "after those days," the New Covenant will then begin for all Jews and for all who live on Earth. Then, the first covenant will disappear. The New Covenant then will be "in their inward parts" and will then be "written in their hearts." It is a Promise!

For us, Gentiles, to claim we are His Chosen, must be quite repugnant to even an agnostic Jewish person. It causes one to wonder how many Jewish people we may have turned away from recognizing that Jesus is their Messiah because of our insistence on such a cruel, judgmental, and erroneous concept through all these centuries of the Church Age. (Our Lord may judge us as presumptuous "imposters.")

The Lord has used Israel's blindness as an example lesson for Christian Gentiles. We see so clearly and vividly what Israel fails to see. We have persecuted and murdered and tortured and reviled and cursed the very ones who, although they are "blind," are responsible for providing *our* clear vision in beholding Messiah. Through their "blindness" we are made to "see."

Gentiles can only be cleansed of sin (become righteous before God) by approaching Him through their "burnt offering," Jesus. But there are some indications that Jews before and after Jesus can and have come to righteousness, through Messiah, by observing the Law. We must surely all agree that multitudes of Jews became so-called Old testament saints under the Law before the time of Jesus. How could they have achieved "sainthood?" Only by keeping the Law and loving the Lord their God with all their heart and with all their soul and with all their might and by loving their neighbors as themselves.

Only God can judge whether or not Jews truly love the Lord and are "keeping-the-Law" in their hearts—which is the only place that matters. Of course, since destruction of the Temple, Jews cannot keep the sacrifices as that part of the Law—except as they may sincerely yearn and mourn for such in their hearts. And, after all, we know each of the sacrifices is a representative "picture" of the Lamb of God—Messiah, Jesus of Nazareth.

Then, if they do earnestly yearn for and await Messiah hopefully (as we yearn for His return), Jews yearn for the same One the Church awaits. They just missed Him when he was in their midst. He might forgive them for failing to recognize or comprehend that He really was their Messiah, but He will not forgive those who do not love Him. ("Agapas" love, that is.)

One of the best sources for answering this question concerning the Jewish approach to salvation can be derived from perhaps the third most famous Jew who ever lived, Paul of Tarsus. (Third after Jesus and Moses.)

> But Paul said: "I am a man which am a Jew from Tarsus" . . .
>
> Acts 21:39

Yes, Paul introduced himself as "a Jew," and yet he was certainly what we would call a "Christian." How could a Jew be a Christian? Well, for one thing, the term "Christian" had not yet been created. Furthermore, his statement demonstrates clearly that Paul considered himself to be a Jew. He did not give up all his "Jewishness" in order to accept Jesus as Messiah. He didn't need to give it up. He was proud to be Jewish.

So many conservative Christian teachers insist that one can no longer be Jewish after accepting Jesus as Messiah. They point so often to a single verse from Paul, in Galatians 3:28, in order to establish this claim, by saying:

> There is neither Jew nor Greek . . . for ye are all one in Christ Jesus.

They omit the middle portion because they really aim to paraphrase this to say: "There is neither Jew nor Gentile because we are all Christians who believe in Christ." The middle portion, which they have omitted, reveals the true context or meaning, however, because it says, " . . . there is neither bond nor free, there is neither male nor female: for ye are all one in Jesus Christ."

Of course we are united in Christ, but we cannot change our worldly status as bonded or free, male or female, and yes, Jew or Gentile. If you were born Jewish you *are* a Jew. And from what we have shown in this study, if you love the Lord your God, you should be proud to be Jewish! (And, if you love Him and if you read and study and believe His Word, you should now understand that Jesus of Nazareth is also Lord!)

Nobody recognized this more than Paul did in his ministry to Jews and Gentiles. Please listen now as Pastor Paul describes his evangelizing technique in 1 Corinthians 9:20–21 (NEB).

> "To Jews I became as a Jew, to win Jews; as they are subject to the Law of Moses, I put myself under the law to win them, although I am not myself subject to it.
>
> To win Gentiles, who are outside the Law, I made myself as one of them, although I am not in truth outside God's law, being under the law of Christ."

Thus, Paul considered that Jews and Gentiles were "different" as people, but both are under God's Law. Similarly he noted, slaves could not change their worldly status as slaves, nor could men or women (then or now!) change their sex, although they were "all one in Christ Jesus." And, notice—Paul says "I am a Jew"—(not "was a Jew")—but not under the Law of Moses—because now he has that "Blessed Assurance!"

Paul also said God looks only for what is in the heart as he writes in Romans 2:29,

> But he is a Jew, which is one inwardly, and circumcision is that of the heart, in the spirit, and not in the letter; whose praise is not of men, but of God.

He expresses a somewhat nonsectarian view in Hebrews 11:6 (NASB) as he describes in the most simple terms how man must come to God.

> And without faith it is impossible to please Him, for He who comes to God must believe that He is, and that He is a rewarder of those who seek Him.

Paul told the "Hebrews" (his brethren) and Gentiles that the Lord is open to any who seek Him and believe Him—have faith in Him. Moreover, Paul seems to have "said-it-all" in Romans 10:12,

> For there is no difference between the Jew and the Greek: for the same Lord over all is rich unto all that call upon Him.

FATHER, FORGIVE US!

Those Jewish people who do attempt to come to God through the Law are really "doing it the hard way." Famous evangelist Hal Lindsey has referred to these choices as Plan "A" and Plan "B." Plan "B" is of course the "easy" way, through Jesus Messiah. Those Jews who have come to Jesus and accepted Him as their "burnt offering" have the Law fulfilled (kept) through Jesus. They have that "Blessed Assurance."

Some conservative Christians express righteous indignation at any idea of Jews being acceptable to God without first accepting Jesus as Messiah: "That is like saying Jesus died in vain!" Of course not! Jesus died for all. The Jewish problem is that they just haven't identified or recognized Jesus, yet. Many Jews have already "accepted" Messiah in their hearts, but they still don't know He is actually Jesus of Nazareth. If they are truly still waiting for Messiah and "keeping" the Law, they may have reached salvation—(*But*, no assurance!) They are just going to be really surprised when they "look upon" and recognize Him who was "pierced" and with those wounds in His hands, standing up there on the Mount of Olives on That Day.

Nevertheless, it seems that the Lord has permitted Jews to come unto Himself through the sacrifices, which we Christians recognize as representing The Lamb of God—Messiah—Jesus. "Why can't they see this?" we ask, impatiently. With even more impatience, we frequently quote from Jesus' words through another famed Jewish writer in John 14:6,

> I am the way, the truth, and the life: no man cometh unto the Father, but by me.

With this we demonstrate unequivocally that Jews (or anyone) can only approach God through Jesus. And this has certainly not been rescinded. The tragedy is that Jewish people are approaching the Lord through Jesus IF they have the Law and repentance for their sins and the love for their Lord in their hearts. They just don't see Jesus reflected in all this, but He is there.

This same Jewish writer gives some light in this direction in one of his epistles, written somewhat later—after he had been preaching the Gospel of Jesus Christ to Jews—in Judea and Samaria.

> Whoever believes that Jesus is the Christ is born of God; and whoever loves the Father loves the child born of Him.

I John 5:1

John says if one loves God, The Father, then he also loves the Son of God—and everyone else who was made by The Father. Some Jews love Jesus—because they love God. (They just don't know it yet.) So, there is no ambiguity here. We must still come to God through Jesus. The Jewish sacrifices mean nothing without Jesus. They never did; because they only formed a "picture" of Him as He "provided Himself—a lamb for a burnt offering."

The Jewish "picture" of this situation is dramatized beautifully at the Passover meal (Seder), although its meaning is hidden from the Jews. The second piece of the three pieces of matzah, the Afikoman, is "broken" and then "hidden away for a time" until after the meal has been consumed. Then, the "broken" piece is searched for and then "found" and eaten as the third cup of wine is taken. The Cup of Redemption! This is the cup that Jesus declined at the Last Supper, saying, " . . . until that day that I drink it new in the Kingdom of God." (Mark 14:25)

Most Christians can immediately see that the broken piece, the second Person of the Triune God, is Jesus. Following this logic, we also can see this with the third cup of wine taken; i.e., "Redemption" is delivered with the recovered (found) broken piece after two "days!" Each previous cup represents passage of one "day" or one thousand years. Messiah is in the Seder. Jewish worshipers just have not seen Him . . . yet! Sadly, they are still waiting for "Elijah" (who appeared in "type" as John the Baptist) and they are still looking for their Afikoman.

Recently, one prominent Protestant body adopted a resolution[23] acknowledging that Judaism has not been replaced by Christianity and that God has not rejected the Jewish people nor has He withdrawn or transferred His covenant. The story of the Shechinah withdrawal appears to reinforce that position. Unfortunately for those Jews who have been persecuted, murdered, and scorned over the years, this story and the Church's resolution arrived 1,900 years late!

Consider the facts presented by this account as well as the resolution mentioned, excerpted as follows:

> This historical denial by the church has led to outright rejection of the Jewish people and to frequent violence. We pray for Divine grace that will enable us, more firmly than ever before, to turn from this path of rejection and persecution to affirm that Judaism has not been superseded by Christianity; that Christianity is not to be understood as the successor religion to Judaism; God's covenant with the Jewish people has not been abrogated. God has not rejected the Jewish people, God is faithful in keeping covenant. . . .

Then, for those who are *still* not convinced that the Lord has *not* cast away His Chosen People, we lead them to these verses written by the Prophet Jeremiah, Chapter 31, verses 35, 36, and 37.

> Thus saith the Lord, which giveth the sun for a light by day, *and* the ordinances of the moon and of the stars for a light by night, which divideth the sea when the waves thereof roar; the Lord of hosts *is* His name.

> If those ordinances depart from before Me, saith the Lord, *then* the seed of Israel also shall cease from being a nation before Me for ever.

Thus saith the Lord; if heaven above can be measured, and the foundations of the earth searched out beneath, I will also cast off all the seed of Israel for all that they have done, saith the Lord.

The Lord is emphatic in these words as He has said, *if* the sun, moon, and stars disappear, *then* Israel will cease forever to be a nation. And, *if* someone can measure Heaven, *then* He will "cast off" *all* of "naughty" Israel—"saith the Lord," AMEN. (Gentiles! Are you listening?!)

Yes, there is "neither Jew nor Greek" as a requirement to receive and accept the Lord's salvation through His Grace. And yes, *both* can only approach the Lord through His Son (the Lord) Messiah. Jewish Believers wait for Messiah to arrive.—Christian Believers wait for Messiah to return. The Father will not reject those who are *still* awaiting Him—if *in their hearts* they are truly waiting for Him.

Messiah—Son of Joseph—and a Carpenter!

An intriguing entry is noted in Talmud, Sukkah 52a, referring to the Scripture in Zechariah 12:12,

> And the land shall mourn, every family apart; the family of the house of David apart, and their wives apart . . .

The narration asks about the cause of this mourning. A second century Rabbi Dosa replies that the reason is the slaying of "Messiah the son of Joseph." (Did you catch that? The "son of Joseph" was slain!) The text justifies such mourning through reference to Zechariah 12:10, as quoted from the Jewish Tenach,

> . . . and they shall look upon Me because they have thrust Him through, and they shall mourn for Him as one mourneth for his only son . . .

A detailed discussion follows concerning the time at which Messiah destroys Satan while the righteous weep and behold Satan, "the Evil Inclination," and ask how they were able to "overcome such a towering hill." Contrastingly, the wicked weep and behold this same "Evil Inclination" and ask why they were not able to "conquer this hair thread." (See also Isaiah 14:15–17.)

A single reference is made to Messiah the son of David, which is certainly acknowledged as the Scriptural geneology of Messiah. In fact, Talmud gives vent to an emotional outburst as the Rabbi pleads, "May He (Messiah) the son of David reveal Himself speedily in our days!"

The Promise of the Son descended from King David is given through several of the prophets, but nowhere is it stated so clearly as from Isaiah 9:6–7,

> ... and His name shall be called Wonderful, Counsellor, The Mighty God, The Everlasting Father, The Prince of Peace.
>
> Of the increase of His government and peace there shall be no end, upon the throne of David, and upon His kingdom, to order it, and to establish it with judgment and with justice from henceforth even for ever ...

It is not understood where this "son of Joseph" tradition originated, because there is no apparent Scriptural reference to such a person. It may be assumed, then, this Messianic view has been handed down through Judaism from the distant past. Notice that Rabbi Dosa is from the second century. Jewish tradition relates that Messiah "the son of Joseph" is to be the "precursor" (forerunner) of Messiah the son of David, who will usher in the Messianic (Kingdom) Age after a period of great devastation on Earth.

Christianity, of course, teaches that Messiah is both "son of Joseph" and "son of David"; although the former is not of the tribe of Joseph, but actually a son of Joseph of Nazareth—a mere carpenter! Christians also teach that John the Baptist was the precursor of Jesus. Furthermore Jesus, as "son of Joseph," is the "precursor" of His own appearance as "son of David" later upon His return to begin the Jewish Messianic Age, which is also the beginning of His Kingdom Age, bringing Glory and Peace on Earth to all men.

Again, Jewish people are just going to be really surprised to see that He is the same One whom they had "thrust Him through." Now, watch what happens next.

Rodkinson's Talmud[28] states later in Sukkah tractate that Jewish tradition considered two Messiahs: one to be "son of Joseph," i.e., from the tribe of Joseph, and the other to be "son of David." Jesus of Nazareth was in fact a "son of David" by virtue of His earthly parentage with Joseph and Mary, but He was most definitely not from the tribe of Joseph. So, now we begin to reach more understanding of Jewish "confusion" concerning Jesus, son of Joseph of Nazareth.

Further confusion is revealed as Rodkinson's states that both, Messiah son of David and Messiah son of Joseph, were to be carpenters! There was this "son of Joseph" who was a carpenter from Nazareth—born in Bethelem—and who was also a "son of David!" Could he actually have been the "precursor" for Himself? Modern Bibles say "craftsmen" or "smiths," but "carpenters" is much more exciting!

Earlier, in Chapter 6, we learned that early Talmudic scholars in Sanhedrin 97a taught that Messiah, Son of David, originally had been expected to appear as Israel's Deliverer at the beginning of the third two-thousand year period after the birth of Adam. This would have been at the start of what we call the first century. After putting all of this together then, at this time one must surely inquire concerning *who* the Rabbis believe to have been "the other Messiah"—the Son of Joseph. You know—the One who was slain.

THE BOTTOM LINE!!! . . . This just cannot get more exciting!

The Talmud reference to "carpenters" is taken from Zechariah 1:20 in the King James translation or from Zech. 2:3 in the Hebrew Scriptures.

> And the Lord shewed me four carpenters.

Rabbi Hanah ben Bizna (third to fourth centuries) explains that these four carpenters are to be identified as: Messiah son of Joseph, Messiah son of David, Elijah, and "The Righteous Priest"—Melchizedek (or Cohen Zedek). Can you see what results now when we realize that two of these four carpenters are actually One person? There are really three "carpenters" in this picture! And yes, "son of Joseph" was slain. (And we still refer to Zechariah as one of the "minor" prophets!)

Did everybody notice how "They" (Elohim) said: " . . . they shall look upon *Me* because they have thrust *Him* through, and they shall mourn for *Him* . . ."? ("Me"? . . . "Him"?) This is another indication of the plurality *and* "Oneness" of The Almighty, "I AM," "WE ARE."

One might ask *why, how,* and by *whom* were these Talmudic traditions originated within Judaism, since many of these items are omitted from Scripture. We can reason that this tradition concerning Messiah, "son of Joseph," for example, may have been given through one of the earlier prophets. The Jews then assumed this meant this precursory Messiah was to be from the tribe of Joseph; whereas, we can see now that He was actually the firstborn son of a man named Joseph and a "son of David" as a bloodline descendant of that favored King.

There were of course many prophets whose words and visions were derived through The Holy One, although some of these were never recorded by the scribes of that day into the Scriptures. As we examine Judaism through the Talmud and Midrash, we can see often the workings of His Holy Spirit in the Law and traditions passed down through ages of Rabbinical thought and custom. Also, as we have seen many times in this work, we will find Messiah "concealed" within the Law and Jewish tradition by using our Christian 20/20 hindsight.

After a Christian once becomes aware of these Jewish "pictures," which the Lord has played out in bittersweet dramas, he can have a much better understanding of the Gospels. He will also develop a more sympathetic understanding of the Jewish vigil for their Deliverer.

I, for one, would like to hear what the scholars have to say after evaluating the secular and Biblical historical account we have presented. We have shown clear evidence that the Glory of the Lord (Shechinah) did in fact withdraw from the Temple forty years after The Crucifixion of Jesus Christ. I leave it to the scholars then to decide what this event really means to Jews and to Christians. It must not be ignored any longer. This event has to have some significance. God Himself wept at this occasion. How can we not want to know about this event and feel what He felt?

11 The Debate Continues

There are a few remaining debate items that emerge with a unique relevance to Jewish perspectives. It is important that Christians should TRY to understand and be sympathetic concerning some of the confusion, doubt, suspicion, and resistance that has caused so many Jewish people to overlook their Deliverer.

SO, WHO BELIEVES IN SIGNS?
One major criticism of this story by "conservative-traditional" teaching is that God would not honor the Temple with His Divine Presence because King Herod was so wicked. That teaching also "assumes" God would not honor Christ-rejecting Judaism by residing in their Temple after The Crucifixion. I intend here to show through the most elementary logic that Shechinah did remain in the Temple for a time after The Crucifixion. I offer this just in case there are still those who doubt or do not understand the meaning of Jesus' own words in Matthew 23:21.

We know from the New Testament that the Judeans (Israelites) were still conducting animal sacrifices during the ministry of the Lord Jesus. God had long ago Promised the sins of Israel would be purified under the Law by the blood of these "burnt offerings." But after the death of Jesus (by "strange coincidence"?) several strange and alarming "signs" occurred in the Temple. More specifically, the signs that had previously assured them of God's approval disappeared entirely; i.e., the westernmost light, crimson strap, etc. In place of these comforting signs, they were faced with the doors of the H'ekhal opening by themselves, the eclipses, the sword over the City, etc.

The priests and the Sanhedrin knew something they had done at that time had drawn the Lord's disapproval. Talmud (Yoma 39) describes and dates these events as "forty years before the Temple was destroyed." Of course, there is no mention of the timing with the crucifixion of that "pretender" in 30 A.D.

Talmud mentions at least one of these "signs" was taken to mean Shechinah was going to depart imminently. The Rabbis must have had some sort of records of similar events ("signs") having occurred just before the Temple Destruction in 586 B.C. Otherwise, how would they have known such a meaning existed when these signs appeared in 30 A.D.—70 A.D.? Then, by elementary logic, this information from the Talmud also indicates that the Rabbis who authored that text were saying Shechinah then dwelled in the Temple; otherwise how could these signs have indicated that he was going to depart?

Of course, you and I now know what happened "forty years before," but the Rabbis apparently never made the connection with their rejected Messiah. Sadly enough, they still haven't made this connection. This is just another of the many reasons why this story must be told.

Yes, Shechinah had been in the Temple probably for about 500 years before Jesus, even though it had certainly been "polluted" many times before and by kings who were far more despicable than Herod. This is further demonstration of God's eternal and infinite love, patience, understanding, and forgiveness of "this stiff-necked people." As discussed earlier, He apparently regards them somewhat like a spoiled-rotten, but favorite child in our large family of nations. We therefore must not be belligerent toward our Father nor resentful toward that favored "spoiled-brat" whom He loves so much.

Now, realizing the Shechinah Glory did reside in the Holy of Holies, we can all the more appreciate the indignation (yes, wrath!) of our Lord Jesus when He referred to "His Father's House" as a "den of thieves." I am certain this was not the first nor the last time the Holy House was defiled by such vermin, and yet Shechinah remained right up until their situation was desperate and "desolate" both times. The Lord Jesus Christ made good on His Promise that their house would be "left desolate" and that "not one stone would remain upon another," but cessation of His recognition of that House did not take place until 66 A.D.

It seems we patronize our Jewish friends when we say:

> Of course we love the Jews.
>
> Some of my best friends are Jews.
>
> But they are lost without Jesus.
>
> We must convert them to be "Christians."

But then we say they are not really God's Chosen people anymore. And next we say Jesus will purify them when He returns and then we will all be Christians. No, we won't—because *they will still be Jews*— fulfilled Jews! And, yes, still His Chosen People!

How can we be so certain "they will still be Jews!" A very simple prophecy is given by Zechariah concerning Jewish/Gentile relations during "those days" when Messiah rules His Kingdom on Earth.

> Thus saith the Lord of hosts; In those days it shall come to pass, that ten men shall take hold out of all languages of the nations, even shall take hold of the skirt of him that is a Jew, saying, "We will go with you: for we have heard that God is with you."
>
> Zechariah 8:23

During "those days" there will be Jews. And they will know their Lord (Jesus) and all Gentiles ("the nations") will also know Him and all will know that He is Jewish!

Some might try to "spiritualize" this verse by saying this is speaking of the present Church Age. (Have you seen anybody following Jews to worship because they have seen that God is with them?) This has not yet happened, but it will happen during "those days." In fact, the entire eighth chapter of Zechariah gives a view of a better world "in those days" when Jews and Gentiles will all worship together under One Lord. Israel will be "a blessing" (verse 13) to all nations "in those days" in Jerusalem as all nations worship One Lord Jesus, who was "pierced" for all nations.

Now the Lord knows I certainly don't know how to "convert" Jewish people, but I pray this story may help some Jews to find their Messiah.

Presence of Shechinah in the Temple does certainly not indicate God's approval of the Jews' failure to recognize their Messiah. (He forgave them on The Cross "for they knew not what they did.") But he most certainly did condemn their disobedience and pleaded: "Return unto Me and I will return unto you." Then, sadly with the Midrash Rabbis' own humble and lamenting admission, " . . . but they did not."

So, by the most elementary logic, again: WHY would those Rabbis "hatch" such a story? It certainly wasn't a proud moment in Jewish history. I am just baffled that they even bothered to record it at all. The fact that Jewish teachers have kept this quiet all these years actually provides credence to affirmation of this story. It makes no sense for them to record a fabrication of that sort.

"THE" UNANSWERED QUESTION
There are a few more thoughts I wish to offer concerning that critical unanswered question as to WHY those Rabbis would have fabricated a false story of this event. What possible motive could they have had? What "gain" for Judaism (or for themselves) could they promote or achieve? How can anyone believe the Jews would conspire to conceive this story as a lie? So far at least, not one critic or doubter of this story has been able to offer even a feeble answer to that burning question.

A few serious, sincere "conservative-fundamental-evangelical" ministers have actually labeled this story as ridiculous—this despite the fact that it was documented by two respectable Jewish authorities who were "on the scene" in Jerusalem at that time. One of these sources, the Rabbis, could be expected to be openly hostile to any connection of this story with Jesus. Those Rabbis of the first century surely had not forgotten about that incident forty years earlier. The other source, Flavius Josephus, is openly sympathetic to Jesus, saying: "He was [the] Christ . . ." and " . . . he appeared to them alive again the third day . . ." (Reference 2 Antiq., 18/63–64.)

Both of these ideologically opposite Jewish sources tell virtually the same story. Yet, the sympathetic source certainly had nothing to gain by "inventing" such a story. Josephus was a Jew, although considered by many modern Jewish people as somewhat of a self-serving "lackey" or even a traitor for the Romans. However, Josephus recorded many wonderful things and many beautiful thoughts about the Lord. (See Appendix C.) Do we, therefore, select as truthful only those incidents that happen to agree with our Latter Day tradition?

And how about the Midrash Rabbis? Does anybody really believe they would fabricate a phony story that would actually glorify Jesus Christ forty years after they had rejected Him? They had not forgotten the incident, but they just didn't make the "connection" of this incident with the fact that His radical followers claimed Jesus had ascended from Olivet forty years before. Therefore, they had no reason to lie.

The fact that this event began just prior to the Feast of Unleavened Bread, as the priests were preparing the Temple for that Holy Season, has important bearing on verification of this story. The "ministrations" of the priests on such occasions were performed by the full body of the twenty-four orders of Aaronic priesthood.

Professor Martin has pointed out that God surely arranged that His withdrawal should be witnessed by this full body of priests in order that they would know for certain this was a "sign" from God.[1] (He knew they were always looking for yet another sign!) Jewish tradition held that when a momentous change in their political or religious system was imminent, this called for a "clear sign" from the Lord. Thus, there was no higher authority in the world to witness the occasion and it was a "clear sign" to all Judeans that this supernatural event did in fact occur. The priests made a public announcement of this fact. (See Appendix A.)

We know this is true also because it was a fulfillment of a prophecy. It had to happen. And it did happen. The Midrash Rabbis were fervently proclaiming this event as fulfillment of Ezekiel's prophecy. This was not a prophecy they looked forward to witnessing. This was an act on the part of the Lord to show His displeasure with their disobedience. (Hasn't anyone noticed that this commentary is in the "Lamentations" portion of the Midrash?)

They were "lamenting" this fulfillment—this event. They didn't enjoy writing this. It certainly doesn't glorify Judaism. There was certainly no reason for them to "make-up" such a story, one which clearly is pointing to their disobedience while at the same time glorifying the Nazarene whom they had caused to be put to death forty years earlier. How does it glorify Jesus? It glorifies Jesus and "I AM" by showing that they both ascended into Heaven from the same point—a dramatic demonstration to those present concerning two of the Divine Personages of the Triune God.

UNDERSTANDING THE COHENS AND THE TRINITY
By demonstrating the close relationship of the "I AM" to Jesus, this story may help some Jewish people overcome one of their chief obstacles to accepting the Divinity of Jesus—the concept of the Trinity. They are taught: " . . . the Lord your God is one God. . . ." Yes, He is one God, but He is also "Elohim." During The Creation (Gen. 1:26) "Elohim" said: "Let us make man in our image, after our likeness. . . ." (Notice, The Creator(s) affirm this plurality of The Creator three times in this single sentence.) This statement, in God's own Words, means "us" and "our" refer to beings of God's same form—after "our" likeness, like "us"—and not like angels, for example. This also means that we humans are like God—except for the present we have been created to be "a little lower than the angels." (Psalms 8:5)

The Lord ("YHWH" or "I AM") is also two other Divine Personages. One is Messiah, His Son (as Himself), and the other is His Holy Spirit (also Himself) who ministered to Israel through the Prophets, delivering His Word to ALL of us through Israel.

Try it this way. Let us say there is the Cohen family, consisting of the father Isaac, the wife Edith, and the children: David, Laurie, Michael, and Elizabeth. They are all equal. They are all one flesh. They are all Cohens. And yet they are each different and separate.

But if one Cohen is grieved, for any reason, ALL of the Cohens are grieved. Likewise, when one has joy—again, for any reason—ALL are joyous. When one is absent, ALL are lonely. If someone offends or insults one Cohen—*any* Cohen—ALL are offended.

If you say you love only Mr. Cohen, he cannot accept this unless you also love his son(s). The Cohens are a very "close" family. One cannot just love one Cohen. You must love them all—because they are One. If you are friendly only to one, you are the friend of none.

Nevertheless, even though the Cohens are One, the father (Isaac) is first—first in everything, above all others. The father is responsible for everything. He pays for everything, even if it is paid "through" his son(s). He "rules the roost." He even has his own private area in his "house," usually a special chair—perhaps even a "room"—a den, or workshop, but private.

But they are still One family. Together they are One. But the father is first. Should you have any doubt about this, his son(s) will be the first to tell you that he is first.

Mr. Cohen would be disappointed in someone who claims to be his friend but refuses to love, accept, and obey his son, even after the son paid the "debt" owed his father by this "friend." But, maybe the friend just didn't realize that was Mr. Cohen's son. Mr. Cohen earlier had told this friend about his son; i.e., how to recognize him, when and where he would "appear," etc.

But, maybe the friend still just did not recognize the son when they met. After all, he was just an "ordinary guy" who walked in off the street one day. He was dressed like a laborer—a "carpenter!" and he said he was from some little "hick" town. Nobody here even knew him! The friend had naturally "assumed" of course the son would be rather an imposing, aristocratic, powerful figure—more like his father, Mr. Cohen.

Well, you and I *now* understand that "ordinary guy" was Mr. Cohen's beloved son, but only Mr. Cohen can judge whether this friend actually made an honest mistake or if he committed an intentional "snub" to the entire Cohen "family." After all, the son has said, "Forgive them, Father, for they know not what they do."

How Many "Gods" Did You Say?

Just as Jewish people have difficulty with the concept of more than one entity as "one" God, some Christians (especially very "young" Christians) may have trouble with the question: "Yes, I know about the Father, Son, and Holy Spirit; but now, who is this 'Shechinah?' Is he saying there are four persons in the Godhead?"

To avoid confusion on this point it is necessary to remind ourselves that God is omnipresent. He is everywhere. But the Shechinah is a visible presence of God, the Father ("I AM," Yahweh, Jehovah, and other identities). So, Shechinah is the Divine Presence of God, the Father—the ONE who spoke to Moses—not a "fourth" deity of any sort. This story should, however, demonstrate more than ever the "Oneness" between The Father and The Son, Jesus. That "Oneness" is demonstrated by the fact that the Father (as Shechinah) punctuated the Ascension of Jesus by ascending from the same point on the Mount of Olives forty years after "the 'stone' was rejected by the builders."

12 Closing Remarks

Assuming you have read all of the preceding chapters and have received a few new blessings, I wish now to leave you with some thoughts that have occurred as a result of facts brought out by this story.

A Messenger's Plea

Please do not ignore this story. Ignoring it would hardly seem likely if you have read through this far. But, please tell others about this beautiful story, even if they won't read it. Stimulate their curiosity. Any Christian or Jew should at least be curious about this story. The sting of rejection and retort is soon forgotten, but the ache of the ignored messenger lingers and remains.

We have pointed out that the Shechinah Event actually played a very important part in God's plan for rescue and preservation of the Jewish and Christian stalwarts who became the remnants to initiate the Church Age. It is indeed ironic that modern "conservatives" of both faiths are embarrassed, thrown off-balance, etc., by this beautiful story—a story which points to why and how their "fore-saints" were alerted to "get out of the camp" before death and destruction inundated Jerusalem and all of Judea.

The more we learn of the Old Testament, Judaic history, customs, the "Law," the more we see of Messiah (hidden) in Jewish culture and religion. Christians, so informed, are then more surely equipped for witnessing the Gospel of Messiah to Jewish people. Knowledge and appreciation of Judaism should also promote better understanding between these two closely linked faiths that are also "closely opposite."

By not emphasizing (even avoiding) the Messianic "pictures" and "types" in the Old Testament, we have cloistered Christianity from the Jews. (And not without considerable help from the Jews themselves, occasionally.) Even more tragically, this "cloistering" of our own Messianic view has further blinded the Jewish people from Messiah, because of something most Christians do not notice. Our Jewish friends are watching us and listening to us, especially if our "walk" demonstrates that we "see" something within Judaism that they do not see. (They are naturally curious.)

We should each be curious. Indeed, my own curiosity about this single event has led me to manifold blessings about the Lord Jesus in my searches through the Bible and all types of Judaica. My hope would be to find a Jewish student who has a similar curiosity about my Faith and about this event.

It is my hope that, if nothing else, this book will have stirred an interest in the Bible. This work has been, after all, a rigorous and vigorous Bible study. Many Christians and Jews encounter only a handful of familiar verses and Bible stories in their Scriptural education from Sunday School and from the pulpit. Great enjoyment and closeness to the Lord can be achieved by disciplining oneself to read the Bible through—yes, cover to cover. Only in that way can you see His story unfold, showing the plight of the Jews, God's forgiveness of "naughty" Israel, subtle appearances of Messiah, etc.

After studying the history, spiritual "pictures," archaeology, Judaism, Laws, prophecies, and other facets, such as those we have addressed, the Bible reader is better equipped for "enjoying" the Bible. The reason for this is simply because the reader then "knows what to look for." Otherwise, for example, if he is not familiar with the prophecies, etc., he could read right through Ezekiel without ever knowing what it is all about.

The Lord wants to speak with you "one on one" through His Word. He doesn't want you to hear Him only through your "Rabbi." "Rabbis" after all, are only human. He wants to talk to you. The Bible is God talking to you! (How many Sunday School teachers or preachers or other "Rabbis" ever told you about the "Dry Bones" prophecy?) See what I mean? (See Ezekiel Chapter 37.)

However, the reader must believe the Bible is God's Word. If you believe, the Lord has Promised many times that He will help you to understand. (See Proverbs 1:7, also 2:1–6) But, in order to read all through the Bible in one year, you must discipline yourself to read about three or four pages every day. Now, that takes about fifteen or twenty minutes. Do you think you could spare fifteen minutes each day for your Creator and your Redeemer? Think about it.

BUT . . . HOW CAN WE BE SURE?

Though some will misunderstand my motives, I say with all humility: The Shechinah Withdrawal could be the most important Biblical event since the Pentecost. I am not the one to make the final conclusion on this possibility, but it does certainly have important bearing on both faiths, on prophecy, and on our outlook and "watching" in these Latter Days.

We have attempted to answer all of the criticism so far received in written and verbal comment from some very highly qualified Christian teachers. At this writing, I have not yet received any scholarly critique from Jewish interests. There can be no doubt that this story is true, both through Scriptural verification and ancient historical records. We have also attempted to display truth through the most elementary logic. Again, it is ironic that some of the most "enthusiastic" doubters are Jewish—yet, the secular (and Biblical!) sources are all Jewish.

My favorite answer to stubborn "resistance" to this story, in the face of what I believe to be very hard evidence, goes like this:

— "Well, why are you so sure the Chicago Bears won Super Bowl XX?"

— "Are you kidding? Everybody knows they won!"

— "Well, were you at the game?"

— "No."

— "Well, do you know someone who was at the game?"

— "No, but I saw it on TV and I read the sports page. So did you."

— "Well, maybe the TV was 'faked.' And the sports writers get things mixed-up all the time."

— "OK. But I haven't seen or heard anyone who claims to have been at that game saying the Patriots won. Therefore, I think it's fair to 'assume' that yes, the Bears won!"

— "BUT . . . GEE!! I thought (hoped) maybe the Patriots won."

— "Nope . . . the Bears!"

That great scholar, Sir Robert Anderson,[3] said it very well:

> There is a point beyond which unbelief is impossible, and the mind in refusing truth must needs take refuge in a misbelief which is sheer credulity.

SOME QUESTIONS FOR THE SKEPTICS

It is natural that anyone would be skeptical upon first hearing this story. After all, it is not every day that some unknown engineer steps out to challenge the thoroughness and perception of nineteen centuries of scholars and learned theologians.

However, documented evidence for this event is much stronger than evidence for many other events of antiquity, including some Biblical accounts. Two sources, who were otherwise fervently dedicated to bitter antagonism, recorded this event in corroborative detail. (This is perhaps the only subject upon which Josephus and the Rabbis of the Second Temple ever agreed.)

Following are some questions offered to assist "skeptics" in their search for TRUTH and to serve as a summary of this glorious event:

— Ask those who insist that only Ezekiel "saw" the Glory withdraw to explain WHY?? Ezekiel stated three times that he saw this event "in the visions of God," while he was actually *in* Babylon seated before some of the elders of Judah.

— Ask them also to explain when Ezekiel's prophecy of the Glory's Withdrawal was fulfilled. The accounts described by Josephus and the Rabbis of the Talmud and the Midrash are the only corroborative documentations we have of such an event. One so-called traditional version would have us believe that only Ezekiel saw that glorious "fire" or "cloud" when He removed from the Temple and went across the Kidron Valley to "the mountain which is on the east side of the City." (Does anybody believe Almighty God would just "sneak" away?!)

— Ask the indifferent skeptic who dismisses or belittles this story or who thinks it is contentious and trivial, to explain why the Lord went to all this bother to appear and to speak and to plead in person with His Chosen after virtually 1,500 years of cloistering Himself from all but the High Priest.

— Ask also those who believe God no longer loves the Jews, to explain why He appeared to them and pleaded with them for three and one-half years.

— Ask those who doubt because Scripture does not record this Event, to explain WHY?? they believe the Temple was destroyed. That event was recorded only by the *same* historians who witnessed and recorded the Shechinah Withdrawal. It is not reported as fulfillment in Scripture.

— Ask those who don't accept the credibility of Talmud and Midrash in this matter, to explain why the first-century Hebrew scribes would ever have "invented" this story by recording, documenting, an event that actually punctuates and glorifies The Resurrection and Ascension of Jesus and that, by their own admission, clearly indicates this was a stinging rebuke from the Lord "because they would not."

— Ask those who don't accept credibility of Josephus, corroborated by his enemies in this matter, why they believe anything else he has written. Flavius Josephus has been proved, archaeologically and/or historically, to be correct most of the time. (This time, too!)

— Ask those who insist that Ezekiel "saw" Shechinah depart (Ezek. 8:3) and that He never returned, to explain how Ezekiel was able to "see" Shechinah return to the Second Temple! (Ezek. 43:2) especially considering the fact that he was still in Babylon and the Temple had certainly not been rebuilt when that vision was given "in the fourteenth year after that the city (Jerusalem) was smitten." (Ezek. 40:1)

— Ask those who have difficulty believing the Divine Presence was in the Second Temple, to explain what the Lord had intended when He told Haggai to exhort Zerubbabel to " ... build the House; and I will take pleasure in it, and I will be glorified ... Yet now be strong ... for I am with you ... and I will fill *this* House with Glory...." (From Haggai 1:8, 2:4, 7)

— If these insist that Jesus, "The Desire Of All Nations," filled the House with His Glory, ask them to explain how Jesus, as a peasant born of the house of David and not a Levite priest, would ever have been permitted to enter the H'ekhal, especially the Holy of Holies or even the Holy Place?

— Ask them to explain who did fill that House with His Glory. (It could only have been the One whom Jesus and Paul said "dwells within.")

— If they "squirm" from this, ask them to explain who was dwelling in the Temple when Jesus said: "... Him that dwelleth therein..." (From Matthew 23:21)

— Also have them explain who "pertaineth" to (belongs to) the Israelites, where Paul said: "... my kinsmen... who are Israelites; to whom pertaineth the Glory..." Not "formerly pertaineth," but now—circa 57 A.D., the time of Paul's letter to the Romans. (From Romans 9:4)

— Try to keep a straight face as you ask the skeptic to explain why God the Father would sacrifice His Son behind the Temple? (west) when all of the other sacrifices were given (east) in front of the Temple?

— If they still "squirm" at this, ask them to explain how the centurion was able to see that "the veil was rent in twain," especially if he were west of the Temple in the vicinity of the Church of the Holy Sepulchre or the Garden Tomb, etc.

— Or, even if he agrees with the Olivet Crucifixion, ask him to explain how the centurion could have seen the torn Veil in the 3 P.M. "ninth-hour" shade, 40 ft. back under the 150 ft. high protico.

— Ask the skeptic to offer some rationale to explain why two out of three Gospel writers reported only that the centurion had seen the Veil torn and then he was terrified and he just up-and-decided that Jesus was the Son of God. Just like that. Just because of a torn drapery? Why was that Veil so important to their report?

— And now, perhaps the most Glorious of all, ask the skeptic to explain why that centurion and his men were "terrified" and were moved to exclaim: "Truly this man was the Son of God." As a former soldier myself, I had often pondered why seeing "those things that were done"—an earthquake, the opened graves, a torn curtain—would "terrify" and move violent, "macho" Roman footsoldiers to suddenly recognize the Divinity of their execution victim. It is incredulous that, even after six hours on that cross, the victim's second unexplainably vigorous shout, "TETELESTAI!" would be likely to inspire them to sudden "conversion." But, after their face-to-face confrontation with Almighty God (Shechinah), they were terrified! And they believed!

So far, nobody has provided any plausible counter-explanations for these questions. Neither do the Scriptures explain all of this; although, the historical accounts presented here certainly are supported by those details and circumstances that are presented in Scripture. Can it be there is only one explanation?

We have proposed sensible answers to these questions, which I, too, had to ask myself. The traditional stories hold no truth, but spawn doubt and skepticism while they are based only on assumptions leading to opinion. It is understood that certain perils exist for any who would buck the tide of traditional opinion. Nevertheless, I submit that we have proved this "entrenched" opinion cannot stand in the light of literal Scripture, recorded history, and simple logic.

I have been critical of both Christian and Jewish conservative "traditionalists." I hope not to convey harshness toward critics, and I invite opponents of the validity of the Shechinah story to investigate Scripture and the factual evidence for themselves.

The Shechinah story tells Jewish people: "Yes, Jesus of Nazareth is Messiah!" It also tells Christians: "But I forgave them at the Cross, remember?" And the Law was not taken away just then; i.e., the sacrifices and the Shechinah were removed only after the passing of a full generation. It is as if God had tested that generation who declined "the time of their visitation" and then He shut down their Temple.

It is my hope that this book will cause people to think! In that way, all persons will more surely reach the truth.

This story rests on three literal Scriptural verses from three different writers with recorded works from three contemporary, indigenous historians of that date. I am open to any who will show me any mistakes in these facts or analyses. "Best-selling writer" Job said:

Teach me, and I will be silent:

And show me how I have erred.

Honest words are not painful,

But what does your argument prove?

Job 6:24, 25 (NASB)

So, That's What "They" Want!

Let us take ourselves back in time to Jerusalem in 66–69 A.D. Can you just imagine that scene? Yes, imagine seeing the Lord Himself, the "fire" and the "cloud"—The "I AM"—up on that mountain top speaking to you. Imagine what you would have felt, had you been there to see Him and to hear Him pleading (with many voices) day and night for three an a half years, pleading to His "naughty children" to repent and return to Him.

This was a startling supernatural event. Why have we never heard of this? Today the bookshelves and racks are top-heavy and overflowing with all the "junk-novels" and paperbacks and all categories of "best-sellers." The secular entertainment industry and journalists are inundating us and choking the TV channels and clogging the aisles of our supermarkets with stories of the "super-natural," extraterrestrial beings, reincarnation, mysticism, terror, science-fiction, celebrity autobiographies, documented "eye-witness" accounts of "Big Foot," "the Abominable Snow-Man," flying saucers, etc., etc.

Women, in the U.S.A. especially, are demonstrating their hunger for "love" by their enthusiastic response to the glut of "junk-novels" and "soap-operas." ("Real-Men" don't watch those, do they?!) Women have been persuaded that their void of what they think is "love" will be filled by this "junk," which is actually a sensual stimulant of sorts. They read about what they think they need—"Love."

Men, we are certainly not much different. Our "macho" search for an elusive "love" is being stimulated (but not satisfied) by the "girlie" magazines, "porno" merchants, etc., in a somewhat less wholesome fashion than that of our distaff side. So everybody, it seems, is looking for love . . . but in all the wrong places.

Our Latter Day culture is literally starving for some kind of assurance, some kind of "link" with the Almighty. (Whoever He is!) They want and need His love, His protection from whatever our "shaky" future holds in store for us. They want to share His knowledge (Whoever He is!) of the future. But, man's nature has not changed much in the past few millennia—because man still wants all of this in a worldly covenant. Man wants it now, but without any commitment from himself to "God."

Man still doesn't realize that the only God who exists has already provided all of these things man is seeking. God has even shared His knowledge of the future with those of us who read and study His prophecies and believe and obey His Word. It's called the Holy Bible. (I often like to refer to it as "The Owner's Manual.")

So, the entertainment industry and the secular journalists have observed and nurtured this "need" in man's hunger for a "God" of some sort; and they are making lots of money filling that need. Then, to satisfy the need, the only commitment required from man is his purse.

Well—so that's what they want! We should give the entertainment/journalism industry a challenge. Let them tell "man" the

Shechinah story if he wants adventure, war, mystery, supernatural phenomena, excitement. They could give them an historical drama "mini-series" that would make "Masada," "Roots," "Shogun," and some of the other "block-busters" seem like day school nap-time stories by comparison. Especially if they showed the violence and carnage at the siege of Jerusalem!

The conspicuous difference that contrasts this story with much of modern popular literature, however, is the fact that this story is true. This really happened—1,900 years ago in Jerusalem—The City of God.

This is a biographical sketch about the most "charismatic," the most all-powerful, THE most beautiful, the most "everything" celebrity of all time—Almighty God, Himself! ("Best-Seller" celebrities will now please leave the stage!)

So, is that what they want? Well, here it is—another of many truelife episodes in the greatest LOVE story ever told. I sincerely pray that men will be privileged to hear this real-life "happening" about Almighty God before He turns the final pages of "His" Story.

So, Now What Should We Do?

There is great temptation now to go out and start witnessing, through this story, to our Jewish friends about how Judaism and Christianity in 30 A.D. and in 69 A.D. "converged at a point" on the Mount of Olives. But don't forget what was noted in the opening chapter of this work—about trying to be a "bridge." (Don't be surprised if you must endure some stress when you are "run-over" and "walked-on" by some.)

Indeed, God does want this story to be told to Jews and Christians. However, we (Christians) must be very gentle and very patient and very careful about *how* we present this bittersweet story to Jewish people. Don't "sock it to 'em" and do not hit 'em over the head with it! God has surely used the Jewish people as an example lesson to us Gentiles. He has used His Chosen People to teach us, but God did not have them do the teaching. He teaches us through their example. We (Gentiles) should, therefore, do likewise by standing back a little so we let this story be, truly, a lesson-from-God, and avoid making it sound like a lesson from a Christian Gentile.

Let's "Get-It-Together"

But why did God wait for so long after Jesus was "offered" until He removed His Divine Presence from the People?

Perhaps God wished to show Israel that He truly did "forgive them for they knew not what they did." And perhaps God wished also to show us Gentiles that He forgave the Jewish people—just as the first Gentiles were first beginning to accept Jesus as their "sin offering" at about that time.

It appears that the Lord tested that last generation before He scattered them among the nations, to give individual Jews at that tragic period one final opportunity to decide whether Jesus was their own "burnt offering." Many did come to realize Jesus was The Anointed as they observed those Temple signs and were finally warned to "scatter" when Shechinah withdrew from the Holy House. These Jews were kept from the Roman slaughter to become a believing remnant who went on to build "The Church" started by Paul and the other Apostles.

Nevertheless, He also preserved a Jewish remnant from the coming generation of those who were still too blind to recognize their Deliverer. This Merciful and Loving Father then laid a "smiting" upon them as He had Promised (Hosea 6:1). Because of their disobedience, He scattered them as a persecuted minority "among the heathen" (Deut. 4:27) as a part of that smiting. But He gave this Promise of His mercy upon individual Jews of future generations in Deuteronomy 4:29–31:

> "But if from thence thou shalt seek the Lord thy God, thou shalt find Him, if thou seek Him with all thy heart and with all thy soul.
>
> When thou art in tribulation, and all these things are come upon thee, even in the latter days, if thou turn to the Lord thy God, and shall be obedient to His voice;
>
> (For the Lord thy God is a merciful God); He will not forsake thee, neither destroy thee, nor forget the covenant of thy fathers which He sware unto them."

Many Jewish people have sought the Lord "with all their hearts," but only God can judge this and only that Jewish individual and the Lord can know if he found God. Christians must stop insisting that Jewish people stop being "Jews" if they genuinely want to find their Lord. Many Jewish people in these "latter days" are finding Messiah Jesus as Lord, but they are finding Him while they remain "Jewish."

Some others, who have not yet found Messiah, may have been

earnestly seeking the Lord, but are still too "Jewish" to see Jesus. Ironically, this may occur partly because we have been too "Christian" in our evangelizing the Jews. They have been watching us. They still haven't forgotten our evangelical approach during the Crusades and the Spanish Inquisition. Neither have they forgotten our "smiting" of their people during the Holocaust.

If you were a Jew, would you seek the Lord your God by becoming a "Christian?" Or would you be proud of your "Jewishness" and your covenantal heritage as a Jew? Some Jewish people may have found "the Lord their God" as Jews (Plan "A"). Many Jewish people have become "Christianized" and have found the Lord. They therefore do have that "Blessed Assurance" (Plan "B"). Those Jews who recently have found the Lord and Messiah as One (Still Plan "B") have also that same "Blessed Assurance" and more—because they are still Jews! These are of course released from the Law and the sacrifices, but they are *still* God's Chosen People. . . . Yes, Jews. Again, if you were Jewish, how would you seek the Lord your God?

Leave the judging of these things to the Lord. Pray that He will teach us how to help Jews find Him. He may "judge" us Christians because we have not really loved the Jewish people by accepting them and even encouraging them to be Jews.

Rev. Vendyl Jones offers an explanation on why we Gentiles should be less judgmental toward Jewish people and how we can improve our understanding of their unique covenantal relationship with God. (Quoting from reference 4, pg. 7–60, ref. Acts 5:33–40):

> Rabbi Gamaliel's words concerning the message of Jesus were: ". . . if this counsel or this work be of men, it will come to naught; but if it be of G-d, ye cannot overthrow it, lest haply ye be found even to fight against G-d. And to him (the Sanhedrin) agreed . . ." What Gamaliel said of the message of Jesus and Christianity can also be said of the Jew and Judaism. If it were of man, or if Christianity had replaced Judasim, it would have long ago come to naught. The very survival of the Jew, Judaism and Israel is the verification of G-d's perseverance of the people of his earthly economy. All the efforts by Christianity to thwart Judaism and the Jewishness of Jesus have been, by the same formula of Gamaliel, "to fight against G-d."

> (Touché Vendyl!)

One would ordinarily expect modern repentant Jewish people to welcome this story. But, as I have explained, this story seems to cause embarrassment for Jews because it confronts them with the fact that their Shechinah ascended to Heaven from the same place as the Gentile Christians' Jesus had ascended forty years earlier.

Then, ironically and paradoxically, even some conservative / fundamental / evangelical Christians are also embarrassed because this story tells a different version of the Shechinah Withdrawal than they quite innocently have been "assuming" and teaching for all these centuries. (The fact that this story is documented only by Jewish sources doesn't add to their enthusiasm, either!) Actually, we just didn't have all of the available information, simply because this report has apparently been somewhat suppressed, although I don't really know why or by whom. (But we certainly know it was for God's Purpose that it should not be told, at least until now. Maybe others have tried it before.)

We should point out that at least one early Christian historian reported the truth concerning the Withdrawal of Shechinah. Eusebius, a native-born Palestinian Christian of the fourth century and a contemporary of Emperor Constantine I, documented and observed the importance of this event[26] and left his works for scholars of the ages to follow. He was Bishop of Caesarea in the early Church. His work has had scant notice outside of the most unbiased scholarly interests, primarily because the Church "establishment" has not wanted to hear this. (It's too "Jewish"!)

Although Eusebius had accurately described the withdrawal of Shechinah from the Temple and had noted that The Crucifixion took place on Olivet, these items from his work have been kept from us by our teachers. This, in spite of the fact that Eusebius is revered by the scholars as "the father of ecclesiastical history!" It seems he was over-ruled by Constantine on these matters after Constantine had employed divination to "discover" these Holy sites in his "visions." The "Church" of course went with Constantine and his mother, Helena. These two early Gentile Holy Land pilgrims "discovered" some of our most popular sites, including "Calvary" and "His Tomb," which are due west of the Temple site at the Church of the Holy Sepulchre. Eusebius, too, has been obscured by the powers of "tradition."

Although this event has been hidden(?), misunderstood(?), or maybe ignored(?) for all these centuries, from God's Word we know also that He does reveal some mysteries to us according to His Purpose:

> He reveals mysteries from the darkness, And brings the deep darkness into light.

Job 12:22 (NASB)

Perhaps now is the time for the mystery of His withdrawal from the Temple to be revealed as an expression of His Eternal Love and His Blessing upon His Church and upon the Believing Remnant of His Chosen. We shall glorify the Lord more by seeking and revealing the truth than by preserving and persisting in error and confusion, "wriggling" and "squirming" to evade or ignore Scripture, fact, and even simple logic.

As we close, it is fitting that we recall from John's Gospel a verse summarizing the central message that I believe the Lord had intended to convey to the world through this Holy Event.

> For God so loved the world, that He gave His only begotten Son, that whosoever believeth in Him should not perish, but have everlasting life.
>
> John 3:16

The Lord has demonstrated through this Event, after having given His only begotten Son, that he did forgive us and that Jesus is in fact His Son. We who profess to be His own, especially, must become aware of this Event, its importance, and its Glory. We can no longer continue to evade or ignore one of His greatest gestures showing his infinite, unequaled and perpetual love for man.

So, now we must swallow our "embarrassment" and "gird up our loins" and get on with it.

It is my sincere hope and fervent prayer that the Lord will permit His Glory to be seen, through this event, by "awakened" Jews, Christians, Muslims, and indeed all mankind before His return.

The Glory of God can be seen everywhere by those who would look for Him in all things.

Appendix A

Josephus (Wars) Excerpt Concerning Departure of the Divine Presence from the Second Temple (66 A.D.)

FROM: *The Works of Josephus*[2]
Translated by William Whiston, A.M.
Hendrickson Publishers—Peabody, Ma
(From: "The Wars of the Jews," Book 6, Chap. 5, 288–300)

The following excerpt from Reference 2 is only that portion which describes the departure of the Glory of the Lord from the Temple, including some other mysterious events that occurred simultaneous with that event.

'Thus, also, before the Jew's rebellion, and before those commotions which preceded the war, when the people were come in great crowds to the Feast of Unleavened Bread, on the eighth day of (Nisan), and at the ninth hour of the night (approx. 3 A.M.) so great a light shone around the altar and the Holy House, that it appeared to be bright day-time; which light lasted for half an hour. This light seemed to be a good sign to the unskillful, but was so interpreted by the sacred scribes as to portend those events that followed immediately upon it. At the same festival also, a heifer, as she was led by the high priest to be sacrificed, brought forth a lamb in the midst of the Temple. Moreover, the Eastern Gate of the inner (court of the) Temple which was of brass, and vastly heavy, and had been with difficulty shut by twenty men, and rested upon a basis armed with iron, and had bolts fastened very deep into the firm floor, which was there made of one entire stone, was seen to be opened of its own accord about the sixth hour of night. Now, those that kept watch in the Temple came thereupon running to the captain of the Temple, and told him of it; who then came up thither and not without great difficulty was able to shut the gate again. This also appeared to the vulgar [ORDINARY PEOPLE] to be a very happy prodigy, as if God did thereby open them the gate of happiness. But the men of learning understood it, that the security of their Holy House was dissolved of its own accord, and that the gate was opened for the advantage of their enemies. So these publicly declared, that this signal foreshewed the desolation that was coming upon them. Besides these, a few days after that feast, on the one-and-twentieth day of the month (Iyar) a certain prodigious and incredible phenomenon appeared; I suppose the account of it would seem to be a fable, were it not related [TOLD] by those that saw it, and were not the events that followed it of so considerable a nature as to deserve such signals; for, before sun-setting, chariots and troops of soldiers in their armor were seen running about among the clouds, and surrounding of cities. Moreover, at that feast, which we call Pentecost, as the priests were going by night into the inner (court of the) Temple, as their custom was, to perform their sacred ministrations, they said that, in the first place, they felt a quaking, and heard a great noise, and after that they heard a sound as of a great multitude, saying, "Let us remove hence. . . ."

Appendix B

Midrash Excerpt Describing the Departure of the Divine Presence from the Second Temple and Jerusalem—66–69 A.D.

FROM: MIDRASH RABBAH
MIDRASH EICHAH RABBATI
PETIKHTA D'EICHAH RABBATI (25)
Introduction to the Midrash of Lamentations (Eichah) Middle Portion of Section (25) Proems

(Bold numbers in the left margin refer to commentary notes by this writer following the end of the Midrash narrative.)

4
5

The Divine Presence moved ten times: From cherub to cherub, from cherub to the threshold of the Temple, from the threshold of the Temple to the cherubim, from the cherubim to the east gate, and from the courtyard to the roof, from the roof to the altar, from the altar to the wall, from the wall to the city, from the city to the Mount of Olives.

- From cherub to cherub, as it is written: (Ezekiel 10:4) 'The Glory of the Lord was raised above the cherub.'

- From the cherub to the threshold of the Temple, as it is written: (Ezekiel 10:4) 'The Glory of the Lord was raised above the cherub where it was, to the threshold of the Temple.'

- From the threshold of the Temple to the cherubim, as it is written: (Ezekiel 10:18) 'And the Glory of the Lord left from above the threshold of the Temple and stood over the cherubim.'

The phrase 'left from' was not appropriate for this sentence: rather, 'came to' was appropriate. Nevertheless, 'left from' was used, instead. Why 'left from?'

6 Quoting Rabbi Akha: 'Like a king who reluctantly must leave his palace, who would leave and come back to caress and kiss the walls of the palace and the pillars of the palace, weeping and saying, "Goodbye, my house–my palace–goodbye, my own precious vessel–goodbye!" In the same way, when the Divine Presence left the Temple, He returned to caress and kiss the walls of the Temple, the pillars of the Temple, weeping and saying, "Goodbye, my Temple–goodbye, house of my kingship. Goodbye, my precious home–goodbye, my precious vessel–goodbye!"

- From the cherubim to the east gate, as it is written: (Ezekiel 10:19) 'And the cherubim took their wings and ... stood at the door of the east gate of the Lord's house; and the Glory of the God of Israel was over them above.'

7
- From the east gate to the courtyard, as it is written: (Ezekiel 10:4) 'and the courtyard was filled with the radiant glory of the Lord.'

- From the courtyard to the roof, as it is written: (Proverbs 25:24)

8 'It is better to live in a corner of the roof than in a large house with a quarrelsome wife.'

- From the roof to the altar, as it is written: (Amos 9:1) 'I saw the Lord standing on the altar.'

- From the altar to the wall, as it is written (Amos 7:7) 'And it came to pass that the Lord stood by a vertical wall.'

9 What is meant by "vertical?" Numerically, "vertical" (in Hebrew) is equivalent to the number "71," which is the Sanhedrin of 71 members and this is what "vertical" means. "And the Lord said I am appointing 71." (Amos 7:8)

- From the wall of the city. Quoting Rabbi Judah, son of Simon:

As it is written: (Micah 6:9) 'The voice of the Lord calls upon the city.'

- From the city to the Mount of Olives. As it is written: (Ezekiel 11:23) 'The Glory of the Lord went up from the midst of the city and stood on the mountain which is east of the city.'

Quoting Rabbi Jonathan: 'Three and one half years the Divine Presence sat on the Mount of Olives, expecting that perhaps Israel would repent, but they did not. And the Divine Presence would declare and say: (Jeremiah 3:14, 22) 'Return, naughty children;' and (Malachi 3:7) 'Return to me and I shall return to you' and, since they did not repent, said (Hosea 5:15) 'I will go back to my place.'

Of that hour it is said: (Jeremiah 13:16) 'Give praise to the Lord before darkness descends. Before darkness descends on the religious judgment. Before darkness descends on prophecy. Before your feet stumble on the mountains of night. And (before) your search for the light in Babylon. And (before) the devastation into deep darkness in Midian. And (before) the obscurely foggy discourses of Greece....'

(Here ends the excerpted Midrash narrative.)

Commentary Notes on Midrash Eichah Narrative.

1. The narrative was translated from the Hebrew, having no generic punctuation code; therefore, brackets, punctuation, quotation marks, etc., have been inserted to improve clarity, flow, and organization of the Midrash material.

2. English translations from the King James Version (KJV), New American Standard Bible (NASB), or New International Version (NIV) have been used as references in this transcript in order to preserve authority and consistency in the Scriptural references quoted here. However, out of respect for the Scriptural quotes in the Midrash as printed and, hopefully, to convey the Rabbi's intended meaning, the Midrash wording is used as closely as possible. For example, in Jeremiah 3:14, 22, "naughty" children is used, as translated from the Midrash, instead of "back-sliding" children or other translations appearing in some modern Bible versions.

3. This translation presents the exegesis from this portion of the Midrash as completely and as accurately and conscientiously as was

humanly possible for the Hebrew translator who assisted in this work. No additions or comments from the translator or this writer are inserted anywhere within this Midrash narrative, although quoted verses from Scripture have been inserted as a convenience to the reader.

4 It should be understood that this does not refer to the present Golden Gate in the City Wall, but refers instead to the East Gate of the Temple; i.e., Nicanor's Gate. (See Sketches 1 and 2.)

At first, one might interpret that Ezekiel is describing the Glory as hovering "above the cherubim" that were over the Ark of the Covenant, or perhaps those cherubim that were carved into the cedar panels of the walls in Solomon's Temple (II Chron. 3:7). This conclusion is incorrect, however, because the prophet makes it very clear in Ezekiel 10:15, 20 and 22 that these are "the same living creatures" he had seen "by the river Chebar." (Ezekiel 1:1, 3 and 3:15)

Additionally, we know from Jeremiah 3:16 and from Josephus (Wars, 5/219) that there was no Ark of the Covenant, no acacia wood cherubim over the Mercy Seat, not even a replica, in the Holy of Holies. Therefore–no wooden cherubim. These were *real* cherubim, attending the Lord at His withdrawal from the Temple. Regardless of whether the Rabbis (priests) saw the cherubim or not, they were describing the movements of the Shechinah and need not have actually seen any Angelic beings in order to have described this event as fulfillment of Ezekiel's prophecy.

5 It has been assumed that Shechinah passed through the open East Gate as He moved "from the Altar to the wall" on the Feast of Pentecost, 66 A.D. The gate, according to Talmud, Sukkah 53b, would have been open since this was a Feast Day. This passing through then, may be interpreted as a fulfillment of Ezekiel 44:3 in which "... He shall go out by the way of the same." (See Chapters 5 and 6.)

It is believed that this refers to the "wall" of the Temple courtyard, rather than the "wall" around the city of Jerusalem. However, it is not clear concerning what is considered as the "city." It may be speculated that there were some dwellings along the route described, on the western slope of the Mount of Olives, in the vicinity of the present sites of the Russian Church of Mary Magdalene and the Church of All Nations, and then on toward the summit. This speculation is somewhat reinforced by a note concerning "city" in Cruden's Concordance as follows:

In Hebrew usage, a collection of permanent human habitations, whether many or few, especially if surrounded by a wall. The word was also used, as now, metaphorically for the people of a city.

Perhaps the most logical explanation is offered by Professor Martin in that Jerusalem's city limits were extended to a "Sabbath day's journey" (Acts 1:12) from the Holy of Holies. Such a distance, 2,000 cubits by Judaic Law, was about half or two thirds of a mile, depending upon the cubit size. This was established, of course, in deference to the crowds of worshipers who could not all live within the city walls, especially on the feast seasons.

An obvious but awkward speculation might be that the Presence moved back over the Temple after reaching the east courtyard wall and then moved westward over Jerusalem ("city") and then moved back across the Temple and across the Kidron Valley to the Mount of Olives. But this would seem to be a somewhat erratic movement which would then require doubling-back again eastward, passing over the Temple, and thence to the Mount of Olives summit. It seems that such an erratic movement would surely have been of enough intrigue that it would have been described either in the Midrash or by Josephus. It therefore appears that the direct passage from the east courtyard wall over the existing dwellings and "legal" (city) limits in the Kidron Valley and on to the summit of Mt. Olivet would be more logical.

6   In this Midrash commentary note, the Rabbi is apparently referring to the subtlety of a nuance in the Hebrew Scripture, which indicates that one is departing of necessity or because of circumstances rather than by choice. (For example: to get out of the way.) The Midrash Hebrew literally says: "Like a king forced to leave his palace. . . . " However, it is neither appropriate nor Scriptural to agree that the Lord could be "forced" to do anything. The Midrash text was therefore modified to read "reluctantly must leave" instead of "forced to leave."

7   It appears that the movements and/or "stops" described in Ezekiel 10: 4 may not be in chronological order, whereas the Midrash locations are implied to be listed chronologically. It is probably not important as to just "when" the Glory filled the courtyard, whether in Ezekiel 10: 4 or later after Ezekiel 10: 19, because from our Biblical knowledge of the Shechinah Glory in the Tabernacle and from the description provided by Josephus we know the brillance was so intense as to fill the entire Temple and appeared to be "bright daytime." (See Appendix A.)

8 This reference to the "roof" by using Proverbs 25: 24 may at first impress one that the Rabbi was stretching things just a bit in order to connect this roof position of the Glory with the Holy Scripture, no matter how remote that connection might be. However, I suppose one could compare Israel, during the Second Temple era, with a "quarrelsome wife," including being confined with her, even in a large house. Considered in this manner then, the verse is not at all far-fetched; in fact, it is surely appropriate. (Perhaps both the Lord and this Rabbi were exhibiting some wry humor even amid the tragedy of this occasion.)

Other not-so-far-fetched verses are Amos 7:7 and 9:1. Initially, each of these verses, in the opening phrases, appears to be "striving" for the connection. However, as one continues through the rest of the verse or perhaps even the next few subsequent verses, there appear "signals" to connect the location of the Divine Presence during the departure with a Scriptual message of judgment on a disobedient and un-repentant Israel. Once again:

> So shall My word be which goes forth from My mouth; it shall not return to me empty, without accomplishing what I desire, and without succeeding in the matter for which I sent it.
>
> Isaiah 55:11 (NASB)

9 The Midrash text explains that "anak," which is the Hebrew word for "vertical" or "plumb-line," is comprised of the same letters of the Hebrew alphabet that also denote the number of seventy-one (71): "aleph"=1; "nouhn"=50; "kahf"=20; or "anak" meaning "vertical." It is then taken by the Rabbi's comment that the passage refers to a "Sanhedrin," because that body was made up of seventy-one Jewish men of high standing and reputation.

As discussed in note 8, one must consider all of Amos 7: 8 and :9 in order to follow this comment:

From verse 8: "... Behold I am about to put a plumb line

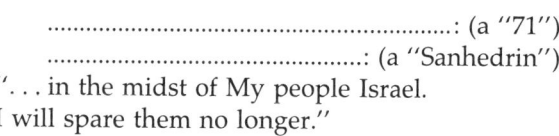

....: (a "71")
....: (a "Sanhedrin")
"... in the midst of My people Israel.
I will spare them no longer."

And verse 9: "The high places of Isaac will be desolated and the sanctuaries of Israel laid waste. Then shall I rise up against the house of Jeroboam with sword."

The implication could be that the Lord, in His displeasure with the Sanhedrin for their poor "shepherding" of His people, will replace them with a new "Sanhedrin" or "71." Also, it carries an additional implication that, just as Hosea had warned Jeroboam and Israel of impending doom almost eight hundred years earlier, Israel would again suffer humiliating desolation at the hands of a pagan conqueror.

A speculation for the "71," or new Sanhedrin, might be "71" survivors of the coming slaughter and the scattering that was to follow the destruction of Jerusalem in 70 A.D. It may be that the Lord selected 71 "roots," unheralded and known only to the Lord. These would begin a long line of new leaders to "shepherd" and "survive" Judaism through the next 2,000 years of scattering, oppression, struggle, and fugitive-like existence. But this is only speculation. Perhaps some scholar can provide a less speculative interpretation of this statement.

A parallel exists in the New Testament in Luke 10:1 when Jesus appoints seventy disciples to spread the Good News. A "Sanhedrin" of sorts was then comprised of seventy plus The One. There was apparently a strong Jewish traditional concept in creating a body of seventy-one men to accomplish the Lord's message to His People. Here again we see Him create a "new Sanhedrin" when His Purpose is not being served by the Temple "establishment."

10 Since the "city limits" of Jerusalem had been extended one Sabbath Limit, or about two thirds of a mile eastward, then the Temple was to be considered as it states: in "the midst of the city."

11 My Hebrew translator informs me that the word used here for "sit" means literally "to-sit-in-mourning" (as for the death of a loved one), not just to be seated casually. Knowing such a detail adds to the drama and pathos of the occasion.

Immediately following where the Lord states: "I will go back to My place," a very exciting prophecy is given in Chapter 6 of Hosea. That continuing portion of the prophecy deals with the timing of Israel's "two days" of suffering after He goes back to His Place. (See "When Did those 'Two Days' Start," Chapter 6.)

12   There is no documented date of the Rabbinical commentaries in the Midrash; however, permit me to speculate as to the time period and what thoughts might be interpreted from the Rabbi's epilogue. It seems likely that this lament was written soon after the "scattering" had taken place, rather than say, several centuries later. This seems evident because the writer admonishes the people to, "Give praise to the Lord before darkness descends." They certainly knew, after the destruction of Jerusalem and the Temple, that even more "darkness" was coming. My view is, therefore, that this might have been written during the first or second century. This view is further reinforced by a statement from *The Encyclopedia Americana* (under **Midrash**) which suggests: "When such writings first arose is not known, but the most flourishing period of midrashic exegesis was from about 100 B.C. to 200 A.D."

In the commentary following the direct comments on Jeremiah's Scriptural statement, the Rabbi makes some remarks which may be a reflection of his own impression of Israel's future plight based on conditions, political and religious, at that time.

First, "your search for the 'light' in Babylon" may refer to some distant hope and yearning for retrieval of the Ark of the Covenant (presumed to be in Babylon, perhaps) in the hope that possession of that precious article might restore Israel and encourage a return of the Shechinah to dwell again with Israel.

Second, "devastation into deep darkness in Midian" may refer to the Rabbi's fear that Judaism would be lost for many Jews who escaped to Midian (Arabia), because they would be under pressures of heathen pagan religions in a land of unfriendly people. (Yes, even 400–500 years before the religion of Islam was born.)

Lastly, "the obscurely foggy discourses of Greece" may have been an apprehensive reference concerning the writings and preachments from those strange but devoted followers of that even more strange Rabbi from Nazareth who, years earlier, was executed for blasphemy. Indeed, these discourses were "obscure" and "foggy" to most of the Jews and, indeed, they were given boldy and vigorously (even to Gentiles) in the Greek language, "even in Jerusalem and in all Judea, and in Samaria, and unto the uttermost part of the earth." (Acts 1: 8)

NOTE: It is of interest that the Hebrew translator of this Midrash text was in no way prejudiced regarding this story. Just like most people, he had never heard of the Shechinah Event nor had he ever read from any other portion of the Midrash. At that time, neither of us was aware of existence of, nor did we have available, the Soncino translation in English. Upon reading this story as he translated, however, my Jewish friend confided that he had been "deeply moved" by its tone and by what it says. (We both had tears of mixed joy and sadness.)

As I have indicated, this translation has certain variations from the Soncino translation, although, the main theme and essential details remain unchanged. It is my opinion that the translation offered here reflects more of the compassion relative to the tragedy and pathos that was felt by the Rabbis who recorded this event and by the Lord our God.

Appendix C

Josephus, "Lover of Truth"
Testimony of the Sages Regarding
Integrity of Flavius Josephus

Some critics and skeptics have doubts concerning the integrity of Josephus as an historian. Since his works are a direct source for this story, we should examine what the sages of historical record have to say about this man. It is my intent that by showing some of what is written concerning his credentials from perhaps the most learned of his critics, we can highlight credibility for Josephus' account of the Shechinah event.

Further testimony as to the integrity of Josephus as an historian is continually being revealed by modern archaeological discoveries. Descriptions of ancient Jerusalem, Caesarea, and especially Herod's fortress at Masada as rendered by Josephus have been shown to be almost faultless. Recent excavations at Masada by Professor Yadin and others have uncovered Herodian works, Roman works and, dramatically, even some artifacts from the zealots who defended so heroically against Roman procurator Silva in 72 A.D.

Direct testimony concerning Josephus' sincerity, his love for the truth, and his love for the Lord is given from his own written statements about God. A fitting summary of his thoughts is derived by scanning the index of Mr. Whiston's work under the word "God." Here is some of what Josephus has to say about God.

> God (the true God), His Presence in the Tabernacle ... His wisdom, and that he cannot be bribed ... His mercy obtained only by religion ... His foreknowledge, and that His decrees cannot be

avoided ... His will is irresistible ... without His will nothing can happen ... that nothing is concealed from Him ... it is dangerous to disobey Him ... whether it is easier to serve God or man ... He uses beasts to punish the wicked ... is not to be imposed on by the wicked ... delights not in sacrifices, but in good men ... is called on in time of danger, by even bad men ... foretells futurities, that men may provide against them ... affords assistance only when the case is desperate ... delights in those that promote His worship ... is by nature merciful to the poor ... is omnipresent ... His bounty the cause of all men's happiness.

Surely, most would agree that Josephus knew God.

Finally, let us briefly review the credentials of his best qualified critic, Joseph Justus Scaliger (1540–1609). This sixteenth century French scholar is, by reputation, perhaps one of the most brilliant men who ever lived. In the introduction to Appendix Dissertation 1 of[2] Mr. William Whiston (translator of Josephus' works) says of Joseph Scaliger: "... perhaps the most learned person, and the most competent judge that ever was, as to the authority of Josephus...."

Joseph Scaliger, according to *Encyclopedia Americana* (1955 ed.), deserves to be called "the father of the science of chronology." It is recorded that Scaliger locked himself in a room and committed to memory the complete works of Homer in twenty-one days. He continued by memorizing the rest of the Greek poets in three months and all of published Greek literature in two years. In addition, he possessed equal skill in twelve other languages.

Although brilliant, Scaliger was evidently somewhat arrogant toward his peers and was persecuted throughout his career, especially after having converted to Protestantism at age twenty-two. The quotation to follow is excerpted from Reference 2 in the Introduction to Appendix Dissertation 1. Hear now an appraisal of Flavius Josephus rendered by this outstanding scholar in the Prolegomena to his book, "De Emendatione Temporum," p. 17:

> Josephus is the most diligent and the greatest lover of truth of all writers; nor are we afraid to affirm of him, that it is more safe to believe him, not only as to the affairs of the Jews, but also as to those that are foreign to them, than all the Greek and Latin writers; and this, because his fidelity and his compass of learning are everywhere conspicuous.

Most anyone would be satisfied with a testimonial of such tone.

Both Jews and Christians owe deep respect and gratitude to Flavius Josephus for having given us such a worthy record of Judaic history, customs, tradition, and religion.

Glossary

Afikoman, or Apikoman–(Greek) "That which comes after." Second matzah wafer, broken at the Passover meal, the Seder.

Apochrypha–Group of fourteen books that were not accepted by the Canonical Council, considered doubtful in authenticity.

Aramaic–Ancient and still actively used Semitic language, very similar to Hebrew, and considered by many scholars to be the same language spoken and written by the Judeans of the first century.

Azazel–(Hebrew) Scapegoat, "he-goat" released to the wilderness after drawing the lot to select the goat for the offering on Yom Kippur.

Berakoth–(Hebrew) Benedictions, title of Talmud tractate.

Centurion–Roman officer commanding unit of one-hundred soldiers.

Chanukah (or sometimes Hanukkah)–(Hebrew) Dedication, for the Feast of Dedication or Festival of Lights, in commemoration of the miraculous burning of the Menorah candlesticks for eight days after the oil had been depleted. This miracle occurred during the re-dedication of the Temple, 167 B.C., after it had been desecrated by Antiochus IV Epiphanes.

Cherubim–(Hebrew) Angelic beings.

City–The City is the City of Jerusalem, the Holy City.

Eastern Gate–Gate to the Court of the Temple Sanctuary, or "Nicanor's Gate" (Sketch 1); not to be confused with the East Gate in the City wall.

Eschatology (or eschatological)–The study of theology and events concerning the "End Times," "Last Days," "Coming of the Lord," etc.

Essenes–Ultra-religious Jewish sect living in the region of the Dead Sea during the first century, called "Herodians" in the Bible.

Eureka–Greek term, meaning: "I have found it!"

Gamaliel–Gamaliel I, highly respected Rabbinical teacher, who instructed Paul of Tarsus in his Jewish religious training.

Gemara–(Hebrew) A completion or learning. A discussion and / or debate of interpretations of the Law and traditions of Judaism.

Hallah–(Hebrew) Dough. Title of Talmud tractate.

Ham–Noah's second son, believed to be ancestor of African peoples.

H'ekhal–The main building of the Temple, comprised principally of the Holy Place and the Holy of Holies. (Earthly dwelling place of the Divine Presence or Shechinah Glory of Almighty God the Father, "I AM.")

Hullin–(Hebrew) Profane, common, unconsecrated. Talmud tractate.

Islam–Religion of followers of the Prophet, Mohammed (Muslims).

Japheth–Youngest son of Noah, ancestor of European peoples.

Josephus, Flavius–Jewish historian. Most respected and renowned of all historians of the first century.

Kingdom Age–(See "Millennial.")

KJV–Abbreviation for the King James Version, early Bible translation.

Kodesh Ha-Kodashim–(Hebrew) Holy of Holies, the inner sanctuary and dwelling place of God (Shechinah) in the Temple.

Maccabees (or "Maccabean")–Pertaining to the Jewish revolt of 167 B.C. led by Judas Maccabeus and his brothers against Syrian oppressor, Antiochus IV Epiphanes.

Matzah (or "matzoh," "mazzah," etc.)–Unleavened bread, similar to soda crackers, eaten at the Passover meal (Seder).

Menorah–Large golden candelabrum with seven candlesticks or "lights," which stood along the south wall of the Holy Place in the Temple. (See Sketch 8.)

Middoth–(Hebrew) Dimensions. Title of a Talmud tractate.

Midrash–A Rabbinical commentary on Jewish Scripture, including all of the Tenach (Old Testament books).

Millennial–Pertaining to the one thousand year reign of Messiah after He arrives at Olivet summit to conquer Israel's enemies.

Miphkad Altar–Place of the sacrifice and burning of the Red Heifer at or near the summit of the Mount of Olives and due east of the Temple.

Mishnah–(Hebrew) To learn. A collection of statements and interpretations (rulings) on the Law and Jewish tradition and listed as the most formal of the entries in the Talmud.

NASA–National Aeronautics and Space Administration, United States federal supervising agency for aeronautical and space sciences.

NASB–New American Standard Bible, modern Bible translation.

NEB–New English Bible, modern Bible translation.

Nisan–(Hebrew) First month on Jewish religious calendar, seventh month of the civil year.

NIV–New International Version, modern Bible translation.

Parah–(Hebrew) Heifer or young cow. Title of Talmud tractate.

Patibulum–Horizontal cross-piece member that supported the arms of the victim in crucifixion.

Pesahim–(Hebrew) Lambs. Talmud tractate dealing with Passover.

Peshitta–Aramaic version of the Bible, having been scrupulously preserved in its original form by the Eastern churches, and having been subjected to very little change over the past nineteen centuries.

Rapture–Term applied in theology to describe the "gathering up" or "taking away" of Believers, particularly Christians, both dead and living; resurrected to be with the Lord just before the seven years of "Tribulation" immediately preceding arrival of Messiah. (Luke 21:36; 1 Corinthians 15:51–57; 1 Thessalonians 4:16–18; Revelation 3:10)

Rosh Hashanah–(Hebrew) New Year. Title of Talmud tractate.

Sanhedrin–Council of seventy-one Jewish elders, comprising the supreme ecclesiastical and secular tribunal to the Jews. Talmud tractate.

Shabbath, or Shabbot–(Hebrew) Sabbath. Title of Talmud tractate.

Seder–(Hebrew) Order; especially the order of the Passover meal.

Shechinah–(Hebrew) Divine Presence. The visible Presence of Almighty God, "Yahweh" or "YHWH" or "I AM," seen by the people of Israel at the Temple or the Tabernacle as a "pillar of cloud by day" or as a "pillar of fire by night." Most English Bible translations refer to the Divine Presence as "the Glory of the Lord."

Shekalim–(Hebrew) Shekels (coins). Title of Talmud tractate.

Shem–Eldest son of Noah, ancestor of Semitic and Oriental peoples.

Sukkah–(Hebrew) Booths. Title of Talmud tractate concerning the Feast of Booths or Feast of Tabernacles.

Suleiman–Sixteenth-century Turkish Sultan and conqueror, Suleiman I.

Talmud–Jewish Rabbinical commentary on the Law and Jewish traditions.

Tenach, or Tanakh–Jewish Scriptures ("Old Testament").

Tetelestai–Greek, meaning: "It is finished." Also: "Paid in full."

Tishri–(Hebrew) Seventh month of the Jewish religious calendar, first month of the civil year.

Torah–First five books of the Hebrew Bible (Old Testament): Genesis, Exodus, Leviticus, Numbers, and Deuteronomy. Usually maintained in scroll form as used in the Temple and in synagogues.

WASP–Acronym meaning "White, Anglo-Saxon, Protestant."

Yoma–(Hebrew) "The Day," specifically The Day of Atonement, Yom Kippur. Title of Talmud tractate dealing with that subject.

Zebahim–(Hebrew) "They that suffer flux." Title of Talmud tractate.

References

1. Martin, Ernest L., *The Original Bible Restored*, 1984—Foundation for Biblical Research, Pasadena, CA., 91102

2. Flavius Josephus, (Translated by William Whiston, A.M.); *The Works of Josephus*, 1987—New Updated Edition, Hendrickson Publishers, Peabody, MA 01961-3473

3. Anderson, Sir Robert, *The Coming Prince*, pp. 129, 1983—(Reprint of the 10th Ed.), Kregel Publ., Grand Rapids, MI., 49501

4. Jones, Vendyl M., *Will The Real Jesus Please Stand?*, 1983—Institute of Judaic-Christian Research, Box 120366, Arlington, TX 76012-0366

5. Keller, Werner (Translated by William Neil), *The Bible as History*, 1956—William Morrow and Company, New York

6. Fleming, James, "The Undiscovered Gate Beneath Jerusalem's Golden Gate," *Biblical Archaeology Review*, 3000 Connecticut Avenue NW, Washington, D.C. 20008, Jan/Feb–1983

7. Kaufman, Asher S., "Where the Ancient Temple of Jerusalem Stood," *Biblical Archaeology Review*, 3000 Connecticut Avenue NW, Washington, D.C. 20008 Mar/Apr–1983

8. Lamsa, George M., *Holy Bible–From the Ancient Eastern Text*, 1984—translated from the Aramaic of the Peshitta, Harper & Row, Publishers, San Francisco, CA

9. *Universal Jewish Encyclopedia*, 1939—published by: Universal Jewish Encyclopedia, New York, NY

10. *Encyclopedia Judaica*, 1972—Keter, Inc., 440 Park Avenue South, New York, NY 10016

11. *The Jerusalem Post*, International Edition, 6 April 1980

12. Martin, Ernest L., *The Place of Christ's Crucifixion*, 1984—Foundation for Biblical Research, Pasadena, CA

13. *Midrash Rabbah*, Third Edition, 1983—The Soncino Press, Limited, 123 Ditmas Avenue, Brooklyn, NY 11218

14. Yadin, Yigael, "The Temple Scroll," *Biblical Archaeology Review*, 3000 Connecticut Avenue NW, Washington, D.C. 20008–Sep/Oct–1984

15. Barkay, Gabriel, "The Garden Tomb–Was Jesus Buried There?" *Biblical Archaeology Review*, 3000 Connecticut Avenue NW, Washington, D.C. 20008, Mar/Apr–1986

16. Frenkley, Helen, "The Search for Roots–Israel's Biblical Landscape Reserve," *Biblical Archaeology Review*, 3000 Connecticut Avenue NW, Washington, D.C. 20008, Sep/Oct–1986

17. Larkin, Clarence, *Dispensational Truth*, 1920—Rev. Clarence Larkin Estate, P.O. Box 334, Glenside, PA 19038

18. Berry, George R., *The Interlinear Greek-English New Testament*, 1976—Zondervan Publishing House, Grand Rapids, MI 49506

19. Berry, George R., *The Interlinear Hebrew-English Old Testament*, 1974—Kregel Publications, Grand Rapids, MI 49501

20. Cruden, Alexander, *Cruden's Complete Concordance*, 1975—Zondervan Publishing House, Grand Rapids, MI 49506

21. *The Babylonian Talmud*, Quincentenary Edition, 1978—The Soncino Press, Limited, 123 Ditmas Avenue, Brooklyn, NY 11218

22. Levitte, Dov, and Wachs, Daniel, "Earthquakes in Jerusalem

and the Mount of Olives Landslide," *Israel–Land and Nature*, Vol. 9, No. 3–Spring 1984

23. "Sixteenth General Synod of the United Church of Christ," Associated Press Release, 1 July 1987

24. Rodkinson, Michael L., *New Edition of the Babylonian Talmud*, 1918—Volume V, pg. 251, The Talmud Society, Boston, MA

25. Martin, Ernest L., *Secrets of Golgotha*, 1988—Academy for Scriptural Knowledge, P.O. Box 25000, Portland, OR 97225

26. Eusebius (Edited and translated by W. J. Ferrar) "The Proof of the Gospel," book VI, Chapter 18, 1981—Baker Book House, Grand Rapids, MI 49506

27. *Halley's Bible Handbook*, 1976—Twenty-Fourth Edition, p. 532, Zondervan Publishing House, Grand Rapids, MI 49506

28. Rodkinson, Michael L., *New Edition of the Babylonian Talmud*, 1918—Volume IV, pp. 79–82, The Talmud Society, Boston, MA

29. *New American Standard Bible* (NASB), 1973—A. J. Holman Company, Division of J. B. Lippincott Co., Philadelphia and New York

30. *The New English Bible* (NEB), 1970—Oxford University Press and Cambridge University Press

31. *New International Version of the Holy Bible* (NIV), 1978—Zondervan Bible Publishers, Grand Rapids, MI

32. *The Encyclopedia Americana*, 1955—Published by Americana Corporation, New York, NY

Index of Biblical References

Note: Some references to Hebrew Scriptural translations do not coincide with verse notations used in some Christian Bibles; however, these exceptions are few and usually of very slight difference from the Christian texts.

Genesis
    1:26, 197
    9:27, 156
    22:2–4, 104
    22:7–8, 104
    22:13–14, 105
Exodus
    3:2, 2
    12:6, 74
    12:46, 75
    12:48, 93
    13:21, 2
    14:13, 119
    19:9, 2
    23:5, 125
    24:11, 84
    26:35–37, 154
    26:36, 67
    29:14, 74
    33:16, 125
    34:29–30, 2
    38:13–15, 74
    40:36–38, 22

Leviticus
    4:11–12; 67, 74
    16:1–17, 34; 2
    16:2, 3
    16:27, 74
    26:44, 125
Numbers
    15:30–36, 74
    Chapter 19; 27, 82
    19:6, 37
    19:9, 74
    19:10, 82
Deuteronomy
    4:7, 109
    4:7–8, 127
    4:27, 208
    4:27–40, 127
    4:29–31, 208
    4:30, 148
    4:33; 147, 148
    4:33–39; 109, 110
    14:2, 180
    30:3, 97

I Samuel
  5:9, 166
  16:12, 111
  17:42, 111
II Samuel
  24:24–25, 10
I Kings
  6:16; 64, 170
  8:10, 162
  9:3–9, 127
  9:6–9, 127
II Chronicles
  2:1, 37
  3:1, 104
  3:7, 217
  5:13–14, 160
Ezra
  6:12; 51, 160
Nehemiah
  Chapters 8–10, 160
  Chapters 8–12, 4
  12:43; 4, 161, 163
Job
  6:24–25, 205
  11:20, 126
  12:22, 210
  33:14, 129
Psalms
  8:5, 197
  Chapter 27; 99
  34:20, 76
  118:26, 57
Proverbs
  1:7, 201
  2:1–6, 201
  25:24; 215, 219
Isaiah
  1:18, 121
  6:10, 128
  9:6–7, 189
  11:12, 10
  13:10, 97

  14:15–17, 188
  27:12–13, 94
  34:4, 97
  43:5–6, 93
  55:11, 219
  59:2, 126
  65:20, 22; 129
Jeremiah
  3:14, 22; 216
  3:16; 3, 217
  Chapter 7, 144
  10:2, 115
  13:16, 216
  Chapter 21, 144
  23:3–4, 93
  23:4, 100
  31:31–34, 181
  31:35–37; 187, 188
Ezekiel
  1:1, 3; 217
  3:15, 217
  Chapters 8–11; 158, 164
  8:1–3, 144
  8:1–4, 158
  8:3; 158, 203
  8:16; 27, 61, 64
  8:16–17, 87
  Chapters 9–11; 51
  9:5, 158
  Chapters 10–11; 6, 7, 11, 144, 176
  10:4; 214, 215, 218
  10:15, 20, 22; 217
  10:18, 214
  10:19; 215, 218
  11:23, 216
  11:24; 6, 158
  26:14, 159
  Chapter 37; 94, 127, 160, 200
  37:22, 160
  Chapters 38–39, 83
  39:2, 83

39:11, 12; 83
40:1; 165, 203
41:2; 83, 85
42:16–20, 44
43:2; 87, 96, 159, 164, 203
43:3; 158, 217
43:4, 87
43:7, 87
44:1–3; 34, 84, 165
44:2–3, 87
44:3, 217
44:6, 7, 13, 14-16; 165
46:1; 65, 86
47:1, 47
47:1–2, 47
47:1–10, 43
47:10, 85
Daniel
    4:34–37, 77
    7:13, 97
    9:24–26; 59, 103
    9:27; 81, 98, 99
    12:1–2, 94
    12:2, 90
    12:4, 172
Hosea
    5:15; 10, 51, 100, 127, 159, 216
    Chapter 6, 220
      6:1, 206
      6:1–3; 100, 101, 127
      6:2, 103
Joel
    2:10, 97
    2:32, 95
    3:15, 97
Amos
    7:7; 215, 219
    7:8; 215, 219
    7:9; 219, 220
    9:1; 215, 219
Micah

6:9, 216
Zephaniah
    3:1–2, 6, 11–13; 78, 79
Haggai
    1:4–8, 161
    1:8, 203
    2:3–5, 161
    2:3–9, 161
    2:4–7, 203
    2:4–9, 51
    2:6–7, 164
    2:7; 4, 163, 168
    2:9, 163
Zechariah
    1:16; 19, 51, 164, 168
    1:20, 190
    2:3 (Hebrew Scripture), 190
    2:6, 97
    8:13, 194
    8:23, 194
    9:9, 57
    11:1, 125
    12:10; 21, 50, 188
    12:12, 188
    13:6; 21, 50
    14:4; 11, 20, 43, 49, 74
    14:5, 43
    14:8, 44
    14:16–19, 44
Malachi
    3:7, 216
Matthew
    5:17; 59, 74
    11:21, 159
    21:9–11, 57
    23:21; 3, 15, 51, 167, 168, 192, 204
    23:24, 146
    23:37, 11
    23:38, 168
    24:2; 58, 160
    24:6–7, 128

24:30, 96
24:44, 99
25:30, 98
26:6–7, 58
26:60–61, 58
Chapter 27, 152
27:45; 114, 173
27:51–54; 61, 74, 151
27:54, 73
Mark
  13:3; 41, 61, 64, 74
  13:8, 128
  13:20, 83
  13:24–27; 96, 97
  14:3; 39, 187
  14:25, 187
  14:50–52, 150
  15:38–39, 151
  16:14, 48
Luke
  6:5, 53
  10:1, 220
  10:13, 159
  11:29, 127
  11:36–38, 53
  12:40, 99
  14:11, 79
  19:40, 57
  19:46–47, 169
  21:9–11, 129
  21:11, 129
  21:26, 98
  21:28, 129
  21:36; 130, 229
  23:44; 114, 173
  23:45–47, 151
  23:53, 74
  24:50, 48
  24:52–53, 51
  24:53, 168
John
  2:16; 51, 169
  3:16, 211
  4:10, 53
  10:16, 108
  10:30, 16
  11:39, 41
  12:1–13, 57
  12:13, 54
  12:14–15, 57
  12:40, 128
  14:6, 186
  14:9, 80
  18:37, 58
  19:19–22, 60
  19:27–29, 150
  19:30–36, 151
  19:31–37, 75
  19:37, 74
  20:4, 62
Acts
  1:8, 221
  1:10–11, 49
  1:11–12, 48
  1:12; 49, 218
  1:13, 48
  5:33–40, 209
  8:39–40, 96
  21:39, 184
Romans
  2:29, 185
  9:4; 3, 51, 167, 168, 204
  10:12, 185
  11:11, 180
I Corinthians
  4:6, 146
  9:20–21, 184
  15:51–57; 130, 229
II Corinthians
  4:6, 147
Galatians
  3:28, 184
Phillipians
  1:21, 179

I Thessalonians
    4:16–18; 130, 229
    4:18, 129
II Thessalonians
    2:13, 180
Hebrews
    11:6, 185
    8:13; 181, 182

I John
    5:1, 186
Revelation
    3:10; 130, 229
    3:20, 124
    11:2, 44
    11:2–3, 99
    19:19–21, 96
    20:4, 102

Index

Note: Several references are omitted from the Index because of their frequent use in the text. These include, for example: archaeology, Ascension, Christian, Holy of Holies, Israel, Jesus, Jewish, Messiah, Mount of Olives, Shechinah, Temple, etc.

A

Aaron (High Priest under Moses), 116, 121, 178, 196
Abraham, xix, 102, 104, 105
Absalom's Pillar, 28 (see Old City map)
Afikoman, 175, 186, 187, 226
Alexander (The Great), 117, 159
Altar (Of Incense), 11, 170 (see Sketches 7 and 8) (Also see "Miphkad Altar")
Altar (Of Sacrifice), 9, 47, 88, 105, 120, 123, 144, 214, 215 (see Sketches 2 and 7)
Anderson (Sir Robert), 202
Anointed, 59, 106, 115, 208
Antichrist (the), 81, 83, 96, 98, 107
Antiochus IV Epiphanes, 118, 144, 226, 228
Aramaic, 68, 105, 121, 155, 168, 226, 229
Araunah (or "Ornan"), the Jebusite, 10

arch, (see "Lower Arch")
Ark of the Covenant, 2, 3, 10, 166, 217, 221
Artaxerxes (King), 59
Ascension (Chapel Of), 10, 24, 26, 42, 43, 154 (Old City) (see Old City map, also Sketches 5, 6 and 9)
ash residue, 38, 39 (see Sketches 9 and 10)
ashes (Red Heifer), 38, 54, 55, 56, 67, 81–83 (Sketches 9 and 10)
Atonement (Day of, Feast of), 2, 3, 58, 74, 76, 86, 91, 92, 96, 99, 100, 119, 121–123, 170, 230
Azazel, 119, 120, 122, 226 (see "scapegoat")

B

Babylon (or Babylonian), xix, 2, 6, 19, 66, 111, 125, 144, 155, 157, 158, 160, 162, 202, 216, 221
Barabbas, 121, 122

Barkay (Gabriel), 63
Barnabus, 102, 182
bedrock, 26, 27
Bethany (village of), 39, 40, 48, 49, 56, 57, 62
"black-ball," 119
Blessed Assurance, 95, 178, 179, 182, 185, 209
Book of Life, 95, 99
bride, 98
bridegroom, 98
bridge, 38, 42, 54, 56, 58, 120, 122 (Sketch 6, see "Azazel" or "Heifer's Gangway")
bullock(s), 67, 74, 121, (see "goats" or "Azazel")
burro (or donkey), 57, 59, 115
burrow, 62

C

Caesarea, 210, 223
Caiaphas (High Priest at trial of Jesus), 53, 56, 59, 76, 77, 119, 165
calendar, xix, 98, 114, 116, 229, 230
Calvary, 74, 106, 210 (see Sketches 9 and 10, also "Gordon's")
candle(s), candlestick(s), 123, 125, 162, 170, 193, 226, 228 (see "Menorah" and Sketch 8)
carpenter, 16, 59, 77, 88, 188–190, 198
cavity, (see "pit" and/or Sketch 10)
cedar, 28, 37, 38, 39, 64, 77, 79, 125, 154, 170, 217
Cemetery (Jerusalem), 62, 63, 171 (Sketches 6, 9 and Old City map)
censer, 86, 170

centurion, 61, 62, 64–67, 69, 73–75, 150, 151, 153, 155, 171, 173–175, 204, 226
Chanukah, 10, 16, 89, 92, 98, 114, 118, 126, 169, 226
character of God, 79, 80
cherubim (or cherub), 73, 214, 215, 217
Church Of All Nations, 217
Church Of The Holy Sepulchre, 60, 62, 63, 171, 204, 210 (see Old City map and Sketch 6)
Church of Mary Magdalene ("Russian" Church), 217 (see Old City map)
"cloud", 2, 4, 7, 15, 22, 106, 109, 116, 158, 160, 202, 205, 229
Cohen family, 197, 198
comet, 112
Constantine I (Emperor), 152, 153, 210
covenant, 22, 127, 161, 167, 181–183, 187, 206, 208
crimson, 28, 38 (also see "red stuff")
Crimson Strap, 76, 120, 121, 125, 162, 193
criticism (Biblical), 48
Crusades, xix, 18, 209
Cruden's Concordance, 217
cubit(s), 27, 30, 39, 40, 43, 44, 49, 218

D

Damascus Gate Bus Station, 62 (see Old City map and Sketch 6)
damsels ("eighty-two"), 67, 155
Daniel (the Prophet), 59, 94, 172
David (King), xix, 77, 111, 188, 189, 203
December (month of), 33, 114

"den-of-thieves", 19, 58, 59, 147, 167, 169
Descent Of The Mount of Olives, 38, 54, 57 (also see Sketch 9)
Desire Of All Nations, 163, 164, 203
divinations, 152
Dome Of The Rock, 10, 11, 30, 36, 44 (Old City map and Sketch 6)
Dome Of The Spirits, 10
Dome Of The Tablets, 10, 11, 14, 24, 26, 34, 37, 39, 41, 42, 44, 47, 51, 62 (see Old City map and Sketches 3, 4, 5)
drought, 129
"dry bones", 160, 200

E

earthquake(s), 42, 43, 61, 65, 69, 73, 128, 150, 151, 164, 171, 173, 174, 204, 213 (also see "quaking")
eclipse, 65, 114, 115, 173
Egypt, 22, 89, 94, 110, 127, 161
El Aqsa, (Islamic mosque), 47 (see Old City map)
elect, 83, 84, 95, 96
Elohim, 4, 16, 190, 197
En Gedi (Israeli village bordering the Dead Sea), 44, 85
Equinox (Vernal), 33
eschatology (or eschatological), 24, 52, 107, 227
Essenes, 56, 152, 227
Et Tur, 11 (village at Olivet summit, see Old City map)
Eusebius (Bishop of Caesarea), xix, 51, 64, 74, 152, 210

F

famines, 128
Feasts, 88, 89, 92, 93, 96, 149, 217, 230 (also "First Fruits", "Jehovah", "Pentecost", "Trumpets", "Unleavened", etc.)
"fire", 2, 4, 7, 15, 22, 73, 106, 109, 110, 116, 148, 158, 174, 202, 205, 229
"Fiddler on the Roof", 128
First Fruits (Feast of), 89, 90, 92
Fleming (Dr. James), 34–37, 41, 42
Flood, xix, 129
food (erub of cooked foods), 40
Foundation Stone (of the Temple), 10, 26

G

Gamaliel (Rabbi), 209, 227
Garden Tomb, 60, 62, 63, 153, 171, 204 (see Old City map and Sketch 6)
Gate (Beautiful), 28, 35, 36 (see Sketches 1, 2, 3, 4, 7)
  (brass or bronze), 26, 35, 65, 68, 84, 112, 113, 149, 212
  (East or Nicanor's), 9, 10, 15, 26, 28–30, 33–36, 56, 62, 65, 67, 75, 84–87, 112, 113, 148–150, 165, 175, 212–215, 217, 227 (see "signs", also Sketches 1–5 and 7)
  (Essene), 56, 152
  (Golden or Suleiman's), 35, 37, 41, 42, 217 (see Old City map)
  (Lower), (see "Lower Arch")
Gentiles 44, 93, 107, 108
Gethsemane, 30, 39, 52, 55, 56, 60, 122 (see Old City map)
goat(s), 67, 74, 105, 119, 121, 123 (see "Azazel" or "bullocks")

Gog & Magog, 83
Golgotha, 54, 55, 67, 74, 150, 175 (see Sketches 9 and 10)
Gordon (General Charles), 152, 153
Gordon's Calvary, 62, 153
Goren (Rabbi Shlomo), 82
graves, 56, 61, 65, 69, 74, 151, 171, 174, 204 (see "tombs", also Sketches 6 and 9)
Greece (or Greek), 184, 185, 188, 216, 221, 224, 226, 227, 230
"greenhouse effect", 129
Gregory XIII (Pope), 116

H
Ham (youngest son of Noah), 156, 227
Hanukkah (see "Chanukah")
Heifer's Gangway Bridge, 38, 42, 54, 56, 58, 119, 122 (Sketch 6)
H'ekhal, 28, 29, 33, 35, 36, 66, 69, 84, 86, 124, 125, 144, 154, 155, 164, 170, 171, 173, 174, 203, 227 (see Sketches 1, 2, 7, 8)
Helena (mother of Emperor Constantine I), 152, 210
Herod('s) (King), 3, 19, 34, 55, 60, 147, 166–169, 192, 193, 223
High Priest (or priests), 28–30, 35, 59, 61, 66, 68, 74, 76, 77, 82, 85, 86, 88, 111, 112, 116–120, 147, 170, 175, 203, 212 (also see Sketch 10)
Hillel II (Rabbi), xix, 116
hinges, 27, 65, 112, 149
Holocaust, 83, 209
Holy Spirit, xv, 92, 98, 106, 178, 191, 197
Hyrcanus (John, High Priest), xix, 112, 117–119
hyssop, 37–39, 77–79

I
Isaac, 104, 105, 220
Islam, xix, 221, 227
Iyar (eighth Jewish month), 112, 213

J
"Jacob's trouble", 84, 97, 101 (also see "Tribulation")
James (the Apostle), 16
James (brother of Jesus), 144
Japheth (second son of Noah), 156, 227
Jehoshaphat, 98 (Valley of, see Sketch 6)
Jehovah (Feast of—see "Feasts")
Jeroboam (King), 220
Jerusalem Post, 27
Jewels, 110, 111
John (the Apostle), 6, 16, 62, 150, 151, 211
Jones (Reverend Vendyl L.), 17, 25, 82, 181, 209
Joseph (of Arimathea), 63
Josephus (Flavius), xiv, xix, 8–10, 15, 25, 26, 28, 30, 35, 51, 85, 108, 110–113, 143, 144, 148–150, 155, 158, 168–170, 195, 202, 203, 212, 217, 218, 223–225, 227
June (month of), 33, 114

K
Kalal, 82
Kaufman (Prof. Asher S.), 8, 10, 11, 24, 25–28, 36, 37, 39, 41–43, 51
Khartoum, 152
Kidron Valley, 9, 14, 28, 42, 43, 49, 56, 64, 69, 174, 202, 218 (see Old City map, Sketches 5 & 6)
Kingdom Age, 84, 90, 93, 98, 100, 101, 107, 108, 164, 189, 194, 227

L

Lamsa Bible, 129, 160, 168 (translated from the Aramaic Peshitta by George M. Lamsa)
landslides, 42, 43
Larkin (Clarence), 106
latrines, 57, 63, 171
Lazarus, 40, 57, 58, 74
Lebanon, 38, 77, 125
leper(s), leprosy or leprous, 33, 39–41, 56–58, 85, 173
Lights (Festival or Miracle of), 114, 226 (see "Chanukah")
logs (for the Altar), 123, 162
lots (drawing of the), 58, 119, 122, 125, 162, 226
Lower Arch (or Gate), 35–37, 41, 42
Luke (the Disciple), 48, 151

M

Maccabees (Apochryphal Book of), xix, 2, 118, 166, 228
Mark (the Apostle), 150, 151
Martin (Prof. Ernest L.), 8, 14, 15, 25, 27, 30, 34, 39, 41, 61, 64, 104, 116, 152, 196, 218
Masada, 207, 223
matzah, 106, 175, 186, 226, 228 (see "unleavened bread")
Megiddo, 98
Melchizedek, 190
Menorah, 123, 226, 228 (see "candlestick", also Sketch 8)
Messiah, Son of David, 93, 95, 97, 103, 164, 188–190
Messiah, Son of Joseph, 188–190
Michael (the archangel), 94, 95
Midian (ancient name of Arabia), 216, 221
millennial (or Millennium), 44, 84, 85, 87, 102, 129, 163, 165, 227, 228

Miphkad Altar, 27–30, 34, 38–43, 52–55, 58, 60, 77, 81, 83, 104, 106, 153, 228 (see Sketches 5, 9 and 10)
Mohammed (the Prophet), xix
Moriah (Mount), 104, 105, 108
Moses, xix, 1, 2, 4, 82, 89, 91, 92, 121, 125, 183–185, 198
Mount of Olives (or "Olivet" —see Sketches 5, 6, 9 and 10)
Muslim(s) (Moslem), xv, xvi, 10, 35, 42, 44, 47, 211, 227

N

nails ("print of the", "spikes", "His wounds"), 68, 143, 186
Nebuchadnezzar (King), 2, 77, 165, 166
Nehemiah, 3, 59, 163
Nicanor's Gate (see "gates", Sketches 1–5 and 7)
ninth hour (or 3 p.m.), 62, 65, 68, 75, 114, 115, 173, 175, 204, 212 (see Sketches 3, 4 and 5)
Nisan (first Jewish month), 9, 89, 98, 114, 149, 212, 229
noise (of the gate), 65, 68, 112, 113, 148

O

omen, 114, 115, 117, 119
oregano, 27, 28, 37
Ornan (the Jebusite, see "Araunah")
Ovid, 20

P

palm branches (or "fronds"), 38, 39, 54, 56
Passover, 9, 65, 74, 75, 89, 92, 93, 98, 106, 116, 121, 175, 186, 226, 228, 229

patibulum, 112, 229
Paul (the Apostle), 3, 6, 48, 77, 102, 143, 146, 147, 167, 179–185, 208, 227
Pentecost (Shavuot), xv, 9, 16, 17, 88, 89, 92, 93, 106, 114, 163, 201, 204, 213
pestilences (or "plagues"), 128
Peter (the Apostle), 16, 62, 106
Phillip (the Apostle), 80, 96
Pilate, 56, 57, 59, 60, 111, 121, 122
Pillar (of "cloud" or "fire"), 2, 229
pit, 67 (also see Sketch 10)
Pompey (Roman conqueror), 145
Pope Gregory XIII, xix, 116
portico (or "porch"), 30, 33, 35, 66, 69, 73, 87, 173, 204 (see Sketches 2 and 7)
prophetic-perfect tense, 158

Q
quaking, 213 (see "earthquakes")
quarrelsome wife, 215, 219

R
rapture, 83, 93, 98, 99, 157, 158, 229
redemption, 129, 187
Red Heifer, 27–30, 34, 36–39, 52, 54, 56, 61, 68, 74, 75, 77, 81–83, 86, 88, 104, 105, 111, 153, 172, 228, 229 (see "ashes")
red stuff, 27, 28, 37, 38
rending-of-the-veil (or "rent-in-twain"), 19, 61, 64–67, 69, 73, 75, 150, 151, 155, 169–171, 173–176, 204 (see "veil")
"Replacement Theology", 17, 145, 181

Resurrection, xv, 62, 92, 93, 107, 115, 148, 164, 174, 203
revolutions (or "rebellions"), 128, 129, 158, 212
river-bottom, 44
"Roots", 103, 207
Rosh Hashanah, 88, 90, 92–96, 98, 99, 116, 229 (see "Trumpets")

S
Sabbath Day's journey (or "limit"), 27, 36, 40, 49, 62, 112, 113, 172, 218, 220
Sanhedrin, 53, 63, 193, 209, 215, 219, 220, 229 (see "seventy-one")
sardonyx, 110, 111
Saul (King), 111
Scaliger (Joseph Justus), 113, 224
scapegoat, 119, 120, 122 (also see "Azazel")
Scapegoat's Gangway, 120, 122, 226 (see Sketch 6)
scarlet, 37, 38, 120–122 (see "red stuff" or "crimson strap")
scattering (or "scattered"), 10, 150, 208, 220, 221
scissoring (or "scissor-step"), 170
Seder, 89, 93, 106, 175, 186, 187, 226, 228, 229 (see "Passover")
"seventy-one", 215, 219, 220 (see "Sanhedrin")
Shavuot, 88, 90
shelf, (see "pit" and/or Sketch 10)
Shem (eldest son of Noah), 156, 229
shepherds, 93, 100
shewbread, 124
shofar, 65 (also see "Trumpets")

side ("hand in His"), 143
siege (or destruction of Jerusalem), 15, 42, 69, 124, 144
"sight-picture", 28–30, 34, 175 (see Sketches 3, 4, 5 and 10)
signs, 9, 109, 110, 124, 127, 128
 (jewels), 110–112
 (in the clouds), 112, 213
 (the "silent" gate), 112, 113
 (eclipses), 114–116
 (the lots), 119, 120
 (crimson strap), 120, 121, 193
 (western candle), 123, 193
 (Altar logs), 123
 (shewbread), 123, 124
 (H'ekhal doors), 124, 193
 (meanings to Judeans), 124–128
 (meanings in today's world), 128–130
Simeon, the Righteous (High Priest), xix, 117–119, 123, 162, 163
Simon (the leper), 39, 56, 58
Sinai, 2, 4, 14, 37, 82, 89, 91
six (in numerology), 89, 102
soil samples, 28, 38
Solomon (King), 54, 127
strap (see "Crimson Strap")
Suleiman ("the Magnificent", Turkish conqueror), 34, 35, 88, 230
sword, 112, 193, 220
synagogue(s), 7, 230

T
Tabernacle, 2, 4, 28–30, 44, 65, 82, 88, 93, 154, 218, 230
Tabernacles (Feast of, also Sukkoth), 44, 91, 93, 106, 229
Tenach, 97, 102, 161, 228, 230 (see "Torah")

TETELESTAI (Greek: "It is finished"; i.e., "Paid in full") 174, 204, 230
Tevyeh, 128
third hour (9 a.m.), 65, 74, 75 (see Sketches 3, 4 and 5)
Thomas (the Apostle), 143
threshing floor, 37
Tishri (seventh Jewish month), 90, 91, 96, 98, 230
Titus (Roman general), 10, 15, 119
tomb(s), 36, 74, 75, 92, 130, 152, 153, 173, 210 (see Old City map and Sketches 6 and 9)
Torah, 18, 103, 121, 230
towels, (used to relay signal), 120
Transfiguration (of Jesus), 16
Tribulation, 83, 93, 95–97, 99–100, 208, 229 (also see "Jacob's trouble")
Trinity (or "Triune"), 16, 106, 107, 148, 196, 197
Triumphal Entry, 38, 41, 53, 54, 57 (also see Sketch 9)
Trumpet(s), (including "Feast of"), 65, 68, 92–94, 96, 98, 100 (also see "Rosh Hashanah")
Tshuvah, 91
"two days", 22, 100–103, 182, 220
Tyre (city of), 159, 160

U
Unleavened Bread (Feast of), 75, 89, 92, 196, 212, 228
Urim (and Thummim), 111
urn, 119
Uzziah (King), 43

V

veil(s) (or "vail"), 5, 19, 29, 33, 34, 36, 61, 62, 64–67, 69, 73–75, 85, 107, 147, 150, 151, 153–155, 169–171, 173–176, 204 (also see Sketches 2, 3, 4, 5, 7, 8)
vision(s), 6, 7, 87, 125, 144, 152, 158, 159, 164, 165, 210
volcanic, 128

W

Wailing Wall, 47 (see Old City map)
wars, 128, 212
Water Gate, 44, 47, 85 (see Sketch 7)
waters (living), 43, 54, 55, 85, 87
weather, 129
"week" (of seven years), 59, 81, 229
"week" of temptation, 101 (see "Tribulation")
Weeks (Feast of, see "Pentecost")
Westernmost candle (see "signs", also Sketch 8)
Whiston (William), 111, 212, 223, 224
winter "rains", 101—"severe", 129
wool, 28

Y

Yadin (Prof. Yigael), 39, 40, 56, 74, 171, 223
Yom Kippur, 2, 6, 86, 90–92, 95, 98, 99, 226, 230 (see "Atonement")

Z

Zakkai (Rabbi Yohanan ben), 125, 178, 179
Zerubbabel (King), 3, 4, 51, 85, 158, 161, 163, 203
Zion (Mount), 104, 161 (see Sketch 5)